SONG OF A LOST CITY

TROY IN MYTH, FICTION AND FACT

R Jay Driskill

RED PIRATE MEDIA

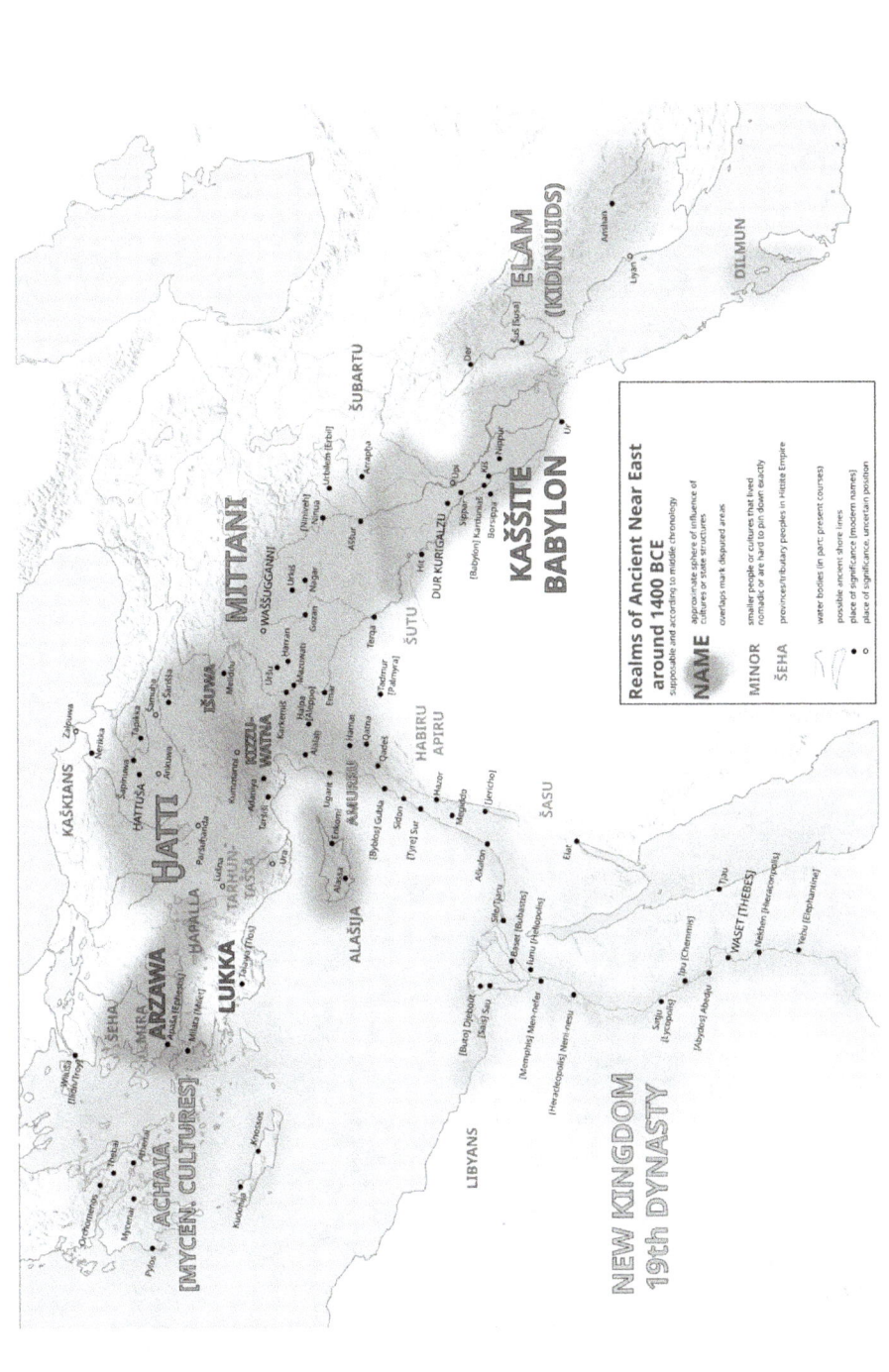

Realms of Ancient Near East
around 1400 BCE
supposable and according to middle chronology

NAME   approximate sphere of influence of
cultures or state structures

overlaps mark disputed areas

MINOR   smaller people or cultures that lived
nomadic or are hard to pin down exactly

ŠEHA   provinces/tributary peoples in Hittite Empire

water bodies (in part; present courses)

possible ancient shore lines

place of significance (modern names)

• place of significance, uncertain position

KAŠKIANS

HATTI

ARZAWA

ŠEHA

SEMIRA

HAPALLA

LUKKA

TARHUN
TAŠŠA

MYCEN. CULTURES]
ACHAIA

ISUWA

KIZZU-
WATNA

WAŠŠUGGANNI

MITTANI

ŠUBARTU

ALAŠIA

AMURRU

HABIRU
APIRU

ŠUTU

ŠASU

DUR KURIGALZU

KAŠŠITE
BABYLON

ELAM
(KIDINUIDS)

DILMUN

LIBYANS

NEW KINGDOM
19th DYNASTY

WASET [THEBES]

CONTENTS

ALSO BY R JAY DRISKILL

Time is a river of vanishing objects and the current is swift. No sooner does anything appear than it has swept by, and another comes in its place, and that too will be swept away.

Marcus Aurelius

PREFACE

I still remember the first time Troy became real to me. It was a cold January evening in 1992, and I was a student at Snead State Community College, huddled in my apartment with a bowl of microwave ramen. The television flickered with images of ancient stone walls as David Wood's documentary "In Search of the Trojan War" began. I'd studied Homer's epics and knew the outlines of Heinrich Schliemann's excavations, but something shifted that night as Wood walked through the ruins at Hisarlık in northwestern Turkey.

"This is it," he said, gesturing to weathered limestone fortifications. "This is Troy."

The simplicity of that statement struck me. Not the Troy of Brad Pitt's gleaming Hollywood production, not the mythical realm of gods and heroes, but an actual physical place where people had lived, loved, fought, and died. A place where the past and present converged in layers of stone and soil. I set aside my cooling noodles and leaned forward, transfixed.

In that moment, I understood what makes Troy unique in human history. It exists simultaneously in multiple dimensions—as an archaeological site in Turkey, as the literary setting for Homer's masterpieces, as a cultural touchstone that has inspired artists for three millennia, and as a complex scholarly puzzle that continues to challenge our understanding of the Bronze Age world. No other ancient site occupies this peculiar intersection of archaeology and imagination, of science and art.

The ruins at Hisarlık contain not one Troy but many—nine major settlements built one atop another spanning more than 4,000 years. Which one was Homer's Troy? Did the Trojan War actually happen? How did a conflict in a distant corner of Anatolia become the foundational narrative of Western literature? These questions have fascinated scholars and the public alike since Schliemann first put spade to soil in 1870.

My own journey with Troy began long before that evening with David Wood's documentary. As a child, I devoured editioned versions of the Iliad, captivated by the rage of Achilles and the tragedy of Hector. In college, I studied Classical Greek, struggling through Homer's intricate hexameters with a dictionary and grammar guide always at hand. Later, as an archaeologist, I examined pottery sherds and architectural fragments from Bronze Age sites across the Mediterranean. But it was that moment in front of my television that crystallized my understanding of Troy's significance—not just as a historical curiosity but as a place where humanity's relationship with its past is uniquely illuminated.

The Convergence of Legend and Reality

What makes Troy extraordinary is the rare convergence of legend and historical reality. Most ancient myths exist in purely literary realms—we have no archaeological evidence for the labors of Hercules or the journey of Odysseus. Conversely, many archaeological sites, while historically significant, lack the rich narrative tradition that brings them to life in the popular imagination. Troy alone stands at the intersection.

When Heinrich Schliemann began digging at Hisarlık in 1870, most scholars considered Homer's Troy to be purely fictional—a literary device rather than a historical place. The prevailing academic wisdom held that the Iliad was valuable as poetry but worthless as history. Schliemann, a businessman turned archaeologist with no formal training, rejected this view. Guided by the ancient texts and his own romantic vision, he set out to prove that Troy was real.

What he found astonished the world. Beneath the surface of an unremarkable hill lay the remains of multiple settlements spanning thousands of years. Though Schliemann's methods were crude by modern standards—he bulldozed through important layers in his haste to find "Priam's Troy"—his discoveries fundamentally changed our understanding of Bronze Age civilization and forced a reevaluation of the relationship between myth and history.

Subsequent excavators refined Schliemann's work with increasingly scientific methods. Wilhelm Dörpfeld in the 1890s, Carl Blegen in the 1930s, and Manfred Korfmann from the 1980s until his death in 2005 each added crucial pieces to the puzzle. We now know that Troy was a significant Bronze Age city strategically positioned to control trade between the Aegean and Black Seas. We know it was destroyed multiple times, including a violent destruction around 1180 BCE that roughly corresponds with the traditional dating of the Trojan War. We know it was likely a Luwian-speaking city called "Wilusa" in Hittite texts, linguistically connected to the Greek "Ilios."

The story of Troy's rediscovery is itself a remarkable tale of archaeological detective work, scholarly debate, and occasional controversy. It's a story of how patient, methodical excavation can bring lost worlds back to light, revealing the complex reality behind legendary events.

From Romantic Quest to Scientific Archaeology

Our understanding of Troy has evolved dramatically from Schliemann's romantic quest to the rigorous scientific archaeology of today. This evolution mirrors the broader development of archaeology as a discipline, from treasure hunting to a sophisticated multidisciplinary science.

Schliemann approached Troy with the Iliad in one hand and a shovel in the other. He was determined to find the Troy of Homer's heroes, and he interpreted everything he found through that lens. When he uncovered a cache of gold objects in 1873, he immediately proclaimed it "Priam's Treasure" and had his wife photographed wearing what he called "the jewels of Helen." This sensationalist approach generated tremendous public interest but distorted the archaeological record.

Wilhelm Dörpfeld, who worked with Schliemann in his later years and continued excavations after his death, brought greater methodological rigor to the site. He recognized that the massive walls and sophisticated architecture of Troy VI (1700-1250 BCE) better matched Homer's description than the much earlier Troy II that Schliemann had favored. Dörpfeld's careful stratigraphic analysis established the sequence of Troy's settlements and connected them to the broader chronology of the Aegean Bronze Age.

Carl Blegen's American expedition in the 1930s further refined our understanding of Troy's history. Using meticulous recording techniques, Blegen documented each layer of occupation in unprecedented detail. He determined that Troy VI had been destroyed by an earthquake, not warfare, and identified the subsequent Troy VIIa (1250-1180 BCE) as the most likely candidate for Homer's Troy. This settlement showed signs of a city under siege—hastily constructed defensive works, houses subdivided to accommodate a larger population, and storage jars embedded in floors for emergency supplies—before being violently destroyed around 1180 BCE.

The most recent major excavations, led by Manfred Korfmann from 1988 until his death in 2005, revolutionized our understanding of Troy's size and significance. Previous excavators had focused almost exclusively on the citadel, the fortified hilltop where the elite lived. Korfmann discovered an extensive "lower city" surrounding the citadel, revealing that Bronze Age Troy was much larger than previously thought—a substantial urban center of 25-30 hectares with a population of 5,000-10,000 people. This discovery transformed Troy from a relatively minor fortress to a significant regional power.

Korfmann also employed cutting-edge technologies—remote sensing, GIS mapping, archaeobotany, and archaeozoology—to build a comprehensive picture of life in Bronze Age Troy. His team's work placed Troy firmly within its historical context as a prosperous trading center at the intersection of Anatolian and Aegean cultural spheres.

Today, archaeologists approach Troy not as a site to be mined for treasures or as a backdrop for Homeric heroes, but as a complex urban settlement that evolved over millennia in response to changing political, economic, and environmental conditions. This scientific approach doesn't diminish Troy's romantic appeal; rather, it enriches our understanding by revealing the actual human community behind the legends.

Why This Book Now

You might reasonably ask why we need another book about Troy. Haven't the stories been told, the ruins excavated, the debates settled? What new perspectives can be offered on a subject that has been studied intensively for over 150 years?

The answer lies in synthesis and timing. The past three decades have seen remarkable advances in our understanding of Troy and its world, but much of this research remains scattered across academic journals, conference proceedings, and specialized monographs inaccessible to general readers. Recent excavations, improved dating techniques, and new interpretations of Hittite texts have transformed our understanding of Bronze Age Troy, yet these discoveries haven't been fully integrated into a comprehensive narrative for non-specialists.

Moreover, we're at a unique moment when archaeological evidence, textual analysis, and cultural studies can be brought together to tell Troy's complete story. Previous works have often focused exclusively on either the archaeological site or the literary tradition, treating them as separate domains. This book weaves together these strands, showing how the physical evidence from Hisarlık intersects with the literary evidence from Homer and other ancient sources, and how both have shaped cultural memory across millennia.

This approach allows us to address questions that cross traditional disciplinary boundaries: How did a historical conflict transform into the epic narrative we know today? What elements of the Trojan War reflect actual Bronze Age warfare, and what elements were later additions? How did the story evolve during the four centuries between Troy's destruction and Homer's composition? Why has this particular ancient site captured the imagination in ways that other equally important archaeological discoveries have not?

By synthesizing archaeological findings, textual analysis, and cultural history, we can now tell a more complete story of Troy than was possible even a decade ago. This book aims to be both an accessible introduction for newcomers to the subject and a fresh perspective for those already familiar with Troy's basic outlines.

Troy and Cultural Memory

Beyond its significance for archaeology and literature, Troy offers a remarkable case study in how human societies preserve memory, create meaning from catastrophe, and transform historical events into enduring narratives. The story of Troy is ultimately about cultural memory—how societies remember, reinterpret, and repurpose their past.

The destruction of Troy around 1180 BCE coincided with a broader collapse of Bronze Age civilization throughout the eastern Mediterranean. This catastrophic period saw the fall of the Mycenaean palaces in Greece, the contraction of the Hittite Empire in Anatolia, and disruptions across the Levant and Egypt. Writing systems were lost, trade networks collapsed, and populations declined dramatically. In Greece, this initiated a "Dark Age" lasting several centuries, during which the art of writing disappeared.

Yet somehow, through this dark age of illiteracy, the memory of Troy survived. The story was preserved through oral tradition, passed down by generations of poets who performed the tales at feasts and festivals. When writing returned to Greece in the eighth century BCE, Homer (or the poets we call "Homer") crystallized this oral tradition into the masterpieces we know as the Iliad and Odyssey.

This process of transmission fascinates me. What begins as historical memory—perhaps accounts from actual participants in a conflict at Troy—gradually transforms into something more universal. Details shift, gods enter the narrative, and the human drama intensifies. Yet archaeological evidence suggests that certain core elements remained remarkably stable—the physical description of Troy's walls, details of Bronze Age weapons and warfare, even specific historical figures whose names appear in both Hittite diplomatic correspondence and Greek epic poetry.

The transformation continues through classical antiquity, as Greek and Roman writers reinterpret Troy for their own purposes. Virgil's Aeneid connects the fall of Troy to the founding of Rome, creating a narrative of renewal from destruction that legitimized Rome's imperial project. During the Middle Ages, European royal families traced their lineage to Trojan refugees, using the ancient story to bolster their political legitimacy.

This pattern of reinterpretation continues into the modern era. Schliemann's excavations were motivated partly by nineteenth-century nationalism, as European powers looked to classical antiquity for cultural validation. Today, Turkey promotes Troy as a heritage site that attracts hundreds of thousands of tourists annually, while contemporary writers and filmmakers continue to adapt the story for new audiences.

Through all these transformations, Troy remains a touchstone for exploring fundamental human concerns: the tension between honor and compassion, the tragedy of war, the relationship between divine will and human agency. Its endurance testifies to its power as a vehicle for cultural memory and meaning-making across vastly different societies.

The Archaeological Detective Story

This book approaches Troy as an archaeological detective story—a case where fragmentary evidence from diverse sources must be carefully assembled to reconstruct events that occurred more than three millennia ago. Like detectives, archaeologists work with incomplete evidence, circumstantial clues, and occasional contradictions. They must interpret what remains while acknowledging what has been lost to time.

The investigation begins with the physical evidence from Hisarlık itself. Each pottery sherd, architectural fragment, and artifact tells part of the story. A layer of burned debris speaks to violent destruction. Arrowheads embedded in walls testify to conflict. Changes in pottery styles reveal shifting trade connections. Human remains—surprisingly rare at Troy—offer poignant glimpses of individual lives cut short.

But physical evidence alone cannot tell the complete story. We must also consider textual sources, beginning with Homer's epics but extending to other Greek and Roman accounts, Hittite diplomatic correspondence, and even Egyptian records that mention conflict in the eastern Mediterranean around the time of Troy's fall.

These diverse sources don't always align neatly. Homer describes events that supposedly occurred four centuries before his time, filtered through generations of oral transmission. Hittite texts mention a place called "Wilusa" that scholars now identify with Troy/Ilios, but they provide only glimpses of its political situation. Egyptian inscriptions describe invasions by mysterious "Sea Peoples" during the period of Troy's destruction but don't specifically mention Troy itself.

Reconciling these disparate pieces of evidence requires careful analysis and sometimes educated speculation. We must consider not only what each source says but also its purpose, reliability, and biases. Homer wasn't writing history in the modern sense; he was composing poetry for performance. Hittite diplomatic correspondence had political objectives that shaped its content. Archaeological evidence can tell us that Troy was destroyed but not always why or by whom.

Despite these challenges, the accumulation of evidence allows us to construct a plausible narrative of Troy's history and destruction. We can say with reasonable confidence that a significant city existed at Hisarlık during the Late Bronze Age, that it was probably the place called Wilusa in Hittite texts and Ilios in Greek tradition, and that it was violently destroyed around 1180 BCE during a period of widespread regional upheaval.

Whether this destruction involved a coalition of Mycenaean Greeks, how long the conflict lasted, and whether it included a wooden horse or a beautiful Helen remains less certain. But uncertainty doesn't diminish the story's power or significance. Indeed, the tension between what we know and what we can only imagine gives Troy its enduring appeal.

Troy Today: Why It Still Matters

Why should we care about a conflict that occurred more than 3,000 years ago in a distant corner of Turkey? What relevance does Troy have for understanding our world today?

The answer lies partly in Troy's role as a witness to one of history's great transitional moments. The destruction of Troy around 1180 BCE coincided with the collapse of the Late Bronze Age international system—a sophisticated network of interconnected states that had dominated the eastern Mediterranean for centuries. This collapse transformed the ancient world, initiating new patterns of migration, trade, and cultural exchange that would eventually give rise to the classical civilizations of Greece and Rome.

Studying this pivotal period helps us understand the fragility of complex societies and the processes through which they collapse and regenerate. The Late Bronze Age collapse has disturbing parallels with contemporary concerns about climate change, resource scarcity, migration, and systemic resilience. Troy stands at the center of this historical inflection point, offering insights into how societies respond to catastrophic change.

Beyond its historical significance, Troy matters because it demonstrates the power of cultural memory to transcend time and space. The story that began with a conflict in Anatolia has become a shared cultural resource that crosses national, linguistic, and temporal boundaries. Concepts derived from the Troy story—the Trojan Horse, the Achilles heel, the face that launched a thousand ships—have become universal metaphors embedded in languages around the world.

This remarkable cultural persistence raises fascinating questions about what makes certain stories endure while others fade. Why did Troy capture the imagination in ways that other ancient sites and conflicts did not? What elements of the narrative give it such universal resonance? How does a story maintain its essential character while adapting to radically different cultural contexts?

Finally, Troy matters because it challenges us to think critically about the relationship between myth and history, between literary representation and archaeological evidence. It reminds us that the boundaries between these domains are often more permeable than we assume. The search for historical Troy doesn't diminish Homer's artistic achievement; rather, it enriches our appreciation of how historical memory transforms into artistic expression.

An Invitation to Discovery

This book invites you to join me on a journey of discovery through Troy's many dimensions. We'll walk the windswept ridge at Hisarlık, where stone foundations mark the outline of a once-thriving city. We'll trace the development of the Troy narrative from its Bronze Age origins through Homer's epics to its modern reinterpretations. We'll examine how archaeological evidence, ancient texts, and cultural traditions complement and sometimes contradict each other, creating a complex picture of Troy's reality and significance.

Our exploration will move between different scales of analysis—from the microscopic examination of soil samples that reveal ancient diet and environment, to the macroscopic view of geopolitical systems that shaped Troy's destiny. We'll meet the archaeologists whose work has transformed our understanding of the site, from Schliemann's romantic treasure-hunting to Korfmann's scientific excavations. And we'll consider how Troy's story continues to evolve in contemporary culture through literature, film, and digital media.

Throughout this journey, I hope to convey both the scholarly rigor that underpins our current understanding of Troy and the sense of wonder that the site still inspires. Troy reminds us that archaeology is not merely the study of ancient objects but a window into the human experience across time—a way of connecting with the hopes, fears, and aspirations of people who lived millennia before us.

The story of Troy is ultimately about the human capacity for cultural transmission across vast stretches of time. It's about how a catastrophic event in a distant corner of Anatolia became transformed into an artistic masterpiece that continues to move us today. It's about the complex interplay between historical reality and imaginative representation that shapes our understanding of the past.

As we explore these themes, I invite you to approach Troy not just as an archaeological problem to be solved or a literary text to be analyzed, but as a place where past and present converge in ways that illuminate both. The stones of Hisarlık and the verses of Homer each tell part of the story. Together, they reveal Troy in all its fascinating complexity—as historical reality, literary masterpiece, and enduring cultural symbol.

The journey awaits. Let's begin.

R Jay Driskill

August 2025

INTRODUCTION: THE ECHO OF ACHILLES' HEEL

Between Myth and Reality

Standing among the windswept ruins of Hisarlik in northwestern Turkey, a visitor today can see fragments of massive stone walls rising from the earth—walls that have witnessed over four millennia of human occupation, destruction, and renewal. These are the stones of Troy, and they carry within their layers one of archaeology's most compelling stories: the quest to separate historical fact from literary legend, to understand how a Bronze Age settlement became Western civilization's most enduring cultural touchstone.

No archaeological site has maintained such a tenacious grip on human imagination across so many centuries. From the moment Homer first sang of Achilles' rage and Hector's courage, Troy has existed simultaneously in multiple realms—as physical place, poetic creation, cultural symbol, and scholarly puzzle. The remarkable fact is not simply that Troy has survived in our collective memory for three thousand years, but that it has remained vibrantly alive, continuously reinterpreted and reimagined by each generation that encounters it.

The persistence of Troy in Western consciousness represents something extraordinary in cultural history. Empires have crumbled, religions have vanished, entire civilizations have been forgotten, yet Troy endures. Why? The answer lies in what we might call the "multidimensional Troy"—the fact that when we speak of Troy, we invoke several distinct yet interconnected realities.

The archaeological Troy sprawls across the mound of Hisarlik, where systematic excavation has revealed at least ten major building phases spanning from approximately 3000 BCE to 500 CE (Korfmann 2004: 23). Here, German archaeologist Heinrich Schliemann first thrust his spade into the earth in 1870, uncovering not one city but a vertical encyclopedia of ancient life—Troy I through Troy X, each settlement built upon the ruins of its predecessor. The physical evidence tells a story of continuous habitation, periodic destruction, and persistent renewal that mirrors the cultural life of the Troy legend itself.

The literary Troy inhabits the pages of Homer's *Iliad*, composed sometime in the eighth century BCE, where heroes and gods walk the same battlefield and human destiny unfolds under divine scrutiny (Powell 2004: 45). This Troy exists in what scholars call "mythic time"—a realm where Achilles can be both historical warrior and timeless symbol, where a ten-year siege can represent both specific conflict and eternal human struggle. When Homer describes Hector's farewell to his wife Andromache, or Priam's supplication to Achilles for his son's body, he creates moments that transcend their Bronze Age setting to speak directly to human experience across all eras.

The symbolic Troy functions as cultural metaphor—shorthand for concepts as varied as doomed love, heroic sacrifice, imperial ambition, and the futility of war. This metaphorical Troy has proven remarkably adaptable, serving Roman imperial propaganda in Virgil's *Aeneid*, inspiring medieval romances, and providing material for everything from Renaissance paintings to modern anti-war literature (Burgess 2001: 12). Each age has discovered in Troy what it needed to find.

The scholarly Troy represents one of archaeology's most fascinating problems—how do we reconcile mythic narrative with material evidence? How do we separate historical kernel from poetic elaboration? This question has driven archaeological investigation at the site for over 150 years and continues to generate scholarly debate today (Latacz 2004: 78).

Understanding Troy's enduring appeal requires us to follow the archaeological detective work that has gradually illuminated the relationship between these different Troys. The story begins with poetry, but it achieves
its modern resonance through the spade and trowel, the pottery sherd and
the carbon date, the patient accumulation of evidence that characterizes
archaeological inquiry.

Homer's *Iliad* established the narrative framework that would captivate
Western imagination for millennia. Composed in the eighth century BCE,
the epic focuses on a few crucial weeks during the tenth year of the Greek
siege of Troy (West 2011: 156). The poet tells us nothing of the war's
beginning—Paris's abduction of Helen, the assembly of the Greek fleet at
Aulis—nor of its end—the wooden horse, the city's fall, the slaughter of
its inhabitants. Instead, Homer concentrates on the psychological drama of
warriors facing death, the tension between individual honor and collective
responsibility, the grief of both victors and vanquished.

What makes the *Iliad* archaeologically significant is not its historical accuracy—Homer was composing poetry, not writing history—but its preservation of cultural memory. The epic contains what scholars call "Dark Age"
memories of an earlier Bronze Age world, memories transmitted orally across
centuries of social upheaval (Morris 1997: 234). When Homer describes
bronze weapons alongside iron ones, or mentions specific details of Bronze
Age warfare and society, he provides tantalizing glimpses of a world that
archaeological excavation has begun to recover.

For the ancient Greeks themselves, the Trojan War represented historical
fact, not fiction. Greek tradition placed Troy's fall around 1184 BCE, and
cities throughout the Greek world claimed connections to the legendary
heroes (Parker 2011: 89). When the fifth-century historian Thucydides wrote
about the war, he accepted its basic historicity while questioning poetic
exaggeration: "The Trojan War did take place, but probably not on the scale
that poets have represented" (Thucydides 1.10.3).

Archaeological investigation of this question began in earnest with Heinrich Schliemann's controversial excavations. Schliemann, a German businessman who made his fortune in various enterprises before turning to archaeology, represents both the possibilities and the problems of nineteenth-century excavation methods (Traill 1995: 67). His techniques were crude by modern standards—he dug massive trenches through the mound, destroying much valuable stratigraphy in his haste to reach what he believed were the Homeric levels. Yet his fundamental insight proved correct: Hisarlik was indeed the site of a major Bronze Age settlement that could plausibly be identified with legendary Troy.

Schliemann's most famous discovery was a cache of gold artifacts he dubbed "Priam's Treasure," after Homer's Trojan king. Though later archaeology has shown that these objects actually date to Troy II (c. 2500-2300 BCE), centuries before any possible historical Trojan War, Schliemann's announcement electrified the world (Easton 1994: 123). Troy was real—not in every detail of Homer's description, but as a place where Bronze Age peoples had lived, fought, and died.

Subsequent excavations have refined and complicated this picture. Wilhelm Dörpfeld, who worked with Schliemann and continued excavating after the older man's death, applied more systematic methods and identified Troy VI as the most likely candidate for Homeric Troy (Dörpfeld 1902: 45). American archaeologist Carl Blegen's excavations in the 1930s revealed that Troy VI had been destroyed by earthquake rather than warfare, leading him to propose Troy VIIa as the historical Troy (Blegen 1963: 178).

The most recent excavations, conducted by an international team under Manfred Korfmann from 1988 until his death in 2005, have revolutionized our understanding of the site (Korfmann 2001: 356). Using modern archaeological techniques including ground-penetrating radar, magnetometry, and computer mapping, Korfmann's team discovered that Bronze Age Troy was far larger than previously imagined. The citadel that earlier archaeologists had excavated represented only the acropolis of a much larger settlement that included an extensive lower city protected by its own fortification system.

This expanded Troy of the Late Bronze Age (Troy VI and VIIa, c. 1700-1180 BCE) emerges from the archaeological record as a significant regional power. The fortification walls, built with massive limestone blocks in a distinctive style, demonstrate sophisticated engineering knowledge (Becks 2006: 234). The citadel contained substantial buildings including what appears to be a palace complex, while the lower city housed workshops, residential areas, and storage facilities. Pottery analysis reveals trade connections extending across the Aegean and into central Anatolia, while animal bones indicate a mixed economy based on agriculture, animal husbandry, and craft production (Korfmann 2004: 167).

Perhaps most significantly, the archaeological evidence suggests that Troy VIIa was destroyed by warfare around 1180 BCE—a date that aligns remarkably well with traditional Greek chronology for the fall of Troy (Latacz 2001: 89). The destruction level contains evidence of burning, hastily buried hoards of valuable objects, and skeletons of individuals who died violent deaths. While this does not prove that Greeks besieged and captured the city, it does indicate that Troy VIIa met a violent end at approximately the right time to be connected with legendary events.

Yet the archaeological Troy differs significantly from Homer's literary creation. The material culture shows Troy was part of an Anatolian, not Greek, cultural sphere. Inscriptional evidence suggests the inhabitants spoke Luwian, an Indo-European language related to Hittite (Hawkins 1998: 45). The city's connections were primarily with other Anatolian settlements and with the Hittite Empire to the east, not with the Mycenaean Greek world across the Aegean. When Homer describes Troy as a Greek-style city ruled by Greek-style kings, he may be projecting his own eighth-century world onto a much earlier and culturally different reality.

This raises one of archaeology's most intriguing questions: what is the relationship between the historical Bronze Age settlement at Hisarlik and the Troy of Greek legend? The answer requires us to think carefully about how cultural memory works, how historical events become transformed into mythic narrative through centuries of oral tradition.

The process likely began with real historical events—perhaps a series of conflicts between Mycenaean Greeks and the inhabitants of northwestern Anatolia during the Late Bronze Age collapse period (c. 1200-1150 BCE). Archaeological evidence from various Aegean sites indicates this was indeed a time of widespread warfare, population movement, and political upheaval (Drews 1993: 234). Troy, as a wealthy city controlling access to the Dardanelles and trade routes between Europe and Asia, would have been a natural target for raiders or conquerors.

Over the centuries that followed, memories of these conflicts would have been preserved in oral tradition, gradually taking on the characteristics that anthropologists observe in heroic poetry worldwide—the compression of multiple events into a single narrative, the elevation of historical figures into legendary heroes, the addition of supernatural elements that explain otherwise inexplicable events (Lord 1960: 156). By the time Homer composed the *Iliad*, what may have begun as historical memory had been transformed into something much richer and more complex—a story that used the past to explore timeless questions about honor, mortality, and human nature.

This transformation from history to myth does not diminish Troy's significance—if anything, it enhances it. The archaeological Troy provides the material foundation, the proof that Homer's story was grounded in real places and real events. But the literary Troy transcends its historical origins to become something larger—a meditation on human experience that speaks across cultural and temporal boundaries.

The Roman appropriation of Troy demonstrates this process clearly. When Virgil composed the *Aeneid* in the late first century BCE, he took the Greek story of Troy's destruction and transformed it into a Roman story of destiny and renewal (Williams 1997: 67). The defeated Trojans, led by the hero Aeneas, become the ancestors of Rome's imperial glory. What had been a Greek victory narrative becomes a Roman origin story, demonstrating Troy's remarkable adaptability as cultural symbol.

This adaptability has continued into the modern era. Medieval Europeans, largely cut off from Greek sources, knew Troy primarily through Latin authors and forged "eyewitness" accounts that portrayed Trojan heroes as chivalric knights (Benson 1980: 123). Renaissance artists found in Trojan themes opportunities to explore questions of love, honor, and political power. Modern writers have used Troy as a lens through which to examine everything from the psychology of warfare to the position of women in patriarchal societies.

What archaeological investigation has added to this cultural conversation is not definitive answers but rather a new dimension of engagement with the Troy story. When we know that real people lived and died at Hisarlik, that real walls were built and destroyed there, that real artifacts were buried in the earth where they waited for modern excavation, we encounter Troy not simply as literary creation but as historical reality—complex, ambiguous, but undeniably real.

The ongoing excavations at Troy continue to refine our understanding of this relationship between archaeological and literary evidence. Each season's work adds new pieces to the puzzle—fragments of pottery that reveal trade connections, building foundations that illuminate urban planning, botanical remains that document ancient diet, written documents that provide glimpses of the languages and cultures of Bronze Age Anatolia (Rose 2014: 234).

Yet for all our scientific methods and sophisticated techniques, the Troy that emerges from archaeological investigation remains tantalizingly incomplete. We can document the city's material culture, trace its trade relationships, analyze its architecture, but we cannot recover the thoughts and feelings of its inhabitants, cannot hear their voices or understand their motivations. For that, we still need Homer—not as historical source but as imaginative guide to the human dimensions of Bronze Age life.

This is perhaps Troy's greatest gift to both archaeology and culture—its demonstration that science and art, evidence and imagination, can work together rather than in opposition. The archaeologist's Troy and the poet's Troy illuminate different aspects of human experience, both necessary for a full understanding of the past. When we stand among the ruins at Hisarlik, we see not just stones and pottery sherds but the setting for one of humanity's greatest stories—a story that began in the Bronze Age but continues to unfold with each new generation that encounters it.

Troy reminds us that the past is never simply past. It lives on in our cultural memory, in the stories we tell about ourselves, in the questions we ask about human nature and human destiny. The wooden horse may have breached the walls of the Bronze Age city, but the idea of Troy has proven indestructible, continuing to inspire archaeologists and poets, scholars and storytellers, all of us who seek to understand how the ancient world shaped the modern one.

As we continue to excavate both the physical remains and the cultural legacy of Troy, we participate in a conversation that spans three millennia—a testament to the power of great stories to transcend their historical origins and speak to the deepest concerns of human experience. In this sense, Troy never truly fell. It lives on, as alive in our imagination as it once was on the windswept plain of northwestern Anatolia.

CHAPTER 1

OF GODS AND MEN

The Divine Origins of the Trojan War

Picture an archaeologist carefully brushing dirt from a bronze spearhead in the ruins of Troy VIIa, circa 1180 BCE. The weapon is real enough—its bronze alloy analyzed, its typology catalogued, its position in the destruction layer precisely recorded. Yet this tangible artifact represents only the beginning of a story that ancient audiences understood as cosmic drama played out between gods and mortals on the plains of Troy.

When we examine the archaeological evidence from the end of the Bronze Age, we find a world convulsed by warfare and destruction. Burned cities dot the landscape from Anatolia to the Aegean, precious objects lie buried in hasty hoards, and entire populations seem to have vanished into the archaeological record (Drews 1993: 48). But the literary tradition preserved by Homer reveals something equally significant: how Bronze Age peoples understood these catastrophic events not as mere political or economic conflicts but as moments when divine will intersected with human history.

To understand the Trojan War as ancient Greeks conceived it, we must think like Bronze Age peoples rather than modern historians. For Homer's audiences, divine causation didn't compete with human motivation—it explained it. The gods didn't replace political and military factors—they revealed the cosmic sig-

21

nificance of earthly struggles. When we excavate the cultural layers of meaning surrounding Troy's destruction, we discover a sophisticated worldview where personal decisions carry consequences across generations and where the actions of kings and heroes reflect the will of immortal powers.

A Wedding to Remember: Bronze Age Royal Marriage and Divine Politics

The divine origins of the Trojan War begin with a wedding feast that, while mythological, preserves authentic memories of Bronze Age aristocratic practices. Recent excavations at Mycenaean palace sites like Pylos and Tiryns have revealed elaborate feasting halls with massive hearths, decorated walls, and clear evidence for large-scale ceremonial dining (Davis and Bennet 1999: 111). When Homer describes divine banquets, he draws on cultural traditions of palatial ceremony that archaeologists can now document in the material record.

The marriage of the mortal hero Peleus to the sea nymph Thetis, preserved in sources like Pindar's eighth Isthmian Ode, establishes the narrative framework for the entire Trojan cycle (Pindar, Isthmian 8.27-35). This divine-mortal union reflects documented Bronze Age practices where aristocratic marriages created political alliances and where religious ceremony legitimized royal power. As anthropologist Walter Burkert observed, "Greek myth preserves in narrative form the social realities of Bronze Age kingship" (Burkert 1985: 120).

The prophecy surrounding this marriage—that Thetis would bear a son greater than his father—reflects ancient Near Eastern royal ideology where divine legitimacy passed through dynastic succession. Hittite texts from Boğazköy contain similar prophecies about royal inheritance, suggesting that such narrative patterns were widespread in Bronze Age court culture (Beckman 1999: 67). Zeus's calculated solution—marrying Thetis to a mortal to ensure her son would be merely the greatest of heroes rather than a threat to divine order—demonstrates the kind of strategic political thinking that characterizes Bronze Age diplomatic correspondence.

But here's where the story becomes archaeologically fascinating: the exclusion of Eris, goddess of discord, from the wedding guest list reflects the real political dangers of Bronze Age court ceremony. Palace archives reveal that slights to important figures could trigger conflicts lasting generations. The golden apple that Eris threw among the remaining guests—inscribed "to the fairest"—introduces the object that will ultimately destroy Troy.

The Judgment of Paris: Material Culture and Cultural Memory

That golden apple provides our entry point into understanding how Greeks preserved Bronze Age memories through mythic narrative. Archaeological evidence from Late Bronze Age sites reveals the central importance of prestige objects in elite culture. Inscribed golden vessels, elaborate jewelry, and ceremonial weapons functioned not just as luxury goods but as markers of status and divine favor (Rehak 1995: 91). When we find such objects in Bronze Age contexts, we're looking at the material foundation for stories like the apple of discord.

The contest between Hera, Athena, and Aphrodite for the golden apple reflects documented tensions within Bronze Age royal households, where competing queens, concubines, and female relatives vied for influence. Linear B tablets from Pylos record offerings to various goddesses, suggesting that religious devotion was closely tied to political allegiance in Mycenaean palace culture (Shelmerdine 1999: 144). Divine competition mirrors earthly rivalry.

Paris's role as judge wasn't arbitrary but reflected Bronze Age legal practices where disputes were submitted to neutral arbiters—often foreign princes or respected elders. The Hittite archives contain numerous examples of such arbitration, including cases where marriage disputes required third-party judgment (Beckman 1999: 156). Zeus's choice of a Trojan prince to judge between Greek goddesses may preserve memory of actual diplomatic practices where international disputes demanded neutral resolution.

Consider the bribes offered by each goddess: kingship from Hera, military prowess from Athena, the most beautiful woman from Aphrodite. These correspond precisely to the three documented sources of Bronze Age royal power—political authority, military success, and prestigious marriage alliances. The fact that Paris chose love over power reflects a narrative pattern found throughout ancient Near Eastern literature, where passion disrupts rational political calculation (Foster 2005: 234).

Helen: Symbolic Capital and Marriage Diplomacy

Helen's departure from Sparta with Paris provides the immediate cause for war, but understanding her significance requires examining both her mythic status and the political realities of Bronze Age marriage diplomacy. As daughter of Zeus and the most beautiful woman in the world, Helen represents what anthropologists call "symbolic capital"—her possession confers legitimacy and prestige that transcends mere political alliance (Bourdieu 1977: 171).

The oath sworn by Helen's suitors to defend her chosen husband's rights reflects actual Bronze Age treaty practices documented in Hittite archives. These texts reveal elaborate oath ceremonies where kings swore to uphold marriage agreements and support allies in case of violations (Beckman 1999: 89). Archaeological evidence from Mycenaean palaces shows that such ceremonies involved ritual feasting, animal sacrifice, and the display of precious objects—exactly the elaborate proceedings described in later Greek sources.

When Helen left Sparta with Paris, she violated more than personal relationships—she shattered the entire network of obligations that held Bronze Age elite society together. As classicist M.I. Finley demonstrated through analysis of Homeric social structures, aristocratic society depended on reciprocal gift-exchange and marriage alliances that created webs of mutual obligation (Finley

1977: 114). Helen's departure with Paris broke these bonds and demanded restoration through warfare.

The enduring ambiguity surrounding Helen's agency—did she go willingly or was she abducted?—reflects the complex legal status of women in Bronze Age society. Linear B tablets suggest that high-status women could own property and exercise religious authority, but their political choices remained constrained by family obligations and dynastic considerations (Shelmerdine 1999: 201). The conflicting traditions about Helen's motivation may preserve memory of actual disputes about women's legal capacity in Bronze Age marriage law.

Prophecies and Divine Planning: Bronze Age Decision-Making

The prophecies that shaped the Trojan War reflect Bronze Age religious practices documented through archaeological and textual evidence. Divination was central to royal decision-making in the Late Bronze Age, as demonstrated by libraries of omen texts found at sites like Mari and Nineveh, and by the prominence of religious officials in Linear B administrative records (Starr 1983: 67).

The prophecy that Troy could not be conquered without Achilles corresponds to patterns found throughout ancient Near Eastern military texts, where specific heroes or sacred objects were deemed essential for victory. The Hittite archives contain similar prophecies about military requirements, suggesting that such traditions were widespread in Bronze Age strategic thinking (Beckman 1999: 178).

Cassandra's gift of prophecy cursed with disbelief reflects documented tension between religious authority and political power in Bronze Age courts. Archaeological evidence from Pylos and Knossos shows that religious specialists held significant administrative positions but remained subject to royal oversight (Shelmerdine 1999: 289). The pattern of ignored warnings found in Cassandra's story parallels actual historical events where religious advisors correctly predicted disasters that rulers chose to ignore.

Perhaps most intriguingly, fragments of the Epic Cycle suggest that Zeus planned the Trojan War as population control—a reflection of Late Bronze Age realities where demographic pressure may have contributed to palatial collapse. Archaeological evidence for agricultural intensification, settlement expansion, and resource depletion in the thirteenth century BCE supports theories that overpopulation contributed to Bronze Age instability (Tainter 1988: 45). Even divine motivations may preserve historical memory.

Divine Factions: Religious Politics in Material Culture

The division of Olympian gods into pro-Trojan and pro-Greek factions reflects the religious politics of Bronze Age interstate relations. Archaeological evidence from cult sites across the Aegean shows that different communities emphasized different aspects of shared religious traditions, often reflecting political alliances and cultural preferences (Marinatos 1993: 156).

Aphrodite's support for Troy and Athena's backing of the Greeks correspond to documented patterns of divine patronage in Bronze Age texts. The Hittite archives record how different gods were invoked to support different sides in conflicts, with elaborate rituals designed to secure divine favor (Singer 2002: 78). When Homer describes divine interventions in battle, he draws on traditions of religious warfare that were central to Bronze Age military culture.

Poseidon's grudge against Troy for being cheated by King Laomedon reflects actual Bronze Age practices where religious and economic obligations were intertwined. Linear B tablets record elaborate temple economies where gods "owned" land, livestock, and craftsmen, and where failure to meet religious obligations could trigger political crises (Killen 1999: 201). The story of Poseidon and Apollo building Troy's walls preserves memory of the massive labor investments required for Late Bronze Age fortification projects.

The Archaeology of Divine Warfare

While we cannot excavate divine interventions, archaeological evidence does illuminate the religious dimensions of Bronze Age warfare. Weapons found in votive deposits show that military equipment was regularly dedicated to gods, while inscribed armor and weapons demonstrate the belief that divine favor was essential for victory (Kilian-Dirlmeier 1993: 134).

The divine armor forged for Achilles by Hephaestus corresponds to elaborate metalworking traditions documented at Bronze Age sites. Analysis of weapons from Troy VIIa and contemporary sites reveals sophisticated metallurgical techniques and artistic decoration that elevated warfare equipment to the level of religious art (Muhly 1985: 67). When Homer describes divinely crafted weapons, he draws on cultural memories of actual Bronze Age metalworking traditions.

Ritual practices associated with Bronze Age warfare—divination before battle, sacrifices for divine favor, elaborate funeral ceremonies for fallen heroes—provide the cultural context for understanding how ancient audiences interpreted divine involvement in the Trojan War. Archaeological evidence from sites like Pylos shows that religious ritual was integral to military organization, not an overlay imposed by later literary tradition (Bendall 2007: 156).

Reading Divine Causation Through Archaeological Evidence

The divine origins of the Trojan War, when examined through archaeological evidence, reveal how Bronze Age peoples understood the relationship between supernatural and natural causation. Rather than seeing these as competing explanations, they viewed divine will as operating through human agency, political calculation, and material circumstances.

This perspective helps explain why Homer's account preserves accurate details about Bronze Age material culture while embedding them in narratives of divine intervention. The bronze weapons, tower shields, boar's tusk helmets, and other military equipment described in the Iliad correspond closely to objects found in Late Bronze Age archaeological contexts (Borchhardt 1977: 89). The religious interpretations reflect how Bronze Age peoples understood these material realities within cosmic frameworks.

When archaeologists uncover evidence for the violent destruction of Troy VIIa around 1180 BCE, we find the material traces of events that Greeks transformed into stories of divine justice, cosmic conflict, and heroic destiny. The burned buildings, scattered weapons, and buried treasures speak to the reality of Bronze Age warfare, while the literary tradition preserves the cultural meanings that ancient peoples attached to these events.

The Enduring Power of Divine Narrative

The enduring power of the Trojan War narrative lies precisely in this combination of material reality and mythic interpretation. Archaeological investigation reveals the historical foundations—real cities, real weapons, real destruction—while literary analysis illuminates the cultural frameworks through which ancient peoples understood these events as moments when human and divine realms intersected.

As we continue to excavate both the physical remains and the textual traditions associated with Troy, we discover that the question is not whether divine causation is "real" in a modern sense, but how Bronze Age peoples used concepts of divine intervention to understand the complex relationships between individual choices, political forces, and historical change. The gods of the Iliad represent not primitive superstition but sophisticated attempts to comprehend how personal decisions carry consequences across generations, how local conflicts reflect cosmic patterns, and how human struggles participate in larger narratives of justice, fate, and meaning.

In this sense, the divine origins of the Trojan War offer us insight not just into ancient religious beliefs but into Bronze Age ways of understanding causation, responsibility, and historical change. When we stand among the ruins of Troy VIIa and imagine the flames that consumed the city around 1180 BCE, we participate in a cultural conversation that began with the first audiences who heard

28

these stories and continues with every reader who encounters Homer's account of gods and heroes struggling on the windy plain of Troy.

The bronze spearhead with which we began tells only part of the story. The complete narrative emerges when we combine archaeological evidence with literary tradition, recognizing that Bronze Age peoples understood their world as a place where divine purposes worked through human actions, where individual choices shaped cosmic destinies, and where the fall of cities like Troy represented not merely political disasters but moments when the eternal patterns of justice, passion, and consequence played out in historical time.

CHAPTER 2
THE FACE THAT LAUNCHED A THOUSAND SHIPS

Helen's Abduction and the Gathering of Forces

In the 1990s, archaeologists working below the ancient citadel of Troy made a discovery that would have thrilled Homer. The bay that the poet describes as sheltering the Greek fleet—a harbor large enough for over a thousand ships—had actually existed in the Late Bronze Age, though three millennia of river silt have since filled it completely (Korfmann 2001: 45). This find illuminates something crucial about the Trojan War stories: they preserve authentic Bronze Age knowledge about real landscapes where real people lived, traded, fought, and died.

The tale of Helen's departure from Sparta and the massive Greek response represents far more than mythic drama. When we excavate the cultural layers embedded in these narratives, we discover sophisticated knowledge about palace diplomacy, marriage politics, and military organization that corresponds remarkably to what Linear B tablets and Hittite archives reveal about how Bronze Age kingdoms actually operated. The transformation of a personal scandal into international warfare preserves authentic memories of how Bronze Age society actually functioned.

A Diplomatic Mission Gone Wrong

Paris's journey to Sparta wasn't a romantic adventure but a formal diplomatic mission, as Apollodorus carefully notes (Epitome 3.3). Recent analysis of Linear B tablets from Pylos and Knossos reveals the elaborate administrative machinery that Mycenaean palaces maintained for receiving foreign dignitaries—detailed inventories of gifts, accommodations, and ceremonial protocols that make diplomacy look like the complex bureaucratic enterprise it actually was (Shelmerdine 1999: 144).

The Late Bronze Age operated through what Eric Cline calls "the first international age," characterized by extensive diplomatic gift-exchange between the Great Kings of Egypt, Hatti, Babylonia, Assyria, and Mitanni (Cline 2014: 89). Troy's participation in these networks is confirmed by archaeological evidence—imported pottery from Cyprus, luxury goods from Egypt, and metallurgical techniques from the Caucasus found at the site demonstrate connections extending from the Baltic amber routes to the Nubian gold mines.

When the Cypria describes Paris arriving with gifts from Troy's eastern trading partners, it preserves accurate memory of how diplomatic missions actually functioned. Archaeological analysis of prestige objects found in Late Bronze Age contexts shows that such gifts served multiple purposes: they demonstrated the sender's wealth and international connections, established reciprocal obligations between rulers, and created networks of alliance that could be activated during military crises (Rehak 1995: 67).

The detail that Menelaus departed for Crete during Paris's visit reflects another documented aspect of Bronze Age royal culture—the constant obligation to attend major ceremonial events in allied kingdoms. Linear B tablets reference royal travel for religious festivals, funeral games, and diplomatic ceremonies, suggesting that such absences were regular features of palace life that sometimes created dangerous opportunities (Davis and Bennet 1999: 178).

The Question Nobody Could Answer: Was Helen Willing?

The ambiguity surrounding Helen's departure—whether willing elopement or forced abduction—reflects genuine complexities in Bronze Age marriage practices that archaeological evidence helps us understand. Linear B tablets record women with various legal statuses: royal wives, concubines, captives, and religious personnel (Shelmerdine 1999: 201). The distinction between legitimate marriage, elopement, and abduction appears to have been as legally and socially complex in the Bronze Age as later literary sources suggest.

Archaeological evidence from Mycenaean palace sites reveals that high-status women could own property, conduct business, and exercise religious authority, but their political choices remained tightly constrained by family obligations and dynastic considerations (Killen 1999: 156). The ra-wi-ja-ja (possibly "captives" or "workers") mentioned in Linear B tablets indicate that seizure of women during raids was a recognized social category, while Hittite diplomatic texts contain complaints about royal women fleeing arranged marriages—suggesting that female elopement, though scandalous, was not unprecedented (Beckman 1999: 234).

Homer's psychologically complex portrayal of Helen—expressing regret while acknowledging her choice to "follow" Paris—corresponds to Bronze Age legal concepts where women's actions could be simultaneously voluntary and constrained by social circumstances. When Helen tells Priam, "Would that evil death had been my pleasure when I followed your son here," she articulates the kind of mixed agency that Bronze Age marriage practices actually involved (Homer, Iliad 3.173-175).

The multiple versions of Helen's story preserved in later sources—Herodotus's account of her detention in Egypt, Stesichorus's phantom Helen—reflect ongoing cultural negotiations about female responsibility that archaeological evidence suggests were already complex in the Bronze Age (Herodotus 2.113-120). Rather than later inventions designed to absolve Helen, these variants may preserve alternative Bronze Age traditions about how to interpret ambiguous cases of marriage, elopement, and abduction.

Sacred Oaths and Bronze Age Treaty-Making

The oath sworn by Helen's suitors to defend her chosen husband's marriage rights wasn't a literary invention but reflects actual Bronze Age treaty practices documented in Hittite archives and referenced in Linear B administrative records. Such oath ceremonies involved elaborate rituals designed to invoke divine enforcement of human agreements—exactly the kind of religious-political hybrid that characterized Bronze Age interstate relations (Beckman 1999: 89).

Archaeological evidence from Mycenaean palace sites shows that such ceremonies required extensive preparation: ritual feasting, animal sacrifice, display of precious objects, and participation by religious officials whose administrative roles are carefully documented in Linear B tablets (Bendall 2007: 134). When Apollodorus describes Tyndareus making all suitors swear to support Helen's chosen husband, he preserves memory of how Bronze Age kingdoms actually created binding military alliances through religious ceremony.

This oath transformed Helen's departure from a personal affront into what Bronze Age peoples would have recognized as a violation of sacred treaty obligations. Linear B tablets record the administrative complexity of maintaining such alliance networks—tracking obligations, coordinating military support, and managing the gift-exchange relationships that sustained diplomatic ties (Shelmerdine 1999: 289). Paris's violation of xenia (guest-friendship) with Menelaus disrupted not just personal relationships but the entire web of reciprocal obligations that held Bronze Age elite society together.

Military Reality Check: Could Greece Really Mobilize 100,000 Men?

The Catalog of Ships in Iliad Book 2, listing 1,186 ships and perhaps 100,000 men, clearly exaggerates the scale of Bronze Age military mobilization by orders of magnitude, but the geographic and political relationships it describes correspond closely to archaeological evidence for Mycenaean political organization (Homer, Iliad 2.494-759). Agamemnon's hegemony over much of the Peloponnese aligns with evidence for Mycenae's prominence in Late Bronze Age Greece, while many locations named in the catalog correspond to known Mycenaean settlements identified through archaeological survey.

Linear B tablets from Pylos provide our best evidence for actual Bronze Age military organization, recording mobilizations of several hundred men rather than tens of thousands (Shelmerdine 1999: 345). The famous o-ka tablets document the complex administrative requirements for equipping and provisioning even relatively small military expeditions—listing bronze weapons, leather armor, chariots, and supplies needed for campaigns. These records suggest that the logistical capabilities described in the Catalog of Ships would have been far beyond Bronze Age administrative capacity.

Archaeological analysis of Mycenaean military equipment confirms both the sophistication of Bronze Age warfare technology and its practical limitations. Bronze weapons found at sites like Mycenae and Pylos demonstrate advanced metallurgical techniques, while Linear B records of bronze allocation show that metal resources were carefully controlled by palace administrations (Kilian-Dirlmeier 1993: 78). However, the quantities involved—measured in kilograms rather than tons—suggest military forces much smaller than epic tradition claims.

The ten-year duration of the Trojan War may reflect the protracted nature of Bronze Age conflicts rather than continuous siege warfare. Archaeological evidence shows that Late Bronze Age wars typically involved seasonal campaigns, extended truces, and gradual wearing-down of enemy resources rather than massive pitched battles (Drews 1993: 156). The pattern of raiding and counter-raiding that the Iliad describes may preserve accurate memory of how such conflicts actually developed over time.

Reluctant Heroes and Bronze Age Military Service

The stories of Odysseus and Achilles attempting to avoid military service reflect documented tensions in Bronze Age military organization between royal obligation and personal preference. Linear B tablets record various categories of military service, including personnel designated as followers of specific nobles and craftsmen with military obligations (Shelmerdine 1999: 367). The administrative complexity suggests that military mobilization involved negotiation and compulsion rather than automatic compliance.

Odysseus's feigned madness, as described by Hyginus, corresponds to documented cases in Bronze Age texts where individuals attempted to avoid military or administrative obligations through claims of incapacity (Hyginus, Fabulae 95). Hittite archives contain legal proceedings involving disputes over military service, suggesting that such resistance was common enough to require formal administrative procedures (Beckman 1999: 145).

The prophecy that Achilles would either live long obscurely or die young gloriously reflects Bronze Age warrior culture documented through archaeological evidence of elaborate burial practices for military elites. The Shaft Graves at Mycenae, Warrior Graves at Pylos, and similar elite burials throughout the Aegean show that martial prowess was the primary path to lasting commemoration in Bronze Age society (Voutsaki 1995: 89). Thetis's attempt to hide Achilles among Lycomedes's daughters preserves memory of the real tensions between maternal protection and warrior ideology that must have characterized aristocratic households.

The detail that Odysseus discovered Achilles by observing his reaction to weapons reflects the central importance of military equipment in Bronze Age elite identity. Archaeological analysis of bronze swords, spears, and shields from

Mycenaean contexts shows that weapons functioned as markers of social status as well as military tools (Borgna 2003: 134). The story preserves accurate cultural knowledge about how deeply martial identity was embedded in Bronze Age aristocratic socialization from childhood.

Divine Consultation and Military Planning

The religious ceremonies surrounding the expedition's departure—omens at Aulis, prophetic sacrifices, divination rituals—correspond to documented Bronze Age practices for seeking divine approval of military ventures. Linear B tablets record elaborate religious preparations for military campaigns, including offerings to specific deities, consultation with religious specialists, and performance of protective rituals (Bendall 2007: 201). War was too important to undertake without divine sanction.

The serpent eating nine sparrows and their mother, interpreted by Calchas as predicting nine years of war followed by victory in the tenth, reflects Bronze Age divination practices documented in Near Eastern texts and referenced in Aegean administrative records. Such omens served both to provide divine sanction for military ventures and to prepare participants psychologically for extended campaigns that might last much longer than initially anticipated (Starr 1983: 156).

The sacrifice of Iphigenia, whether literal or symbolic, represents the kind of extreme religious obligation that Bronze Age warfare could require. Archaeological evidence from cult sites across the Aegean shows that human sacrifice, while rare, was practiced during periods of crisis when normal offerings seemed insufficient to secure divine favor (Marinatos 1993: 178). The story preserves memory of how military necessity could override normal social relationships, establishing the moral ambiguity that would characterize the entire conflict.

Navigation Challenges and Naval Logistics

The expedition's initial error in landing at Mysia rather than Troy reflects genuine navigational challenges of Bronze Age seafaring. Without precise maps or sophisticated navigational instruments, identifying specific coastal locations required local knowledge that long-distance expeditions typically lacked (McGrail 2001: 234). The Mediterranean was a big place when you were navigating by landmarks and dead reckoning.

Archaeological analysis of Bronze Age ships and harbors reveals the logistical complexity of maintaining large fleets. Mycenaean pottery found throughout the Aegean traces maritime trade routes that connected Cyprus, Crete, and the mainland, while harbor installations at sites like Pylos show the infrastructure required for naval operations (Wedde 2000: 156). The mention of supply ships from Lemnos reflects real understanding of how extended military campaigns required established bases and regular provisioning from secure territories.

Recent geomorphological studies at Troy have confirmed that the bay Homer describes as sheltering the Greek fleet actually existed in the Late Bronze Age, providing natural harbor facilities that would have been essential for such an expedition (Korfmann 2001: 89). This discovery demonstrates how accurately epic tradition preserved Bronze Age geographic knowledge across centuries of oral transmission.

Troy's Strategic Advantages

Archaeological excavation at Troy has revealed the formidable defensive position that faced any attacking force. The massive stone walls of Troy VI/VIIa, up to five meters thick with sophisticated towers and gates, represent some of the most impressive Bronze Age fortification architecture in Anatolia (Becks 2006: 145). The city's location on a hill overlooking the Dardanelles provided both defensive advantage and control over crucial trade routes connecting the Black Sea with the Mediterranean.

Linear B tablets and Hittite diplomatic texts reveal the alliance systems that protected major Bronze Age settlements. The Alaksandu Treaty between the Hittite king and the ruler of Wilusa (almost certainly Troy) establishes military obligations that would have provided Troy with powerful backing against foreign aggression (Beckman 1999: 178). When Homer describes Troy's numerous allies arriving from across Anatolia, he preserves memory of how Bronze Age warfare actually involved competing alliance networks rather than simple bilateral conflicts.

The protracted nature of the siege reflects Bronze Age military technology's limitations. Archaeological evidence shows that effective siege equipment—catapults, battering rams, siege towers—had not yet been developed (Drews 1993: 234). Bronze Age armies could starve out defenders or capture cities through treachery, but direct assault on well-fortified positions was extremely difficult and costly.

Women in Charge: Palace Administration During Wartime

While epic poetry focuses on male warriors, Linear B tablets reveal that women assumed crucial administrative roles during periods of male absence. Female religious officials, textile supervisors, and landholders documented in palace archives suggest that kingdoms could function effectively under female leadership when men departed for military campaigns (Shelmerdine 1999: 401). Penelope's management of Odysseus's household during his twenty-year absence reflects real Bronze Age administrative practices rather than poetic invention.

Clytemnestra's response to Agamemnon's departure—taking Aegisthus as lover and plotting revenge for Iphigenia's sacrifice—corresponds to documented cases where royal women exercised political agency during their husbands' military campaigns. Hittite texts reference similar situations where queens assumed power and pursued independent political agendas that sometimes conflicted with their husbands' policies (Beckman 1999: 267).

Archaeological evidence from Bronze Age Greece shows no significant disruption in settlement patterns or economic activity that might indicate massive military mobilization. This suggests that the Trojan War, if historical, involved elite warriors rather than mass armies—exactly the kind of limited conflict that Bronze Age administrative systems could actually support without collapsing domestic society.

Social Memory and Archaeological Truth

The transformation of Helen's departure into a decade-long war preserves sophisticated Bronze Age knowledge about diplomacy, military organization, religious practice, and interstate relations that archaeologists can now verify through material evidence. The cultural practices described in epic tradition—elaborate gift-exchange, oath-bound alliances, palace administration, divine consultation—accurately reflect how Bronze Age societies actually functioned.

Rather than pure fiction, these stories represent what anthropologists call "social memory"—cultural knowledge about past practices transmitted through narrative tradition across generations. The details that seemed most fantastic to earlier scholars—the complexity of diplomatic protocols, the religious dimensions of military planning, the administrative requirements for extended campaigns—prove most accurate when compared to Bronze Age archaeological evidence.

When we stand among the ruins of Troy VIIa and examine the arrowheads embedded in the walls, the burned buildings, and the hasty burials that mark the city's violent end around 1180 BCE, we encounter the material remains of events that Greeks transformed into the greatest story of their civilization. The archaeological evidence provides the historical foundation while the literary tradition preserves the cultural meanings that Bronze Age peoples attached to these traumatic events—the understanding that personal choices carry consequences across generations, that political conflicts reflect cosmic patterns, and that human struggles participate in larger narratives of justice, fate, and historical change.

The bronze spearheads and pottery sherds tell us that something violent happened at Troy around the time tradition claims. The epic poems tell us how Bronze Age peoples understood what violence meant—not just as political or economic conflict, but as the moment when divine justice, human passion, and historical necessity intersected on the windy plain below the walls of Ilios.

CHAPTER 3
NINE YEARS OF SIEGE

Wrath and Its Consequences

You're sitting in a Bronze Age palace hall, firelight flickering off painted walls, as a bard begins the greatest war story ever told. But instead of starting with ships launching from Greece or armies gathering on distant shores, he plunges you directly into the ninth year of the siege, when the Greek coalition itself teeters on the edge of collapse. This is Homer's genius—the Iliad begins not with the war's origin but with its most devastating internal crisis.

"Sing, goddess, of the anger of Peleus' son Achilles and its devastation, which put pains thousandfold upon the Achaeans, hurled many strong souls of heroes to Hades, and made their bodies prey for dogs and all birds, and the will of Zeus was being accomplished..." (Homer, Iliad 1.1-5). These opening lines establish everything we need to understand about this epic: divine forces shape human events, heroic anger carries catastrophic consequences, and individual choices serve larger cosmic purposes that mortals can barely comprehend.

Archaeological evidence from Bronze Age Greece reveals the historical context that makes Homer's story so compelling. Linear B tablets from Pylos and Knossos document the complex administrative systems required to maintain royal coalitions, track military obligations, and manage the tribute relationships that held Bronze Age alliances together (Shelmerdine 1999: 144). When that system breaks down—as it does in the Iliad's opening—the consequences cascade far beyond personal relationships.

A Quarrel Over Captives: Honor, Authority, and Bronze Age Politics

The catalyst for the Iliad's action might seem minor to modern readers—a dispute over captive women awarded as war prizes. But this conflict cuts to the heart of Bronze Age aristocratic society. When plague strikes the Greek camp, the seer Calchas reveals it stems from Apollo's anger over Agamemnon's refusal to return Chryseis, daughter of Apollo's priest, who had been awarded to Agamemnon as his share of the spoils. Forced to return her, Agamemnon demands Briseis, Achilles' prize, as compensation.

Linear B tablets reveal how thoroughly Bronze Age palace culture was organized around such status distinctions. Administrative records from Pylos carefully track the allocation of captive women, livestock, and luxury goods to various palace officials according to their rank and service (Killen 1999: 201). The system wasn't just about wealth—it was about publicly recognizing each person's value and contribution to the community's success.

Agamemnon's seizure of Briseis violates more than personal property rights. As Gregory Nagy observes, "The Iliad presents a conflict between two divergent models of leadership: Agamemnon's hierarchical authority based on political position versus Achilles' authority derived from martial excellence" (Nagy 1979: 26). This tension between institutional power and individual prowess would have resonated powerfully with the Iliad's original audiences in early Archaic Greece, a society transitioning from Bronze Age monarchies toward the emerging city-state system.

Achilles' response—withdrawing from battle and asking his divine mother Thetis to convince Zeus to favor the Trojans until the Greeks recognize his value—represents more than wounded pride. Archaeological evidence suggests that

Bronze Age military coalitions depended heavily on the voluntary participation of warrior elites who could choose to withdraw their support if slighted (Drews 1993: 156). Achilles exercises a real political option that his Bronze Age audiences would have understood immediately.

The Tide Turns: Duels, Mass Combat, and Divine Intervention

With Achilles absent, Homer showcases other heroes on both sides while revealing the war's fundamental dynamics. Book 3 presents what should be a decisive moment—single combat between Menelaus and Paris, the wronged husband and the abductor, fighting to resolve the entire conflict. Menelaus clearly dominates: "Menelaus struck Paris on his helmet's ridge, but the spear shattered there. Then Menelaus drew his silver-studded sword, raised it high, and brought it down on Paris's helmet ridge. But the sword shattered into three, four pieces, falling from his hand" (Homer, Iliad 3.362-366).

But just as victory seems within reach, Aphrodite intervenes, whisking Paris away to safety and nullifying the agreement. This pattern—divine intervention preventing decisive outcomes—recurs throughout the poem, suggesting that the war serves larger cosmic purposes that individual combat cannot resolve. Archaeological evidence from Bronze Age conflicts shows that single combat between champions did occur in ancient warfare, as documented in Hittite, Egyptian, and Mesopotamian texts, though probably not with the frequency Homer describes (van Wees 1994: 134).

The Iliad alternates between these focused duels and panoramic views of mass combat that capture warfare's chaotic brutality. Homer employs vivid, often gruesome imagery that medical researchers have noted for its anatomical accuracy (Saunders 1999: 67). A typical description reads: "Antilochus was first to kill a Trojan warrior, valiant Echepolus, son of Thalysias, fighting among the front ranks. He struck him on his helmet's crest, the bronze spearpoint lodged in his forehead, pushing through the bone. Darkness covered his eyes, and he collapsed like a tower amid the fierce struggle" (Homer, Iliad 4.457-462).

These detailed death scenes—hundreds appear throughout the poem—serve multiple purposes beyond mere gore. They emphasize the war's human cost, showcase the heroes' lethal skills, and paradoxically immortalize the fallen through poetic memory. As James Redfield notes, "The hero gains immortality precisely by dying memorably" (Redfield 1975: 156).

Heroes Step Forward: Aristeia and Bronze Age Warfare

With Achilles absent, Homer employs a structural device called aristeia—extended sequences highlighting particular heroes' excellence in battle. These episodes reveal the depth of the Greek forces while maintaining dramatic tension about whether anyone can truly replace Achilles.

Diomedes' aristeia in Book 5 proves especially significant because Athena grants him permission to attack gods supporting Troy: "She removed the mist from his eyes that was there before, so he might distinguish well both god and man. And she commanded him: 'If Aphrodite daughter of Zeus enters battle, you may wound her with sharp bronze'" (Homer, Iliad 5.127-132). Diomedes subsequently wounds both Aphrodite and Ares—an extraordinary achievement that emphasizes both the unprecedented scale of divine involvement in this conflict and the Greeks' potential even without their greatest warrior.

Archaeological evidence supports Homer's portrayal of Bronze Age elite warriors as remarkably skilled fighters. Analysis of weapons found in Mycenaean graves reveals sophisticated metallurgy and craftsmanship, while skeletal remains show evidence of extensive combat training from youth (Kilian-Dirlmeier 1993: 134). The detailed martial descriptions in the Iliad reflect genuine knowledge of Bronze Age military technology and fighting techniques.

Ajax, son of Telamon, emerges as the Greeks' defensive bulwark—a towering figure whom Homer describes carrying "his shield like a tower—bronze with seven layers of ox-hide, which Tychius crafted for him, the best of leatherworkers, who lived in Hyle" (Homer, Iliad 7.219-221). In Book 7, Ajax duels Hector to a draw, with both warriors exchanging gifts afterward in a remarkable show of mutual respect amid relentless violence. Such moments of heroic courtesy reflect documented Bronze Age practices where elite warriors maintained codes of honor even during warfare (Beckman 1999: 234).

The Embassy: When Honor Cannot Be Bought

By Book 9, the Trojans have gained such momentum that they threaten the Greek ships themselves—which would strand the entire expedition in enemy territory. Agamemnon finally acknowledges his error and sends an embassy offering extraordinary compensation: seven tripods, ten talents of gold, twenty cauldrons, twelve horses, seven women of Lesbos, the return of Briseis with an oath she remains untouched, one of his daughters in marriage, and seven populated cities as dowry.

This lavish offer addresses material compensation but completely fails to restore Achilles' compromised honor. His response cuts to the heart of the heroic value system: "I hate like the gates of Hades the man who hides one thing in his mind and speaks another. But I will speak what seems best to me. Neither Agamemnon nor the other Achaeans will persuade me, since there appears to be no gratitude for fighting tirelessly against the enemy. Equal portion goes to he who hangs back and he who fights his hardest; the same honor attends both coward and hero, and death comes alike to the idle man and to him who accomplishes much" (Homer, Iliad 9.312-320).

Achilles' rejection reveals how deeply the social contract has been violated in his view. Linear B tablets show that Bronze Age society operated through complex networks of reciprocal obligation, where contributions were carefully tracked and publicly acknowledged (Shelmerdine 1999: 289). The incident has forced Achilles to question this entire system—why risk death when honor can be arbitrarily stripped away? As James Redfield observes, "Achilles' wrath is directed not just at Agamemnon but at the social system that enables Agamemnon's behavior" (Redfield 1975: 197).

Night Operations: The Dolon Episode

Book 10 presents a distinctive episode that illuminates different aspects of Bronze Age warfare. Odysseus and Diomedes undertake a night reconnaissance mission, encountering Dolon, a Trojan scout who reveals valuable intelligence before they kill him: "Newly arrived are the Thracians, led by Rhesus, son of Eioneus. His horses are the most beautiful and largest I have seen, whiter than snow, and swift as the wind. His chariot is adorned with gold and silver, and his armor, golden and gigantic, is a wonder to behold—more fitting for immortal gods than for mortal men" (Homer, Iliad 10.435-441).

Acting on this information, they infiltrate the Thracian camp, killing thirteen men including King Rhesus, and steal his magnificent horses. Archaeological evidence suggests such night raids were indeed part of Bronze Age warfare. Linear B tablets from Pylos record defensive measures against "watchers by the sea," indicating real concerns about surprise attacks (Shelmerdine 1999: 345). The episode also reflects the multiethnic nature of the Trojan alliance, with contingents from across western Anatolia and Thrace—a detail archaeology confirms through the diverse material culture found in Late Bronze Age Troy (Becks 2006: 67).

This night operation highlights the diverse fighting styles within the Greek force. Not all warfare is conducted through frontal assault and heroic duels—strategic thinking, stealth, and intelligence gathering play crucial roles in Bronze Age military success.

The Turning Point: Patroclus and the Crisis

As Trojan success continues, the Greeks face complete disaster. By Book 12, Hector has breached the wall protecting the Greek ships, and Books 13-15 describe desperate fighting as the Trojans nearly succeed in setting fire to the Greek fleet—which would have stranded the entire expedition in enemy territory with no means of escape.

This crisis prompts Patroclus, Achilles' closest companion, to request permission to enter battle wearing Achilles' armor: "Give me your armor to wear on my shoulders, and perhaps the Trojans might take me for you and withdraw from fighting, allowing the warlike sons of the Achaeans, exhausted as they are, to breathe again" (Homer, Iliad 16.40-43). Achilles consents but with a crucial warning: "Obey this command I place upon your heart: do not, in the pride and glory of fighting, lead our men toward Troy, lest one of the ever-living Olympian gods enters the fray—Apollo especially loves them. Return once you've brought safety to the ships" (Homer, Iliad 16.87-91).

Patroclus's intervention initially succeeds brilliantly. The Trojans, mistaking him for Achilles, retreat in disarray as Homer describes with one of his most powerful similes: "As when from the high peak of a great mountain Zeus, the cloud-gatherer, stirs a dense cloud, and all the peaks and high ridges and valleys appear, as the sky breaks open from heaven, so the Danaans, having driven hostile fire from their ships, breathed again, though there came no pause in the battle" (Homer, Iliad 16.297-302).

Patroclus kills twenty-seven named Trojans, including Sarpedon, Zeus's own son. But his success leads to fatal hubris—he pursues the Trojans to Troy's walls, ignoring Achilles' warning. There, Apollo strikes him, disarming him, Euphorbos wounds him from behind, and Hector delivers the killing blow.

This sequence creates the central pivot of the entire epic. As Marshall Sahlins noted, "Achilles' withdrawal from battle represented a withdrawal from the social contract; Patroclus's death brings him back into human community through grief and shared purpose" (Sahlins 2004: 134). The news transforms Achilles' wrath, redirecting it from Agamemnon to Hector and setting up the climactic confrontation.

Divine Craftsmanship: New Armor and Return to Battle

News of Patroclus's death plunges Achilles into overwhelming grief that his divine mother Thetis witnesses firsthand. She obtains new armor for him from Hephaestus, including the famously elaborate shield depicting scenes of both peace and war—essentially a microcosm of human existence beyond the battlefield (Homer, Iliad 18.478-608). Archaeological evidence from Bronze Age Greece reveals the sophisticated metalworking techniques that make such divine craftsmanship believable to ancient audiences (Muhly 1985: 156).

Achilles formally reconciles with Agamemnon, who provides all the promised gifts, but this gesture is now completely secondary to his driving purpose: vengeance against Hector. His return to battle in Book 20 proves cataclysmic: "As ravaging fire rages through deep glens of a parched mountain and the thick forest burns, and the wind driving it whirls flames in all directions, so Achilles raged everywhere with his spear like a demon, pressing after those he killed, and the black earth ran with blood" (Homer, Iliad 20.490-494).

Achilles's rampage includes a supernatural battle with the river god Scamander, who becomes choked with Trojan corpses. This extraordinary confrontation emphasizes Achilles's near-divine status while foreshadowing his inevitable mortality—even the greatest heroes cannot transcend human limitations indefinitely.

The Duel of Duels: Achilles versus Hector

The Iliad builds inexorably toward the confrontation between Achilles and Hector. Before their duel, Homer provides a poignant scene in Book 6 of Hector's farewell to his wife Andromache and infant son Astyanax—a humanizing portrait that makes his fate all the more tragic when it finally arrives.

When they meet in Book 22, Hector initially flees, circling Troy's walls three times before divine intervention forces him to stand and fight. Archaeological evidence from Troy VI/VIIa reveals the massive fortification walls that would have made such a chase both possible and dramatically visible to defenders and attackers alike (Becks 2006: 145). Their duel, when it finally comes, is brief but climactic: "Achilles rushed at him, heart full of savage wrath... He eyed Hector's handsome body, seeking where it might best yield. All the rest of his flesh was protected by bronze armor... but where the collarbones divide the neck from shoulders, the throat appeared, where destruction of life comes quickest. There, as Hector charged, shining Achilles drove his spear" (Homer, Iliad 22.312-326).

After killing Hector, Achilles commits his most controversial act—refusing proper burial and dragging Hector's body behind his chariot: "He pierced the tendons of both feet from heel to ankle, threaded ox-hide thongs through them, and bound them to his chariot, leaving the head to drag. Mounting his chariot, lifting the famous armor, he whipped the horses to a run, and they flew willingly. Dust rose around the dragged body, dark hair spread wide, and the head once so handsome lay in the dust" (Homer, Iliad 22.396-403).

This desecration violates sacred funeral customs documented throughout the Bronze Age Mediterranean and represents Achilles at his most savage. As Emily Wilson observes, "Achilles's treatment of Hector's body is not just an insult to Hector but a rejection of the customs that make human community possible" (Wilson 2019: 234).

The Ransom of Hector: Compassion and Closure

The Iliad could have ended with Achilles's revenge, but instead continues to a more complex and ultimately more satisfying conclusion. In Book 24, guided by Hermes, King Priam enters the Greek camp to ransom his son's body. The elderly king kneels before Achilles and kisses "the hands that had killed so many of his sons"—a gesture of extraordinary courage and humility.

This remarkable scene culminates in a moment of shared grief that transcends the ethnic and political divisions driving the war: "So he spoke, and stirred in Achilles a longing to weep for his father. Taking the old man's hand, he gently pushed him away. And the two remembered: Priam, huddled at Achilles' feet, wept loudly for man-slaying Hector, while Achilles wept for his father, and then again for Patroclus. The sound of their mourning filled the house" (Homer, Iliad 24.507-512).

Achilles agrees to return Hector's body and grants an eleven-day truce for proper funeral rites. The poem ends not with triumph but with Hector's funeral—a somber recognition of mortality that unites Greek and Trojan in common humanity. Archaeological evidence from Bronze Age burial practices confirms the central importance of proper funeral rites in maintaining cosmic and social order (Cavanagh and Mee 1998: 89).

Beyond the Iliad: The War's Conclusion

Though the Iliad concludes with Hector's funeral, the Trojan War continued. Our knowledge of subsequent events comes from other sources—the Epic Cycle poems (now mostly lost except for summaries), Greek tragedies, Virgil's Aeneid, and later compilations (Davies 1989: 67). These sources describe several crucial developments: Penthesilea and the Amazons arriving to aid Troy, Memnon of Ethiopia leading reinforcements, the death of Achilles from Paris's arrow guided by Apollo, the contest for Achilles' arms between Ajax and Odysseus, the summoning of Philoctetes and Neoptolemus to fulfill prophecies, the theft of the Palladium, and finally the construction of the Trojan Horse that enabled the city's capture.

Archaeological evidence from Troy VIIa shows clear signs of violent destruction around 1180 BCE—burned buildings, unburied bodies, bronze arrowheads embedded in walls, and evidence of hasty attempts to repair fortifications (Korfmann 2001: 89). This destruction coincides with broader upheaval throughout the Eastern Mediterranean during the Late Bronze Age collapse, when interconnected civilizations fell like dominoes across the region (Cline 2014: 156).

Archaeology Meets Epic: Material Evidence and Literary Truth

How does Homer's account align with archaeological evidence? Excavations at Hisarlik reveal that Troy VI, a prosperous city with impressive walls, was destroyed by earthquake around 1300 BCE (Becks 2006: 134). The subsequent settlement, Troy VIIa, was indeed destroyed by warfare around 1180 BCE, with clear evidence of fire, violence, and desperate final resistance.

Material culture confirms aspects of Homer's Bronze Age world. Linear B tablets from Mycenaean Greece mention names found in the Iliad, including possible references to "Atreus" and "Achilles" (Chadwick 1976: 89). Hittite diplomatic texts describe conflicts in western Anatolia involving kingdoms called "Ahhiyawa" (possibly "Achaea") and "Wilusa" (likely Troy/Ilios) (Beckman 1999: 178).

The Tawagalawa Letter from a Hittite king discusses a renegade named Piyamaradu conducting raids along the Anatolian coast—potentially preserving a historical kernel that evolved into the Troy legend (Bryce 2006: 234). As Trevor Bryce suggests, "The Trojan War tradition may have conflated several historical conflicts between Mycenaean Greeks and western Anatolian powers over a period of generations."

Homer's depiction of siege warfare aligns with Late Bronze Age realities. Without effective siege engines, Bronze Age armies relied on blockade, trickery, or internal betrayal to take walled cities—exactly the pattern the Iliad describes (Gabriel 2005: 156). The detailed anatomical accuracy of wound descriptions suggests the poet drew on extensive observation of combat injuries (Saunders 1999: 134).

The Human Cost Beyond Heroes

While focusing on aristocratic warriors, the Iliad acknowledges war's broader human impact. Homer gives voice to ordinary soldiers, captive women, and civilian victims whose suffering provides emotional weight to the heroic narrative. Archaeological evidence from Troy VIIa supports this portrayal—unburied remains, evidence of hasty food preparation, and signs of nutritional stress all suggest a population under siege (Korfmann 2001: 134).

The poem's treatment of captive women reflects historical realities. Linear B tablets document female slaves identified by their cities of origin, confirming that enslavement of women from conquered territories was standard Bronze Age practice (Shelmerdine 1999: 401). The administrative matter-of-factness of these records contrasts sharply with Homer's psychological exploration of these women's trauma.

Conclusion: The Siege as Cultural Memory

The Trojan War's enduring significance stems from Homer's artistic achievement but also from the historical catastrophe it reflects—the collapse of Bronze Age civilization. As Eric Cline observes, "The fall of Troy marks the end of an era. Whether or not it happened exactly as Homer describes, it represents a historical watershed" (Cline 2014: 234).

The Iliad transforms this historical disaster into an exploration of timeless human questions: the nature of heroism, the cost of pride, the tragedy of conflict, and the possibility of compassion even between enemies. By focusing on a few weeks within a ten-year siege, Homer creates a microcosm that captures warfare's essence across time and cultures.

Modern archaeological work continues refining our understanding of Troy and its fall. Recent excavations have identified a substantial lower city outside the citadel, confirming Homer's description of Troy as a major urban center rather than just a fortress (Korfmann 2001: 67). Evidence of international connections through pottery and trade goods supports the Iliad's depiction of Troy as a wealthy, cosmopolitan city embedded in Bronze Age trade networks.

The siege of Troy—whether understood as historical event, cultural memory, or literary creation—remains a foundational narrative of Western civilization. In its unflinching portrayal of both war's glory and its devastation, the Iliad continues to speak to contemporary experiences of conflict. As Caroline Alexander writes, "The Iliad accepts violence as an inescapable aspect of human existence but never glorifies war itself. Its enduring power lies in its honest reckoning with both the allure and the cost of warfare" (Alexander 2015: 289).

The story reminds us that archaeological evidence and literary tradition need not be opposed. Together, they provide complementary perspectives on a pivotal moment when history became legend, and legend illuminated universal truths about courage, loss, honor, and the tragic beauty of human mortality played out against the backdrop of Bronze Age civilization's end.

CHAPTER 4

THE WOODEN HORSE AND THE FALL OF A CITY

Deception, Destruction, and the End of an Age

Picture archaeologist Heinrich Schliemann standing among the ruins of Troy in 1870, holding what he believed was Priam's treasure—golden cups and jewelry gleaming in the Anatolian sunlight. He was convinced he had found proof of Homer's greatest story, though we now know his "Priam's Treasure" dated to a much earlier period. Yet Schliemann's passionate belief captures something essential about Troy's enduring power: this ancient city represents the moment when heroic legend crashes into brutal historical reality, when the age of heroes ends in flames and the world fundamentally changes.

The final phase of the Trojan War gives us history's most enduring image of military deception—the Trojan Horse. This cunning stratagem marks the transition from the heroic single combat of the Iliad to the harsh realities of Bronze Age siege warfare, where cleverness often proved more effective than courage. Archaeological evidence from across the Late Bronze Age Mediterranean confirms that Troy's fall wasn't an isolated event but part of a civilizational collapse that would reshape the ancient world (Cline 2014: 156).

The Wooden Horse: Ancient Innovation or Poetic Metaphor?

The Trojan Horse story comes to us not from Homer's Iliad, which ends with Hector's funeral, but from later sources—fragments of the lost Epic Cycle, especially the Little Iliad and the Sack of Troy, plus Virgil's dramatic account in the Aeneid. According to these sources, after Achilles' death from Paris's arrow guided by Apollo, the Greeks found themselves at a strategic dead end. Direct assault had failed for a decade, and Troy's massive walls—which Homer calls "god-built"—remained as impregnable as ever.

The solution attributed to Odysseus demonstrates the evolution of siege warfare in the Late Bronze Age. As Virgil describes it: "They build a horse of mountainous size, through Pallas's divine art, and weave planks of fir over its ribs... they pretend it's a votive offering: this rumor spreads. They secretly hide the best of their warriors in its dark flanks, filling the vast cavern of its womb with armed men" (Virgil, Aeneid 2.15-20).

Archaeological evidence confirms that deception played crucial roles in Late Bronze Age warfare. The Hittite "Apology of Hattusili III" describes using false retreats to lure enemies into ambushes, while Egyptian records detail similar tactical ruses (Beckman 1999: 234). Neo-Assyrian royal inscriptions similarly describe infiltration tactics against walled cities, with Mursili II recording how he "sent men inside the city secretly, and they opened the gates" (Bryce 2005: 167).

While no direct evidence confirms a literal wooden horse, several plausible historical interpretations exist. Some scholars suggest the horse might symbolize a siege engine—perhaps a battering ram with a horse-shaped protective covering—used to breach Troy's gates (Strauss 2006: 145). Others propose it represented a ship, since the Greek word for ship planks was the same as that for cavalry formations. Most intriguingly, the horse might symbolize an earthquake, since Poseidon was god of both horses and earthquakes, and Troy VI shows clear evidence of seismic destruction (Rose 2014: 89).

The 2nd-century CE geographer Pausanias offers a rationalist interpretation: "Anyone who does not consider the Trojans completely foolish must have realized that the horse was a siege engine that broke down the city wall" (Pausanias 1.2 3.8). This reflects ancient attempts to find historical truth within mythological narratives—a process archaeologists continue today.

Whatever its historical basis, the Trojan Horse represents the triumph of mētis (cunning intelligence) over biē (brute force)—a theme that resonates throughout Greek literature and reflects real Bronze Age military thinking where strategic deception often determined outcomes.

Ignored Warnings: Cassandra and Laocoön

The myth emphasizes that Troy's fall wasn't inevitable—clear warnings came but went tragically unheeded. Two figures stand out as prophets of doom whose insights couldn't prevent catastrophe: Cassandra and Laocoön.

Cassandra, Priam's daughter, had received Apollo's gift of prophecy but been cursed so no one would believe her predictions when she rejected the god's advances. When she warned about the horse, her fellow Trojans dismissed her as mad. Aeschylus captures her anguish in the Agamemnon: "Apollo, Apollo! God of the ways, my destroyer! For you have destroyed me, and utterly, this second time" (Aeschylus, Agamemnon 1080-1082).

Laocoön, priest of Poseidon, similarly warned against bringing the horse inside with the famous line preserved in Virgil's Aeneid: "Timeo Danaos et dona ferentes" ("I fear the Greeks, even when bearing gifts") (Virgil, Aeneid 2.49). His punishment was swift and terrible—two enormous sea serpents emerged from the sea and crushed him and his sons to death, an event the Trojans fatally misinterpreted as divine punishment for his skepticism rather than confirmation of his warning.

The famous Hellenistic sculpture group of Laocoön and his sons, discovered in Rome in 1506 and now in the Vatican Museums, dramatically captures this moment. The writhing figures locked in mortal struggle with the serpents embody the agony of foresight without power to change fate—a central theme in Greek tragedy (Spivey 2013: 167).

These unheeded warnings reflect a psychological truth about catastrophic events that archaeologists recognize in the Bronze Age collapse: often, signs of impending disaster are visible but ignored due to wishful thinking, political expediency, or simple human inability to accept unwelcome truths. The Trojans, exhausted by ten years of war, saw what they wanted to see—an opportunity for peace—rather than the threat before them.

The Sack of Troy: Archaeological Evidence for Bronze Age Warfare

With Greek warriors hidden inside the horse and the rest of the army feigning retreat to Tenedos, the Trojans pulled the wooden structure into their city as a victory trophy. According to Virgil, the Greek warrior Sinon, who had pretended to be a deserter, released his comrades under cover of night. They opened the city gates for the returning Greek army, and systematic slaughter began.

What followed aligns perfectly with Bronze Age warfare practices documented through archaeological evidence. Destroyed cities throughout the Eastern Mediterranean during the Late Bronze Age collapse reveal a consistent pattern: systematic slaughter of fighting-age men, enslavement of women and children, ritual desecration of sacred spaces, and comprehensive looting followed by fire (Drews 1993: 189).

Priam's fate—slaughtered at the altar of Zeus Herkeios—reflects common practice of killing enemy leaders in ritualized contexts. Virgil's description captures both the political necessity and religious significance: "Thus Priam's fate was sealed: this was his end, by destiny appointed—to see Troy burnt, and Pergama in ruins, he who was once the magnificent ruler of so many Asian lands and peoples" (Virgil, Aeneid 2.554-558).

Archaeological evidence from palatial centers destroyed during this period, such as Ugarit in Syria and Pylos in Greece, shows similar patterns of deliberate desecration of royal and religious spaces (Yon 2006: 134). The violation of temples during Troy's fall, most notably Ajax the Lesser's assault on Cassandra in Athena's sanctuary, corresponds to evidence of destroyed cult objects and burned sanctuaries at multiple Bronze Age sites.

The fate of Trojan women, divided as prizes among Greek commanders, reflects harsh realities of ancient warfare. Linear B tablets from Pylos document women identified by their cities of origin working as textile producers, confirming that enslavement of conquered populations was standard practice (Shelmerdine 1999: 401). Homer foreshadows this reality when Andromache laments to Hector: "For me it would be better to sink beneath the earth when I have lost you, for there will be no other comfort when you have met your doom, only grief" (Homer, Iliad 6.410-413).

Archaeological Evidence: Troy VIIa and the Bronze Age Collapse

The destruction layer at Troy VIIa, dated to approximately 1180 BCE, shows evidence remarkably consistent with literary tradition. Archaeologists have found bronze arrowheads embedded in walls, unburied human remains, valuable items abandoned suggesting hasty flight, and extensive fire damage throughout the settlement (Korfmann 2001: 189). While this cannot definitively prove the Trojan War as described in epic poetry, it confirms that Troy experienced violent destruction consistent with the traditional timeframe.

Recent excavations under Manfred Korfmann and Ernst Pernicka have revolutionized our understanding of Troy's size and importance. Rather than a small fortress, Troy VI/VIIa was a substantial urban center of approximately 25-30 hectares with an estimated population of 5,000-10,000—definitely a city worth fighting over (Rose 2014: 134). The discovery of a substantial lower city beyond the citadel confirms Homer's descriptions of Troy as a major urban center rather than just a hilltop fortress.

Material evidence demonstrates Troy's importance as a commercial hub. Its strategic location controlling access between the Aegean and Black Seas made it a natural trade center and potential target for conflict. Pottery and artifacts reveal connections with both Mycenaean Greece and Hittite Anatolia, consistent with Troy's literary depiction as a wealthy, cosmopolitan city embedded in international networks (Becks 2006: 167).

This destruction coincides with the broader Late Bronze Age collapse that devastated civilizations throughout the Eastern Mediterranean between 1200-1150 BCE. As Eric Cline demonstrates, this was a period when "interconnected civilizations fell like dominoes" across the region (Cline 2014: 156). Troy's fall, whether caused by Greek invasion, internal rebellion, earthquake, or some combination of factors, was part of this larger pattern of systemic collapse.

Survivors and Diaspora: Aeneas and Cultural Transmission

Not all Trojans perished in the city's destruction. The most famous survivor, Aeneas, carried his father Anchises on his shoulders and led refugees from the burning city. His escape was prophesied and divinely sanctioned, as he was destined to establish a new Troy. Virgil's Aeneid traces his journey to Italy, where his descendants would eventually found Rome—transforming military defeat into ultimate cultural victory.

This narrative of cultural transmission through diaspora reflects actual population movements during the Late Bronze Age collapse. Archaeological evidence shows displaced groups establishing new settlements throughout the Mediterranean, often carrying distinctive cultural practices from their homelands (Yasur-Landau 2010: 89). The Sea Peoples mentioned in Egyptian records may represent such diaspora populations fleeing the collapse of their original societies.

Intriguingly, Hittite texts mention conflicts in western Anatolia involving kingdoms called "Ahhiyawa" (possibly the Achaeans) and "Wilusa" (likely Troy/Ilios). These documents also reference a rebel leader named Piyama-radu who conducted coastal raids before fleeing by sea—a potential historical parallel to mythical Trojan refugees (Bryce 2006: 234).

Other Trojan survivors in myth established settlements across the Mediterranean. Antenor, who had advocated returning Helen, supposedly founded Patavium (modern Padua) in northern Italy. Helenus, a prophetic son of Priam, established a kingdom in Epirus. While not historically verifiable, these foundation myths reflect the Mediterranean-wide impact of population movements following Bronze Age civilizational collapse.

Divine Retribution: The Troubled Returns

If Troy's fall represented Greek triumph, the aftermath revealed the war's true cost. The Nostoi ("Returns") poems, largely lost except for fragments, detailed the disastrous journeys home faced by Greek heroes—divine punishment for their excesses during Troy's sack.

Odysseus's ten-year journey home, immortalized in Homer's Odyssey, represents the most famous troubled return. His wanderings through supernatural dangers symbolize the psychological and spiritual difficulties of transitioning from war to peace—a theme with remarkable contemporary relevance for veterans of modern conflicts (Shay 2002: 156).

Other Greek leaders faced similar or worse fates. Ajax the Lesser, who violated Athena's sanctuary, was shipwrecked and drowned after boasting he had escaped divine punishment. Agamemnon returned home to be murdered by his wife Clytemnestra and her lover Aegisthus—a story that became the subject of Aeschylus's Oresteia trilogy. Diomedes found his wife unfaithful and was forced into exile in Italy.

Even Menelaus, who regained Helen, was blown off course to Egypt and struggled eight years to return home. Only Nestor, noted for his piety and wisdom, had an uneventful journey back to Pylos—perhaps because Linear B tablets suggest Pylos itself was destroyed during this period, making his "successful" return tragically ironic (Shelmerdine 1999: 456).

These difficult returns reflect both historical realities and psychological truths. Historically, the Late Bronze Age collapse disrupted established maritime routes and political systems, making travel genuinely hazardous. Psychologically, the stories acknowledge the difficulty of reintegrating warriors into peaceful society—a challenge documented across cultures and time periods.

The Trojan Horse as Universal Metaphor

The Trojan Horse has transcended its original context to become a universal metaphor for deception and infiltration. Its enduring relevance speaks to the central role of strategic deception in warfare throughout history.

Ancient military manuals consistently emphasized stratagems over direct confrontation. The 4th-century BCE military writer Aeneas Tacticus devotes substantial attention to defending against deception, suggesting its prevalence in Greek warfare (Hunter 2010: 89). His contemporary Xenophon records numerous instances of successful military ruses in his accounts of Greek campaigns.

The Horse represents what military theorists call "getting inside the enemy's decision cycle"—exploiting their expectations and turning strengths into vulnerabilities. Troy's massive walls, its primary defense, became irrelevant when the Trojans themselves breached them by bringing the horse inside (Strauss 2006: 178).

The psychological dimension remains equally relevant. The Trojans' willingness to believe what they wished to be true—that the Greeks had departed—illustrates cognitive biases that continue to shape military and political decision-making. As Thucydides observed, "It is a habit of mankind to entrust to careless hope what they long for, and to use sovereign reason to thrust aside what they do not desire" (Thucydides 1.84.3).

In our digital age, the metaphor has gained new relevance through "Trojan horse" malware that disguises harmful code within seemingly beneficial programs. This modern application captures the essence of the ancient stratagem: exploiting trust to bypass defenses.

Troy in Cultural Memory: From History to Symbol

Whether or not events matching Homer's narrative occurred precisely as described, the Trojan War held profound significance in ancient cultural memory. By the Classical period, Troy's fall had become a foundational event marking the boundary between the heroic age and historical time.

For Greeks, the Trojan War represented both their greatest achievement and a cautionary tale about hubris. Athens' 5th-century BCE naval empire was explicitly framed as continuation of the pan-Hellenic expedition against Troy. The Athenian treasury at Delphi featured scenes from the Trojan War, visually linking contemporary Athenian power to heroic precedent (Hurwit 1999: 167).

For communities throughout the Mediterranean claiming Trojan ancestry—including Rome—Troy represented cultural resilience and divine destiny. Virgil has Jupiter proclaim about the Romans: "For these I set no limits, world or time, but give empire without end" (Virgil, Aeneid 1.278-279).

Troy's fall transcended its historical context to become a universal symbol of catastrophic civilizational collapse. When later cities fell—from Athens to Jerusalem to Constantinople—chroniclers inevitably compared these events to Troy's destruction. The image of Troy in flames became the archetypal urban disaster against which all subsequent city falls were measured.

Conclusion: Between Myth and History

The fall of Troy occupies a unique position at the intersection of myth, history, literature, and archaeology. While we cannot definitively prove or disprove specific events from the poetic tradition, archaeological evidence confirms that Troy was a significant Bronze Age city that suffered violent destruction around the traditionally accepted date of the Trojan War.

The enduring power of the Troy story lies in its multidimensional truth. As historical narrative, it preserves cultural memory of the turbulent end of the Bronze Age. As literature, it explores timeless themes of heroism, hubris, divine justice, and human suffering. As cultural symbol, it provides a framework for understanding civilizational rise and fall that remains relevant today.

The Trojan Horse specifically represents both historical siege tactics and deeper truths about human psychology—our vulnerability to deception when it aligns with our desires. Laocoön's warning remains relevant: "Whatever it is, I fear the Greeks, even when bearing gifts"—caution that applies to contexts far removed from ancient warfare.

Perhaps most significantly, Troy's fall reminds us that no civilization, however magnificent, is immune to downfall. The Trojans' fatal error wasn't simply accepting the horse but succumbing to hubris—believing their walls impregnable, their victory assured, and their civilization eternal. In our own era of complex global challenges, Troy's fall continues to resonate as both warning and reflection on the fragility of human achievement.

When we stand among the ruins of Troy today, looking out over the Dardanelles where Greek ships once anchored, we see not just the remains of an ancient city but a window into one of history's great turning points. Whether the wooden horse was literal siege engine, poetic metaphor, or cultural memory of multiple conflicts, it symbolizes the moment when the Bronze Age world of heroes and kings gave way to a new era—one we can trace through archaeological evidence of destruction, displacement, and ultimately renewal across the ancient Mediterranean.

As Horace observed, "Captive Greece took captive her fierce conqueror" (Horace, Epistles 2.1.156). Troy's fall may represent a Greek military victory, but the story's preservation and elaboration reflect a deeper conquest—the power of narrative to transform historical events into enduring cultural touchstones that continue to shape our understanding of both past and present. In the end, Troy's greatest victory may be its immortality in human memory, achieved not through military triumph but through the eternal power of story itself.

CHAPTER 5

AFTERMATH AND DIASPORA

The Divergent Paths of Victory and Defeat

S tanding among the ruins of Troy VIIa today, you can still see the blackened stones that bear witness to the city's violent end around 1180 BCE. But as archaeologists have learned, every ending is also a beginning. The flames that consumed Priam's citadel didn't just destroy—they illuminated two divergent paths stretching across the Mediterranean world. On one path walked the defeated Trojans, carrying their gods and memories toward new homelands. On the other, the victorious Greeks discovered that triumph often carried consequences as severe as defeat itself.

This isn't just poetry—it's cultural memory encoded in myth, reflecting real population movements and political upheavals that archaeologists can now trace through material evidence. The aftermath narratives of the Trojan War reveal how Bronze Age peoples understood the complex relationships between victory and suffering, migration and cultural transmission, divine justice and human agency (Wilson 2019: 234). These stories transformed the historical chaos of the Late Bronze Age collapse into meaningful frameworks for understanding how civilizations rise, fall, and transform.

Aeneas: From Defeated Prince to Imperial Ancestor

Among Troy's survivors, none achieved greater posthumous fame than Aeneas, whose journey from the burning city to the shores of Italy established the mythological foundation for Rome's imperial destiny. Though relatively minor in Homer's Iliad—described as a respected Trojan commander and son of Aphrodite—Aeneas's significance expanded dramatically as his story became intertwined with Roman identity (Williams 1973: 89).

Virgil's canonical account in the Aeneid, composed during Augustus's reign (29-19 BCE), draws on much older traditions while serving contemporary political purposes. The poet describes how divine visitation instructed Aeneas to flee on Troy's final night: "The gods who made this realm great in the past have withdrawn their protection... Escape, dear son, from these flames. The enemy holds our walls; Troy falls from its high place. Enough has been given to Priam and your homeland. If Troy could be defended by any right hand, it would have been defended by mine. Troy entrusts to you her sacred objects and household gods; take them as companions of your fate" (Virgil, Aeneid 2.320-330).

This divine mandate transforms Aeneas from defeated warrior to cultural courier, carrying not just his family but Troy's religious and cultural essence to a new homeland. The iconic image of Aeneas fleeing Troy—bearing elderly Anchises on his shoulders, leading young Ascanius by the hand, carrying the sacred Penates—became the archetypal representation of pietas, dutiful respect toward gods, country, and family (Gruen 2011: 156).

Archaeological evidence confirms historical connections between western Anatolia and central Italy during the Late Bronze Age and Early Iron Age, suggesting migrations that might have inspired the Aeneas legend. Etruscan art from the 6th century BCE depicts scenes from Aeneas's story, indicating the tale's circulation in Italy centuries before Virgil's literary treatment (Torelli 1989: 234). Recent excavations at Lavinium, traditionally founded by Aeneas, have revealed cult deposits and inscriptions that suggest genuine ancient connections to the Trojan prince (Castagnoli 1977: 145).

Aeneas's journey from Troy to Italy—with stops in Thrace, Crete, Epirus, Sicily, and Carthage—maps a geography of cultural transmission across the Mediterranean that corresponds to documented Bronze Age trade routes and settlement patterns. At each location, Aeneas attempts to establish a new settlement, only to be redirected by divine signs or obstacles. This pattern reflects the historical reality of multiple failed colonization attempts that characterized ancient migration movements (Malkin 1998: 178).

The Carthage episode, where Aeneas engages in doomed romance with Queen Dido, serves multiple narrative functions beyond entertainment. It establishes the mythological origin of historical enmity between Rome and Carthage while demonstrating Aeneas's transformation from Trojan warrior to Roman founder—willing to sacrifice personal happiness for collective destiny. When Mercury delivers Jupiter's rebuke, Aeneas's response reveals his evolution: "I am not pursuing Italy of my own free will" (Virgil, Aeneid 4.361).

This reluctant acceptance of fate distinguishes Aeneas from the self-determined Greek heroes of Homeric epic, establishing a distinctly Roman heroic model centered on submission to divine will and sacrifice for community good. As historian Ronald Syme observes, "The Aeneas legend offered Augustus the perfect mythological framework for his program of moral and religious renewal—connecting his regime to both heroic Trojan ancestry and divine favor" (Syme 1958: 234).

The Trojan Diaspora: Seeds of Civilization

While Aeneas dominates survivor narratives, ancient tradition preserved accounts of other Trojans who escaped to found settlements throughout the Mediterranean. These secondary migration myths often served local political purposes, connecting cities and peoples to prestigious Trojan heritage while explaining cultural similarities across distant regions.

Antenor, the Trojan elder who had advocated returning Helen to prevent war, reportedly led refugees called the Heneti to northern Italy, founding Patavium (modern Padua). Strabo records this tradition: "It is said that Antenor and his children escaped here with a group of Heneti who had been expelled from Paphlagonia, and that they settled at the head of the Adriatic, where they drove out the Euganean people who inhabited the region" (Strabo, Geography 5.1.4).

Archaeological evidence confirms significant cultural connections between Anatolia and the Veneto region during the Early Iron Age, potentially providing historical basis for this migration myth. Analysis of burial practices, pottery styles, and metalworking techniques reveals eastern Mediterranean influences that appear in northern Italy during the period traditionally associated with the Trojan War's aftermath (Bietti Sestieri 1997: 156).

Other Trojan diaspora narratives include Helenus, Priam's prophetic son, establishing "Little Troy" (Buthrotum) in Epirus after Greek capture, and various companions of Aeneas separating from his expedition to found their own settlements across the western Mediterranean (Malkin 1998: 201). These dispersed Trojan communities created a mythological network spanning the Mediterranean, explaining cultural similarities and political relationships between regions.

As archaeologist Jan Driessen observes, "These foundation myths provided ancient cities with prestigious origins while simultaneously explaining the presence of shared cultural elements across geographically distant regions" (Driessen 2001: 89). The Trojan diaspora narratives collectively transformed military defeat into cultural victory through dissemination—Troy's physical destruction enabled the spread of its essence throughout the Mediterranean world.

The Nostoi: When Victory Becomes Curse

If Trojan survivor narratives centered on new beginnings born from catastrophe, the Greek heroes' return stories (nostoi, "returns") explored the disruptive consequences of victory and violence. Despite achieving their decade-long objec-tive, most Greek leaders returned to find their households and kingdoms pro-foundly altered by their absence. These narratives reveal a moral economy where violence inflicted at Troy demanded reciprocal suffering (Nagy 1999: 167).

The most infamous return belongs to Agamemnon, commander of the Greek forces, whose homecoming to Mycenae ended in murder. As dramatized in Aeschylus's Oresteia trilogy, Agamemnon returned to find his wife Clytemnes-tra embittered by his sacrifice of their daughter Iphigenia and engaged in an affair with Aegisthus. The royal couple murdered Agamemnon in his bath, initiating a cycle of vengeance that would consume the House of Atreus.

Aeschylus presents this murder as divine retribution for excessive violence during Troy's sack. The Chorus warns: "The gods are not blind to those who kill many. The black Furies eventually wear down and bring to nothing the man who prospers unjustly" (Aeschylus, Agamemnon 461-463). Archaeological ev-idence from Mycenae shows the palatial system collapsed around the traditional date of the Trojan War's end, with signs of destruction and abandonment that suggest historical disruptions inspiring these tales of troubled returns (French 2002: 134).

Odysseus's ten-year wandering journey home to Ithaca, immortalized in Homer's Odyssey, represents the most famous troubled return. Delayed by di-vine hostility, particularly from Poseidon, and various supernatural encounters, Odysseus finally returns to find his household besieged by suitors pursuing his wife Penelope. After secretly entering his palace, he slaughters the suitors and reclaims his position. The Odyssey presents Odysseus's extended return as punishment for his role in Troy's destruction, particularly the blinding of Poseidon's son Polyphemus (Nagy 1999: 234).

Other prominent nostoi include:

Menelaus: Though he successfully recovered Helen, his return journey lasted eight years, including extended stays in Egypt and other Mediterranean loca-tions. This prolonged wandering, despite having achieved his personal objective, suggests a pattern where even "justified" violence required atonement (Heubeck 1989: 156).

Ajax the Lesser: After violating Cassandra in Athena's temple during Troy's fall, Ajax was shipwrecked during his return. When he boasted of surviving despite the goddess's anger, Poseidon split the rock where Ajax clung and drowned him. This direct divine punishment for sacrilege established clear moral frameworks about excessive violence (Gantz 1993: 678).

Diomedes: Though initially returning successfully to Argos, Diomedes found his wife Aegialeia unfaithful, reportedly influenced by Aphrodite's anger over her wounding during the war. Forced to flee, Diomedes established cities in southern Italy, transforming his troubled nostos into a secondary foundation narrative (Malkin 1998: 245).

Neoptolemus: Achilles's son, notorious for brutality during Troy's sack, met violent death either at Delphi (killed at Apollo's altar as divine retribution) or in conflict with Orestes over Hermione. As Jonathan Burgess notes, "Neoptolemus's fate completes a pattern where the most violent participants in Troy's destruction themselves die violently" (Burgess 2001: 167).

The nostoi collectively present a moral framework where military victory carried spiritual and psychological costs. Archaeological evidence throughout the Greek world shows significant disruption during this period—the Mycenaean palatial system collapsed, literacy temporarily disappeared, and many sites show destruction or abandonment (Cline 2014: 234). While these changes likely resulted from complex historical processes rather than specific mythological events, they provided historical context making tales of troubled returns plausible to ancient audiences.

Divine Justice and Historical Memory

The post-Trojan War narratives reveal sophisticated theological frameworks where divine forces both punish and guide human actors. Several key themes emerge that reflect Bronze Age religious understanding:

Proportional Retribution: The suffering experienced by Greek heroes often corresponds directly to their wartime actions. Ajax's drowning punishes temple violation; Agamemnon's murder avenges Iphigenia's sacrifice; Odysseus's wanderings balance his role in Troy's destruction (Parker 1983: 178).

Purification Through Suffering: Many nostoi narratives present the heroes' trials as necessary purification for blood-guilt incurred at Troy. This appears explicitly in Aeschylus's formulation "pathei mathos" ("learning through suffering") and implicitly in the transformative journeys of figures like Odysseus and Aeneas (Goldhill 1992: 134).

Transferrence of Sacred Power: Multiple aftermath narratives involve moving sacred objects—the Trojan Palladium, Penates, cult statues—from Troy to new locations, suggesting divine favor could transfer between civilizations. This theological concept provided religious legitimacy for emerging political entities claiming Trojan heritage (Scheid 2003: 89).

As religious historian Walter Burkert notes, "These theological frameworks transformed historical disruptions into meaningful narrative patterns, suggesting that even catastrophic events served divine purposes within a moral cosmos" (Burkert 1985: 234).

Archaeological Evidence for Mythical Journeys

Archaeological discoveries provide intriguing potential connections to the mythological aftermath narratives, though direct confirmation remains elusive. Material evidence reveals patterns that broadly align with the geographic and chronological frameworks of these stories:

Western Mediterranean Connections: Excavations at sites in southern Italy, Sicily, and Sardinia reveal increasing Eastern Mediterranean influences during the Early Iron Age (10th-8th centuries BCE), including architectural techniques, pottery styles, and religious practices that could correspond with mythological migrations of Trojan and Greek heroes (Ridgway 1992: 156).

Etruscan Trojan Interest: Etruscan art and burial practices show particular fascination with Trojan narratives, with numerous depictions of Aeneas's flight appearing centuries before Virgil's literary treatment. These artistic representations suggest early circulation of Trojan migration myths in central Italy (Torelli 1989: 234).

Philistine Origins: Archaeological evidence indicates the Philistines who settled in the Levant around Troy's traditional fall brought Aegean cultural elements. Some scholars connect this historical migration with myths about Greek heroes settling in the region after the war (Yasur-Landau 2010: 167).

Cypriot Evidence: Cyprus shows particularly strong evidence for new connections with both the Aegean and Levant during this period, corresponding with various traditions about both Greek and Trojan settlements on the island (Karageorghis 1998: 234).

As archaeologist Carolyn Aslan suggests, "While we cannot archaeologically 'prove' specific mythological journeys, material evidence confirms significant population movements and cultural transmissions during this period that broadly align with the geographic framework of the nostoi and Trojan diaspora narratives" (Aslan 2006: 145).

Literary Processing of Historical Trauma

The aftermath of the Trojan War provided rich material for ancient authors exploring themes of justice, trauma, cultural identity, and the relationship between human action and divine will. Major literary treatments demonstrate how these narratives served as mechanisms for processing collective historical memory:

Homer's Odyssey: Beyond chronicling Odysseus's return, the epic explores how war transforms both individuals and communities. Odysseus returns physically and psychologically altered, while his household has developed new power dynamics during his absence. The poem's exploration of recognition between long-separated individuals serves as metaphor for post-war reconciliation (Schein 1996: 178).

Aeschylus's Oresteia: Using Agamemnon's murder as its central narrative, this trilogy examines how cycles of violence can transform into systems of justice. The progression from personal vengeance to civic legal process reflects Athens's own political evolution during the 5th century BCE (Goldhill 1992: 234).

Euripides's Trojan Women: Focusing on Troy's immediate aftermath from captured women's perspective, this tragedy explores war's devastating civilian impact. Produced during the Peloponnesian War after Athens's brutal treatment of Melos, the play offers pointed critique of imperial violence (Croally 1994: 156).

Virgil's Aeneid: Beyond chronicling Aeneas's journey, Virgil explores how trauma can transform into purpose. Aeneas carries psychological burden of witnessing Troy's destruction while bearing responsibility for preserving its essence. The poem's famous phrase "forsan et haec olim meminisse iuvabit" ("perhaps someday it will help to remember even these things") suggests painful memories can eventually serve constructive purposes (Williams 1973: 267).

As literary scholar Jonathan Shay observes in his study of combat trauma, "These ancient narratives offered mechanisms for societies to collectively process the psychological and social disruptions caused by warfare—creating meaning from suffering and establishing moral frameworks for understanding violence's consequences" (Shay 1994: 189).

The Trojan War in Historical Context

The mythological accounts gained credibility from their correspondence with actual developments during the Late Bronze Age collapse and subsequent Early Iron Age (approximately 1200-800 BCE). This period witnessed widespread migration, new political formations, and cultural transmissions that provide historical context for the mythological narratives:

Sea Peoples Activity: Egyptian records describe invasions by confederated maritime groups around 1177 BCE, coinciding with Troy's traditional fall. Some scholars suggest connections between returning Greek warriors of myth and these historical Sea Peoples (Cline 2014: 134).

Foundation of Western Greek Colonies: Beginning around the 8th century BCE, Greek city-states established colonies throughout the Mediterranean. These historical colonization movements may have been retroactively connected to the heroic generation through nostoi narratives (Malkin 1998: 234).

Emergence of New Political Entities: Bronze Age kingdoms' collapse created opportunities for new formations. The Philistines in the Levant, Etruscan civilization in Italy, and various Greek poleis emerged during this transitional period (Drews 1993: 178).

As archaeologist Susan Sherratt suggests, "The Trojan War aftermath narratives provided a heroic framework for understanding these complex historical processes—attributing migrations, political changes, and cultural transmissions to specific heroic individuals rather than impersonal historical forces" (Sherratt 1998: 234).

Cultural Legacy and Political Legitimacy

The narratives of Trojan survivors and returning Greek heroes profoundly influenced Mediterranean and European cultural development in several key areas:

Political Legitimacy: Throughout antiquity, ruling families and cities claimed Trojan or Greek heroic ancestry to enhance prestige and legitimize authority. The Roman Julian clan's claim to descent from Aeneas represents the most successful example, but similar claims appeared throughout the Mediterranean world (Gruen 2011: 234).

Colonial Narratives: Greek and Roman colonization movements frequently employed nostoi and Trojan diaspora frameworks to justify territorial claims and explain cultural connections between distant regions. As historian Irad Malkin notes, "These myths created 'networks of memory' that integrated new settlements into existing cultural frameworks" (Malkin 1998: 156).

Literary Paradigms: The return and foundation narratives established enduring patterns influencing countless subsequent works. The nostoi pattern of departure-trial-return became fundamental narrative structure in Western literature, while the Aeneid established the "national foundation epic" as distinct genre (Hardie 1986: 234).

Models of Heroism: The contrasting heroic models—Odysseus's adaptability, Aeneas's pious duty, Agamemnon's flawed leadership—provided reference points for discussions of virtue and leadership throughout Western intellectual history (Galinsky 1996: 178).

Conclusion: The War That Never Ended

The mythological aftermath of the Trojan War reveals sophisticated ancient understanding of war's complex consequences. Far from presenting simplistic victory narratives, these traditions acknowledge how violence transforms both perpetrators and victims, creating ripple effects extending across generations and geographies.

The parallel journeys of figures like Odysseus and Aeneas—one returning to reclaim his original home, the other journeying toward new homeland—represent complementary responses to warfare's disruptions. Together, they establish frameworks where military conflict functions as both ending and beginning, destruction and creation.

The enduring power of these aftermath narratives stems from their psychological and historical resonance. They address universal questions about how individuals and societies recover from trauma while simultaneously preserving cultural memory of actual historical disruptions during the Late Bronze Age collapse.

As historian Erich Gruen observes, "These myths demonstrate remarkable sophistication in their recognition that military victory often carries costs as severe as defeat, while catastrophic loss can sometimes contain the seeds of renewal and even greatness" (Gruen 2011: 345).

When we excavate the destruction layers at Troy today, examining the burned buildings and scattered artifacts that mark the city's violent end, we're looking at more than archaeological evidence—we're seeing the moment when history transformed into legend, when Bronze Age reality became the foundation for millennia of cultural imagination. The scattered Trojans and returning Greeks, carrying the psychological and spiritual consequences of their decade-long conflict, collectively demonstrate how warfare's true impact extends far beyond battlefields, reshaping identities and redirecting historical trajectories in ways that continue reverberating through time.

The fall of Troy represents not an endpoint but a transition—the moment when ancient memory becomes future destiny, when the catastrophe of one civilization creates conditions for others to emerge. In this sense, the Trojan War never truly ended; its aftermath continues unfolding through the cultural, political, and literary legacy it generated—a legacy that remains vibrant in our contemporary understanding of warfare, trauma, migration, and the eternal human struggle to create meaning from chaos.

CHAPTER 6

HOMER'S LEGACY

How Epic Poetry Shaped Three Millennia of Understanding

Picture Heinrich Schliemann in 1876, standing over a golden death mask at Mycenae, declaring "I have gazed on the face of Agamemnon!" He was wrong about the mask's date—it actually predated the Trojan War by centuries—but his passionate conviction captures something profound about Homer's enduring power. For nearly three millennia, the Iliad and Odyssey have functioned as the primary lens through which Western civilization has viewed Troy, creating a literary framework so compelling that it has often overshadowed archaeological and historical evidence.

This isn't just about poetry influencing culture—it's about how a masterful work of art can become so embedded in human consciousness that it shapes the very questions we ask about the past. When archaeologists dig at Troy, when historians analyze Bronze Age conflicts, when artists create new works about ancient warfare, they're all operating within parameters largely established by Homer's epic vision. Understanding this influence is crucial for understanding not just Troy itself, but how we construct our relationship with the ancient world (Nagy 1996: 89).

The Making of a Masterpiece: How Homer's Troy Came to Be

Before examining the poems' massive cultural influence, we need to understand their origins. The Homeric epics emerged from centuries of oral bardic poetry that likely preserved memories of Bronze Age conflicts long before being written down. Most scholars place the composition of the Iliad and Odyssey in their current form around the 8th century BCE—approximately four centuries after the traditional date of the Trojan War (West 2011: 156).

The gap between events and composition is crucial for understanding what these poems actually represent. They're not Bronze Age journalism but Iron Age poetry that artfully combines genuine historical memories with later cultural perspectives. Linguist Calvert Watkins has identified archaic formulaic phrases that appear to date to the Bronze Age, embedded within clearly later compositional frameworks—suggesting the poems preserve ancient kernels of tradition within evolved narrative structures (Watkins 1995: 234).

The textual history reveals their cultural significance from antiquity. When scholars at the Library of Alexandria like Zenodotus and Aristarchus created critical editions in the 3rd century BCE, they faced hundreds of variant versions, demonstrating both the poems' widespread circulation and their perceived importance (Nagy 1996: 134). As Gregory Nagy notes, "The very existence of these editorial projects shows that by the Hellenistic period, the Homeric poems were already considered foundational cultural documents worthy of preservation and scholarly attention."

Few ancient works received such consistent attention across so many centuries. When the Byzantine Empire preserved classical texts through the medieval period, Homer topped their priority list. Renaissance humanists treated the poems as essential cultural patrimony. This unbroken chain of transmission ensured that Homer's vision of Troy would dominate Western understanding for millennia.

The Homeric Lens: How Epic Poetry Shaped Archaeological Practice

Homer's influence on Troy extends far beyond literature into the realm of archaeological practice itself—with fascinating and sometimes problematic results. When Heinrich Schliemann began excavating at Hisarlık in the 1870s, he explicitly framed his project as an attempt to validate Homer's historical accuracy. His methodology was fundamentally shaped by his desire to find the Homeric Troy, leading him to interpret findings within a Homeric framework even when evidence suggested otherwise (Traill 1995: 167).

Schliemann's approach created patterns that persisted well into the 20th century. He identified architectural features according to Homeric descriptions, labeled artifact assemblages with Homeric names, and consistently prioritized evidence that aligned with the poems while downplaying contradictory findings. When he discovered what he called "Priam's Treasure"—a cache of gold objects from Troy II—he ignored the fact that this level dated to around 2300 BCE, far earlier than any possible Trojan War (Easton 1994: 134).

This Homeric gravitational pull continued with subsequent excavators. Wilhelm Dörpfeld's identification of Troy VI as "Homer's Troy" in the 1890s and Carl Blegen's later reassignment of this designation to Troy VIIa in the 1930s both accepted the basic premise that one archaeological layer must correspond to the Homeric city (Blegen 1963: 156). Even modern excavations led by Manfred Korfmann frequently framed their findings in Homeric terms, despite Korfmann's own cautions about direct correlations.

As archaeologist Susan Sherratt observes, "Schliemann's archaeological methodology reveals more about his devotion to Homer than about Bronze Age Troy, frequently stretching evidence to fit Homeric expectations" (Sherratt 2000: 89). This created what we might call "the Homeric filter"—a tendency to evaluate archaeological discoveries primarily by how well they align with the epic poems rather than on their own material terms.

The influence extends beyond Troy itself. The identification of Mycenaean civilization as representing "Homer's Greeks" established interpretative patterns that sometimes projected Homeric social structures onto archaeological evidence without sufficient justification. Material discoveries that align with Homeric de-tails—like boar's tusk helmets or tower shields mentioned in the poems—receive disproportionate attention, while features absent from Homer often remain un-derstudied (Morris 1997: 234).

Troy as Symbol: The East-West Paradigm

Homer's portrayal of the Trojan War established a paradigmatic vision of East-West conflict that has resonated throughout Western cultural history with profound political consequences. Though the Iliad presents a nuanced view where individual Trojans like Hector appear sympathetically, it nevertheless es-tablishes a fundamental opposition between Greek and Trojan identities that later interpretations would simplify into civilizational clash.

This framework proved remarkably durable and adaptable. Classical Athenian orators invoked the Trojan War as precedent for their conflicts with Persia, casting themselves as the new Achaeans fighting eastern barbarians. Alexander the Great explicitly modeled his Asian campaigns as reenactment of the Trojan War, visiting Troy to sacrifice at supposed tombs of Homeric heroes and claiming to complete what his ancestors had begun (Bosworth 1988: 145).

Roman writers brilliantly inverted the paradigm while maintaining its basic structure. By claiming descent from Trojan refugees through Aeneas, they posi-tioned themselves as both victims of Greek aggression and ultimate victors who would rule the Mediterranean world. Virgil's Aeneid transforms the Trojans from defeated easterners into founders of western empire—a remarkable ideological reversal that maintained Homer's framework while completely reorienting its implications (Hardie 1986: 234).

During the Renaissance and Enlightenment, European powers repeatedly in-voked Homeric parallels in their conflicts with the Ottoman Empire. The Greeks fighting for independence in the 1820s explicitly framed their struggle as resum-ing the ancient conflict, while European supporters saw themselves as aiding the descendants of Homer's heroes against modern Trojans. As historian Edith Hall observes, "The Homeric framework provided ready-made narrative that allowed Europeans to conceptualize modern geopolitical tensions as continuations of ancient cultural oppositions" (Hall 1989: 156).

This pattern continues today in surprising ways. Political rhetoric about "clashes of civilizations" often unconsciously echoes Homeric paradigms, while archaeological discussions of Troy frequently employ language that recalls ancient East-West dichotomies despite scholarly awareness of their limitations.

Literary Legacy: Homer's Troy Through Three Millennia

The literary influence of Homer's Troy extends throughout Western literary history, establishing patterns and themes that countless authors have adopted, adapted, and challenged. This influence reveals both the poems' extraordinary creative power and their remarkable adaptability to changing cultural contexts.

Classical Responses: In the ancient world, Homer's account quickly became definitive, marginalizing alternative traditions. Greek tragedians like Aeschylus, Sophocles, and Euripides based numerous plays on Trojan cycle episodes, consistently working within Homer's framework while occasionally challenging specific aspects. Euripides's Trojan Women (415 BCE) maintains Homer's basic narrative while shifting focus to Trojan women's suffering, transforming a narrative of heroic achievement into one of tragic loss (Croally 1994: 234).

Roman authors similarly worked within the Homeric paradigm while adapting it to their cultural context. Virgil's Aeneid represents the most significant response, accepting Homer's portrayal of Troy's fall while creating a continuation that transforms defeat into foundation for Roman imperial destiny. As Richard Thomas notes, "Virgil's genius lies in his ability to simultaneously honor the Homeric account while completely reorienting its historical significance" (Thomas 2001: 167).

Medieval Transformations: Medieval European literature demonstrates Homer's remarkable adaptability. Though direct knowledge of Homeric texts was limited in Western Europe before the Renaissance, derivative accounts preserved the basic narrative while introducing modifications aligned with medieval sensibilities. Works like Benoît de Sainte-Maure's Roman de Troie (c. 1160) transformed the Trojan narrative into chivalric romance, introducing anachronistic elements like knights and courtly love while maintaining Homer's character framework (Baumgartner 1994: 145).

As medievalist C.D. Lewis observes, "Medieval Troy was simultaneously ancient and contemporary, historical and fictional. Authors felt free to adapt details while treating the core narrative as historical truth—precisely the approach Homer himself likely took to earlier traditions" (Lewis 1969: 234).

Renaissance and Beyond: The Renaissance reintroduction of Homer's original texts dramatically influenced literary portrayals. Shakespeare's Troilus and Cressida (c. 1602) reveals this influence's complexity, combining elements from Homer, medieval romances, and Chaucer to create a cynical deconstruction of heroic values. As Janet Adelman notes, "Shakespeare uses the Trojan setting to explore disillusionment with traditional heroic ideals, creating deliberately jarring contrast between elevated epic language and petty, often sordid behavior" (Adelman 1973: 156).

Modern Reimaginings: Contemporary novelists continue reinterpreting the Trojan narrative, often giving voice to marginalized perspectives. Works like Christa Wolf's Cassandra (1983), Marion Zimmer Bradley's The Firebrand (1987), and Madeline Miller's The Song of Achilles (2011) maintain Homer's basic framework while critiquing its assumptions and filling its silences. As Emily Wilson observes, "These modern retellings reveal both the enduring power of Homer's vision and its limitations—the perspectives it privileged and those it obscured" (Wilson 2019: 234).

Educational and Cultural Foundations

Homer's portrayal of Troy served as an educational cornerstone throughout Western history with profound cultural consequences. In classical Athens, recitation and analysis of Homeric passages formed the core of formal education. Students memorized extensive passages, analyzed heroic behavior, and learned moral lessons from epic examples (Clarke 1968: 134).

Roman educational practices continued this tradition, with Homeric texts serving as primary material for teaching Greek language and cultural values. As Quintilian noted, "Homer alone is nearly sufficient for developing every faculty required in students of rhetoric" (Quintilian, Institutio Oratoria 10.1.46). This educational centrality ensured that generation after generation of Mediterranean elites shared a common framework for understanding Troy based primarily on Homeric accounts.

Renaissance humanists revived this educational model with renewed enthusiasm. Erasmus wrote, "From Homer we learn not merely grammar and vocabulary but the entire range of human wisdom" (Erasmus, De Ratione Studii). This educational prominence meant that European intellectual elites across centuries possessed intimate familiarity with Homer's Troy, making Homeric references and parallels fundamental to educated discourse (Grafton 1991: 167).

Beyond formal education, public performances and artistic representations continually reinforced Homer's vision. From rhapsodes performing Homeric recitations in ancient agoras to Renaissance paintings of Trojan scenes to modern film adaptations, visual and performative traditions have consistently reinforced the primacy of the Homeric framework (Ford 2002: 234).

Archaeological Challenges and Reconciliations

Modern archaeology has revealed numerous inconsistencies between Homer's Troy and material findings, creating productive tensions that have advanced our understanding of both the poems and the archaeological site. These challenges don't invalidate Homer but rather illuminate the complex relationship between literary tradition and historical evidence.

Chronological Mismatches: The material culture Homer describes combines elements from different historical periods, creating what Emily Vermeule called "a deliberate archaizing amalgam" rather than historically accurate portrait of any single era (Vermeule 1986: 89). Bronze weapons dominate Homeric descriptions, yet by the traditional Trojan War date, iron technology was emerging. Political geography better reflects 8th-century BCE conditions than Late Bronze Age realities.

Material Contradictions: Specific Homeric details frequently contradict archaeological evidence. Homer describes Troy as wealthy in horses, yet steep terrain around Hisarlık is poorly suited for horse breeding. The massive walls Homer describes find no exact archaeological parallel in appropriate layers. As Manfred Korfmann acknowledged, "There is no single archaeological layer at Troy that perfectly matches Homer's description. The poet created a composite image drawing on traditions from multiple periods" (Korfmann 2004: 156).

Historical Context Issues: Hittite texts, providing our most contemporaneous written sources for the region, make no mention of a conflict matching Homer's description, despite documenting numerous other regional conflicts. As Trevor Bryce notes, "The silence of Hittite sources regarding a major conflict at Troy/Wilusa during this period represents a significant challenge to accepting the Homeric account at face value" (Bryce 2006: 234).

Productive Synthesis: Contemporary scholarship has moved beyond simple questions of whether Homer is "true" or "false," developing nuanced approaches that recognize both historical elements and literary nature. Many scholars now approach the poems as preserving cultural memories of historical events while transforming them through centuries of oral transmission (Sherratt 2000: 167).

This approach recognizes that oral traditions can preserve memories across centuries while inevitably transforming them. Elements like massive walls, chariot use, and certain weapon types may reflect genuine Bronze Age memories, while other elements clearly reflect later contexts. As Susan Sherratt suggests, "The poems likely contain kernels of historical memory embedded within layers of later additions, making them neither purely fictional nor straightforwardly historical" (Sherratt 2000: 189).

The Homeric Paradox: Inspiration and Limitation

Perhaps the most fascinating aspect of Homer's influence is how it has simultaneously inspired and constrained our understanding of Troy. Without Homer, Troy might remain just another excavated Bronze Age settlement rather than a site of extraordinary cultural significance. The poems have inspired archaeological investigations that have dramatically expanded our understanding of Bronze Age Mediterranean cultures, regardless of how closely findings align with specific Homeric details.

Yet this same influence has created interpretative biases that sometimes prevent us from seeing Troy on its own material terms. The gravitational pull of Homer continues to influence even scientifically rigorous investigations. Excavators may resist direct Homeric correlations in technical publications while employing Homeric frameworks when communicating with the public (Bryce 2006: 267).

As archaeologist Ian Morris argues, "The Homeric filter has created persistent biases in Bronze Age archaeology, prioritizing certain research questions and interpretative frameworks while marginalizing others. We continue to excavate in Homer's long shadow" (Morris 1997: 234).

Beyond True and False: Homer's Enduring Relevance

The tension between Homeric accounts and archaeological evidence has proven extraordinarily productive, generating research questions and methodological innovations that might otherwise never have emerged. As Susan Allen notes,

"Without Homer, Troy might remain just one of many excavated Bronze Age settlements rather than a site of extraordinary cultural significance" (Allen 1999: 156).

Modern approaches increasingly treat Homer not as a historical source to be verified or debunked but as a cultural phenomenon that illuminates how societies construct relationships with their past. The poems present not merely a narrative of events but profound exploration of human experience—the tragedy of war, complexity of heroism, interplay of divine and human causation, tension between individual excellence and communal responsibility.

These themes transcend questions of historical accuracy, giving the poems relevance across cultures and centuries. As Emily Wilson observes, "Homer's Troy persists not because it perfectly matches archaeological Troy but because it perfectly captures essential human experiences and conflicts. The poems' emotional and philosophical truth transcends their historical accuracy or inaccuracy" (Wilson 2019: 267).

Conclusion: The Conversation Continues

After three millennia, Homer's portrayal of Troy remains the foundation through which most people understand the site and its significance. Despite archaeological evidence that complicates specific Homeric details, the poems continue shaping public perception, scholarly discourse, and artistic representation of Troy. This enduring influence testifies to the extraordinary literary power of Homer's vision.

Perhaps the most remarkable aspect is how Homer's influence has created productive dialogue between literature and archaeology, poetry and history. The tension between Homeric accounts and material evidence has generated far richer understanding than either approach alone could provide. As Manfred Korfmann acknowledged, "The dialogue between Homer and archaeology has been the most productive force in Trojan studies, pushing both literary scholars and archaeologists to refine their methods and conclusions" (Korfmann 2004: 234).

Homer's Troy thus represents more than an ancient city or literary setting—it embodies the complex relationship between memory and history, narrative and evidence, that characterizes all human attempts to understand the past. Troy's greatest significance may lie not in whether Homer "got it right" but in how his powerful vision has inspired three thousand years of questioning, investigation, and imagination.

As we continue excavating, analyzing, and interpreting both the physical site and literary tradition it inspired, we participate in a conversation that began with Homer—a conversation about how to remember the past, understand human conflict, and find meaning in traumatic events that shape both individual lives and entire civilizations. In this sense, Homer's influence on Troy extends far beyond archaeology or literature into the realm of human meaning-making itself, ensuring that his vision will continue shaping our understanding for generations to come.

CHAPTER 7
HEINRICH SCHLIEMANN

The Man Who Found Troy

Picture Heinrich Schliemann in 1873, standing in a massive trench he'd carved through the ancient mound at Hisarlık, Turkey, holding what he believed were the golden treasures of King Priam himself. The German businessman-turned-archaeologist was wrong about almost everything—the date, the historical context, even the circumstances of discovery—yet his passionate conviction that Homer's Troy was real and findable would transform archaeology forever. In the annals of archaeological history, few figures embody such contradictions: part romantic visionary, part rigorous investigator, part destructive treasure hunter, part scientific pioneer.

Schliemann's story illustrates both the promise and perils of archaeology's heroic age, when spectacular discoveries competed with spectacular mistakes, and when one person's obsession could reshape our understanding of the ancient world. His excavations at Hisarlık launched not only modern Aegean archaeology but also a century and a half of scholarly debate about the relationship between Homer's literary Troy and archaeological reality (Traill 1995: 89).

From Business Success to Archaeological Obsession

Heinrich Schliemann's path to Troy began in 1822 in the small German town of Neubukow, where his father served as a Protestant minister. The boy's fascination with ancient Troy supposedly began at age seven when his father gave him a children's history book containing an illustration of the burning city. As Schliemann later recalled in his autobiography: "With great grief I gazed on the walls of Troy in this picture, and said, 'Father, did you ever see Troy?' 'No,' he answered. Then I exclaimed, 'Father, if such walls once existed, they cannot possibly have been completely destroyed; vast ruins of them must still remain, but they are hidden away beneath the dust of ages'" (Schliemann 1881: 1-2).

This oft-repeated anecdote—likely embellished or entirely invented by the adult Schliemann—nonetheless captures the romantic conviction that would drive his later archaeological endeavors. From childhood, supposedly, Schliemann approached Troy not as mythology but as historical reality waiting rediscovery (Traill 1995: 45).

Before fulfilling this dream, however, Schliemann first needed to acquire the financial means for such ambitious undertaking. His early life reads like a 19th-century business adventure novel. After receiving only rudimentary education, he worked as a grocer's apprentice at fourteen, became a cabin boy on a ship bound for Venezuela (only to be shipwrecked off the Dutch coast), and found employment in Amsterdam, where he demonstrated extraordinary aptitude for languages (Allen 1999: 67).

Working as a correspondence clerk for a trading firm, Schliemann developed methodical approaches to language acquisition that allowed him to master Dutch, English, French, Spanish, Portuguese, Italian, Russian, Swedish, Polish, and eventually Greek and Latin. By his own account, he could learn a new language in six weeks—a skill that proved crucial to his subsequent business career.

Moving to St. Petersburg in 1846, Schliemann established himself as an indigo merchant before making his fortune during the Crimean War as a military contractor. Further success in California, where he profited from banking and investments during the Gold Rush, established him as a wealthy international businessman by his early forties (Easton 1984: 134).

Yet commercial success never displaced his childhood fascination with Homer and Troy. In 1868, at age 46, Schliemann liquidated his business interests and dedicated himself to archaeology, determined to prove that Homer's epics described historical events and places. As he wrote to a friend, "I am now free to follow the dream of my life, the discovery of Troy" (Schliemann 1875: preface).

The Homeric Detective: Locating Troy Through Literature

Schliemann's approach to archaeology was inseparable from his devotion to Homer. Unlike many contemporary scholars who viewed the Iliad and Odyssey as purely literary creations, Schliemann maintained almost religious conviction that Homer's epics preserved genuine historical memories of Bronze Age Greece. "I have worked solely to vindicate the truth of that immortal poem," he wrote of the Iliad, and this conviction guided his archaeological methodology from the outset (Schliemann 1874: xiii).

Before beginning excavations, Schliemann immersed himself in Homeric studies, traveling throughout Greece and Turkey following routes described in the epics. He married young Greek woman Sophia Engastromenos, partly because he believed she embodied the classical Greek ideal and could assist his archaeological work. Most significantly, he became convinced that the traditional location of Troy at Bunarbashi (favored by many contemporary scholars) was incorrect, and that the true site lay at Hisarlık, a hill in northwestern Turkey (Meyer 1936: 89).

This conviction wasn't entirely original to Schliemann. British diplomat Frank Calvert, who owned part of the Hisarlık site, had already conducted small excavations there and believed it might be Troy. Schliemann, however, would pursue this identification with unprecedented resources and determination. As Calvert later wrote, somewhat bitterly, "Mr. Schliemann came, saw, and appropriated to himself my discovery" (Allen 1999: 156).

Archaeological evidence now confirms that Schliemann and Calvert chose correctly—Hisarlık is almost certainly the site of Bronze Age Troy. But their reasoning was based primarily on literary analysis rather than material evidence. They compared Homer's geographic descriptions with the actual landscape, noting that Hisarlık's position overlooking the Dardanelles matched the Iliad's portrayal of Troy's strategic location controlling access between Europe and Asia.

Revolutionary Methods, Questionable Results

In 1870, Schliemann began excavations at Hisarlık, working initially on land owned by Calvert before obtaining official firman (permit) from the Ottoman government to expand his work. His approach was characterized by boundless enthusiasm but limited scientific methodology. As archaeologist William Calder III later observed, "Schliemann dug like a prospector, not an archaeologist" (Calder 1972: 234).

This assessment, while harsh, captures fundamental truth about Schliemann's early work. Rather than the careful, stratigraphic approach that would later characterize scientific archaeology, Schliemann employed hundreds of workers to remove vast quantities of earth as quickly as possible, driving massive trenches through the center of the mound. His goal was simple: reach what he believed were Homeric layers of the site, regardless of what might be destroyed in the process.

Modern archaeologists cringe at Schliemann's methods. His great north-south trench destroyed countless artifacts and obliterated stratigraphic relationships that could have revealed how the site developed over time. As excavation director Manfred Korfmann noted more than a century later, "Schliemann's trenches are like archaeological black holes—we can never recover the information his methods destroyed" (Korfmann 2004: 67).

Yet the results were undeniably dramatic. By 1873, Schliemann had identified nine distinct cities built one atop another at Hisarlık, revealing that the site had been continuously occupied for over three millennia. He immediately identified the second city from the bottom (Troy II) as Homer's Troy, largely because it showed evidence of violent destruction that he attributed to the Greek sack described in epic poetry.

"I have proved that in a remote antiquity there was in the plain of Troy a large city, destroyed of old by a fearful catastrophe," he wrote triumphantly (Schliemann 1874: 325). This conclusion seemed to validate his Homeric quest, but it contained a significant chronological error. The burned city he identified as Homer's Troy actually dated to approximately 2400-2200 BCE—roughly a millennium too early for the traditional dating of the Trojan War.

This mistake exemplifies how Schliemann's determination to find Homer's Troy sometimes led him to force evidence to fit his preconceptions—a problem that continues to challenge archaeologists today.

"Priam's Treasure": Discovery, Drama, and Deception

If Schliemann's methods were questionable, his results were undeniably spectacular. On May 31, 1873, near the end of his second season at Hisarlık, Schliemann claimed to have made the discovery that would secure his place in archaeological history—a cache of gold objects that he immediately dubbed "Priam's Treasure."

The circumstances of this discovery, as recounted by Schliemann himself, read like adventure fiction. While his workers were at lunch, Schliemann and his wife Sophia supposedly spotted a copper object gleaming in the soil. Recognizing its potential importance, they allegedly excavated the area themselves, uncovering spectacular assemblage of gold, silver, bronze, and copper artifacts: diadems, earrings, bracelets, rings, buttons, vessels, weapons, and the famous "Jewels of Helen"—two gold headbands with pendants and earrings.

Schliemann's account was characteristically dramatic: "In excavating this wall further and directly by the side of the palace of King Priam, I came upon a large copper article of the most remarkable form, which attracted my attention all the more as I thought I saw gold behind it... In order to withdraw the treasure from the greed of my workmen, and to save it for archaeology... I immediately had 'paidos' [lunch break] called... While the men were eating and resting, I cut out the treasure with a large knife" (Schliemann 1874: 323-324).

This narrative, emphasizing the personal heroism of Schliemann and his wife, captivated public imagination. Here was tangible proof, it seemed, that Homer's Troy was real—that legendary kings and their golden city were historical facts rather than poetic inventions.

The reality was considerably more complex. Modern analysis reveals that the treasure almost certainly didn't belong to anyone named Priam, as it dated to Troy II (c. 2400-2200 BCE), roughly a millennium before the traditional Trojan War. Moreover, subsequent examination of Schliemann's field notes and correspondence suggests the discovery was neither as sudden nor as personal as his published account claimed. The treasure appears to have been found over several days, with workers present, rather than in a single dramatic moment (Traill 1995: 167).

Most problematically, Schliemann smuggled the treasure out of Turkey in violation of Ottoman law, which stipulated that half of all archaeological finds belonged to the government. This action, which he freely admitted in his publications, damaged his relationship with Turkish authorities and established troubling precedent of archaeological imperialism that continues to haunt the discipline.

Despite these ethical and methodological problems, the discovery of "Priam's Treasure" transformed both Schliemann's reputation and public perceptions of Troy. When he published his findings in "Trojanische Alterthümer" (1874), complete with photographs and drawings of spectacular gold artifacts, Schliemann became international celebrity. The treasure was exhibited in London and Berlin, drawing enormous crowds and generating unprecedented public interest in archaeology.

Academic Backlash and Scientific Evolution

The scholarly response to Schliemann's discoveries was far more mixed than enthusiastic public reception. From the beginning, professional archaeologists and classicists expressed serious reservations about both his methods and interpretations.

Rudolf Virchow, prominent German physician and anthropologist who visited Hisarlık in 1879, praised Schliemann's energy but criticized his hasty excavation techniques, noting that "important evidence has been irretrievably lost" (Virchow 1881: 45). British archaeologist Alexander Conze similarly lamented that "Schliemann has done much damage through his impetuous and unskilled digging" (Conze 1882: 234).

Even more pointed criticism came from those who questioned Schliemann's identification of Hisarlık as Troy. French scholar Victor Bérard dismissed Schliemann's claims entirely, arguing that "Homer's Troy is a poet's creation, not a place to be found with a spade" (Bérard 1894: 67). Others accepted that Hisarlık might be an ancient settlement but rejected specific identification with Homer's Troy.

The most substantive criticisms concerned Schliemann's tendency to force archaeological evidence to fit Homeric narratives. As British archaeologist Arthur Evans (later famous for excavations at Knossos) observed, "Schliemann found at Hissarlik what he went to find—neither more nor less" (Evans 1884: 156). This tendency was particularly evident in Schliemann's naming practices, dubbing architectural features "Priam's Palace" or "The Scaean Gate" with little evidence beyond their general location.

Schliemann responded to these criticisms with mixture of defensive bluster and genuine scientific improvement. His later excavations at Troy, conducted in collaboration with more methodologically rigorous Wilhelm Dörpfeld, showed significant improvements in technique and documentation. He also modified some of his more extreme claims, eventually acknowledging that the "Burnt City" he had initially identified as Homer's Troy might be too early for traditional dating of the Trojan War.

Yet he never abandoned his fundamental belief in the historical reality of Homer's epics or his conviction that he had discovered the physical remains of Troy. As he wrote shortly before his death in 1890, "I may have made errors in details, but the great fact remains: Troy has been found" (Schliemann 1890: preface).

The Schliemann Paradox: Pioneer and Problem

Heinrich Schliemann died on December 26, 1890, leaving behind complex and contested legacy. His work at Troy (and later at Mycenae and Tiryns) had transformed public understanding of Bronze Age Greece, bringing unprecedented attention to a period previously known primarily through myth and poetry. Yet his methods had destroyed valuable archaeological evidence, and many of his specific interpretations would be revised or rejected by subsequent scholarship.

The immediate impact was to establish Hisarlık definitively as the location of historical Troy. Whatever doubts scholars might harbor about his methods or conclusions, the sheer volume of material he uncovered made it impossible to dismiss the site as insignificant. As archaeologist Carl Blegen later observed, "Schliemann may not have found Homer's Troy, but he found Troy for Homer" (Blegen 1963: 12).

More broadly, Schliemann's excavations helped establish archaeology as discipline that could meaningfully engage with questions of historical and literary significance. By demonstrating that sites previously known only through texts could be physically located and excavated, he helped bridge the gap between philology and material culture studies that had previously characterized classical scholarship.

Schliemann also played crucial role in popularizing archaeology for mass audiences. His dramatic narratives, spectacular finds, and personal charisma made Bronze Age archaeology accessible to the public in unprecedented ways. As C.W. Ceram noted in "Gods, Graves, and Scholars," "Schliemann gave archaeology the character of adventure, of a great treasure hunt, and thus won for it the interest of millions who would otherwise never have heard of Mycenae or Troy" (Ceram 1951: 67).

This popularization had both positive and negative consequences. It generated public support and funding for archaeological research that might otherwise have remained niche scholarly pursuit. But it also established problematic expectations about archaeological discovery, emphasizing spectacular treasures over more mundane but often more historically significant aspects of material culture.

Revisions and Vindications: Troy After Schliemann

Subsequent excavations at Troy have significantly revised Schliemann's findings while building upon his foundational work. Wilhelm Dörpfeld's excavations in the 1890s employed more rigorous methodology and identified Troy VI as a more likely candidate for Homer's city, based on its impressive fortifications and appropriate dating. Carl Blegen's work in the 1930s further refined the chronology, suggesting Troy VIIa (destroyed around 1180 BCE) as the most probable setting for any historical Trojan War.

Manfred Korfmann's excavations from 1988-2005 revolutionized understanding of Troy's size and importance, revealing that the Bronze Age settlement was much larger than Schliemann had imagined—a substantial urban center rather than just a hilltop fortress. These discoveries validate Schliemann's basic insight that Hisarlık was indeed a major Bronze Age site worthy of Homer's epic treatment (Rose 2014: 134).

We now know that Schliemann's "Burnt City" (Troy II) dates to the Early Bronze Age, roughly a millennium before the traditional Trojan War. His "Priam's Treasure" belonged to anonymous Early Bronze Age rulers whose names and stories are lost to history. The Troy that might have inspired Homer's epic was either Troy VI (destroyed by earthquake around 1300 BCE) or Troy VIIa (destroyed by warfare around 1180 BCE).

Yet these revisions have built upon rather than erased Schliemann's foundational work. As archaeologist Susan Heuck Allen notes, "Every archaeologist who has worked at Troy since Schliemann has been in dialogue with his findings, whether affirming, revising, or rejecting them" (Allen 1999: 234). This ongoing conversation testifies to the enduring significance of his discoveries, whatever their limitations.

Lessons from the Pioneer: The Schliemann Legacy

The story of Heinrich Schliemann and Troy offers important lessons about archaeology's development as scientific discipline. His combination of romantic vision and empirical investigation, literary inspiration and material discovery, personal ambition and scholarly contribution created template for archaeological practice that subsequent generations would both emulate and critique.

His flaws serve as cautionary tales for modern archaeologists: the destruction of evidence through hasty excavation, the smuggling of artifacts, the forcing of data to fit preconceptions. Contemporary archaeological practice emphasizes careful stratigraphic excavation, international cooperation in artifact management, and hypothesis testing rather than confirmation bias—all responses to problems exemplified by Schliemann's work.

But his achievements remain foundational to our understanding of the ancient Aegean: the location of Troy, the demonstration of Bronze Age wealth and complexity, the integration of textual and material evidence. As classicist Emily Vermeule observed, "Schliemann was wrong about many things, but he was magnificently right about the most important thing: that Homer's world had a historical reality that could be recovered through archaeology" (Vermeule 1986: 45).

Perhaps most importantly, Schliemann established productive tension between literary and archaeological approaches to the ancient world that continues to characterize classical scholarship. By insisting on historical reality behind Homer's epics, he forced both archaeologists and classicists to grapple with complex relationships between text and artifact, memory and history, that define our understanding of Bronze Age Mediterranean.

Conclusion: The Hero's Journey

The story of Heinrich Schliemann and Troy illustrates how archaeology itself often mirrors the mythic patterns it seeks to investigate. Like hero from Greek epic, Schliemann embarked on quest driven by unwavering conviction, overcame obstacles through determination and resourcefulness, achieved spectacular triumphs, and left complex legacy that continues inspiring both admiration and criticism.

His excavations at Hisarlık marked watershed moment in Bronze Age Mediterranean archaeology, transforming Troy from poetic landscape into physical reality that could be touched, measured, and analyzed. Whatever his methodological shortcomings, this achievement fundamentally altered our relationship to Homer's epics and to the ancient world they describe.

When we examine artifacts from Schliemann's excavations today—housed in museums from Berlin to Athens to Istanbul—we're looking at both archaeological evidence and cultural artifacts that embody the tensions between romantic vision and scientific method, between literary inspiration and material proof, that continue to define classical archaeology. His story reminds us that the greatest archaeological discoveries often emerge from the passionate conviction that the past can be recovered, even when the methods for recovery remain imperfect.

As we continue to excavate, analyze, and interpret the physical remains of Troy, we remain in conversation with Schliemann—sometimes affirming his insights, sometimes correcting his errors, but always building upon the foundation he established. In this sense, his legacy, like Troy itself, represents complex layering of history and interpretation, achievement and controversy, that continues shaping our understanding of the ancient world and the discipline that studies it.

Chapter 8

CHAPTER 8: WILHELM DÖRPFELD AND THE REFINEMENT OF TROY

The Systematic Revolution

I n the spring of 1882, a tall, methodical German architect named Wilhelm Dörpfeld arrived at Hisarlık to join Heinrich Schliemann's excavations. The contrast between these two men could hardly have been more striking. Where Schliemann had been impulsive and dramatic, Dörpfeld was measured and precise. Where Schliemann relied on intuition and literary inspiration, Dörpfeld brought technical training and scientific rigor. This unlikely partnership would transform not only our understanding of Troy but revolutionize the very practice of archaeological excavation.

Standing at the edge of Schliemann's great trench, which had carved through the heart of the ancient mound like a massive wound, Dörpfeld must have recognized both the archaeological treasure and the methodological disaster before him. Here lay the remains of one of history's most famous cities, but excavated with techniques that destroyed as much evidence as they revealed. As British archaeologist Colin Renfrew later noted, "Schliemann had the vision and passion that discovered Troy, but it was Dörpfeld who gave us the framework to understand what Schliemann had found" (Renfrew 1980: 134).

From Architecture to Archaeology: The Making of a Methodologist

Wilhelm Dörpfeld initially joined Schliemann's expedition as an architectural expert, having previously worked at the prestigious German excavations at Olympia under the direction of Ernst Curtius. His background in architecture proved crucial for interpreting the complex stratigraphy of Troy, where multiple cities had been built one atop another over millennia. Unlike Schliemann, who had cut through layers with minimal documentation, Dörpfeld understood that the relationships between walls, floors, and foundations could reveal the sequence of construction and destruction that told Troy's story (Easton 1991: 78).

Their collaboration was not always smooth. Schliemann, accustomed to being the unquestioned authority at his excavations, sometimes bristled at Dörpfeld's methodological interventions. Yet the older man recognized his colleague's expertise. In a letter to archaeologist Rudolf Virchow in 1883, Schliemann wrote: "Dörpfeld's architectural knowledge has been invaluable. He sees patterns in the walls that I would have missed entirely" (Schliemann 1884: 45).

By the time of Schliemann's death in 1890, Dörpfeld had become his most trusted collaborator and designated successor. More importantly, he had begun introducing systematic approaches that would transform Troy from a treasure hunting ground into a scientific excavation. When Dörpfeld returned to Troy in 1893 for his own independent campaign, he was ready to apply these revolutionary methods fully.

The transformation Dörpfeld brought to Trojan archaeology reflected broader changes occurring throughout the discipline in the late 19th century. Archaeology was beginning its evolution from romantic antiquarianism toward scientific methodology, borrowing techniques from geology, architecture, and art history to create more rigorous approaches to understanding the past (Daniel 1981: 156).

The Stratigraphic Revolution: Reading Troy Layer by Layer

Dörpfeld's most significant contribution to Trojan archaeology was his sys-tematic application of stratigraphic principles—the study of archaeological layers and their chronological relationships. Stratigraphy had been developing as a concept throughout the 19th century, borrowed from geology where it explained the formation of rock layers over time. But Dörpfeld was among the first to apply it rigorously at a complex urban site where human activity had created an intricate sequence of construction, destruction, and rebuilding (Harris 1979: 89).

"Before Dörpfeld," explained archaeologist Martha Sharp Joukowsky, "ex-cavators often focused on finding objects rather than understanding contexts. Dörpfeld recognized that the position of artifacts within layers was as impor-tant as the artifacts themselves" (Joukowsky 1980: 234).

At Troy, Dörpfeld meticulously documented the sequence of settlements, identifying nine major phases of occupation spanning from the Early Bronze Age to the Roman period. He labeled these settlements Troy I through Troy IX, creating a chronological framework that, with modifications, remains in use today. This systematic approach revealed Troy's remarkable history in a way that Schliemann's treasure-focused excavations never could have achieved.

Dörpfeld demonstrated that the site had been continuously occupied for over 4,000 years, with each successive settlement rebuilding on the ruins of its predecessor. This extraordinary longevity helped explain why Troy occupied such an important place in ancient memory—it had been a significant settle-ment for millennia, not merely during the brief period described by Homer.

More importantly, Dörpfeld's stratigraphic work corrected one of Schlie-mann's most significant errors. Schliemann had identified Troy II—a wealthy Early Bronze Age settlement—as Homer's Troy, primarily because of the rich gold treasures he discovered there. Through careful analysis of architectur-al relationships and pottery sequences, Dörpfeld demonstrated conclusively that Troy II dated to approximately 2500-2300 BCE, roughly a thousand years before the traditional date of the Trojan War (Dörpfeld 1902: 67).

Instead, Dörpfeld proposed that Troy VI—a much larger and more impressive settlement dating to the Late Bronze Age (c. 1700-1250 BCE)—was the most likely candidate for Homer's city. This identification aligned much better with the traditional dating of the Trojan War to the late 13th or early 12th century BCE.

Architectural Analysis: Reconstructing Troy's Built Environment

If stratigraphy provided the chronological framework for Dörpfeld's work at Troy, his architectural documentation supplied the spatial dimension. As an architect by training, Dörpfeld brought unprecedented precision to recording Troy's built environment, creating detailed plans that allowed later scholars to understand how the city had developed over time.

Dörpfeld's architectural drawings were remarkable for their era. He created detailed plans of each building phase, documenting wall alignments, construction techniques, and spatial relationships with mathematical precision. These drawings allowed archaeologists to understand not just what buildings existed, but how they related to each other and how the city's organization had evolved through time (Dörpfeld 1902: 134).

For Troy VI—the settlement he identified as Homer's Troy—Dörpfeld documented a sophisticated urban center with massive fortification walls, large houses, and evidence of systematic planning. The fortifications were particularly impressive, built of carefully dressed limestone blocks and sloping inward to resist both earthquakes and siege warfare. At some points, these walls reached a thickness of five meters, lending archaeological credence to Homer's repeated description of "strong-walled Troy."

Inside these fortifications, Dörpfeld uncovered large megaron-style houses with central hearths, similar to those found at Mycenaean sites in Greece. This architectural similarity supported the idea of cultural connections between Troy and the Mycenaean world—providing the likely historical background for the conflict described in the Iliad (Blegen 1963: 89).

Archaeological evidence from Dörpfeld's excavations also revealed signs of catastrophic destruction. Troy VI showed clear evidence of damage consistent with a major earthquake, including toppled walls and structural collapses. The subsequent settlement, Troy VIIa, appeared to have been destroyed by fire, with burned debris and collapsed buildings throughout the excavated areas.

These observations led Dörpfeld to refine his identification of Homer's Troy. In his major publication "Troja und Ilion" (1902), he suggested that while Troy VI represented the wealthy, well-fortified city described in the Iliad, the actual destruction by the Greeks might have occurred during the Troy VIIa phase, after the city had been weakened by earthquake damage.

Material Culture and Regional Connections

Beyond stratigraphy and architecture, Dörpfeld made significant contributions to understanding Troy's material culture and its connections to the wider Mediterranean world. Unlike Schliemann, who had focused primarily on precious metals and spectacular finds, Dörpfeld recognized the chronological and cultural significance of everyday objects, particularly pottery.

Working with ceramic specialists, Dörpfeld established the first systematic pottery sequence for Troy, documenting how ceramic styles changed through time and how they related to pottery traditions at other sites. This ceramic chronology allowed him to correlate Troy's development with contemporary settlements throughout the Aegean and Anatolia, placing the city within its broader regional context (French 1999: 156).

Particularly significant was Dörpfeld's identification of Mycenaean pottery in the Troy VI and VIIa levels. This imported Greek pottery confirmed direct contact between Troy and the Mycenaean world during the Late Bronze Age—precisely the period when the Trojan War was traditionally believed to have occurred.

The presence of this pottery supported the historical plausibility of Greek-Trojan interactions, if not necessarily a war on the scale described by Homer.

Dörpfeld also documented local Trojan pottery traditions, demonstrating that while Troy maintained connections with the Greek world, it remained culturally distinct. This observation aligned perfectly with Homer's portrayal of Troy as a separate kingdom with its own language and customs, albeit one familiar with Greek practices and capable of diplomatic and military interaction.

In his field notes from 1894, Dörpfeld wrote: "The pottery tells us two important stories: that Troy was connected to the wider Aegean world through trade and cultural exchange, and that it maintained its own distinct identity. Both aspects support the historical plausibility of Homer's account" (Dörpfeld 1894: field notes).

Methodological Innovation: Creating Archaeological Science

Perhaps Dörpfeld's most lasting contribution was methodological. He established standards for archaeological documentation that transformed the discipline from treasure hunting into scientific inquiry, creating practices that remain fundamental to archaeological work today.

Dörpfeld insisted on detailed field notes, regular photography of excavation progress, and precise measurements of architectural features. He maintained stratigraphic sections showing the relationships between layers and carefully recorded the provenance of every artifact. These practices, now standard in archaeological fieldwork, were revolutionary in the late 19th century when most excavations produced little more than treasure lists and anecdotal accounts (Lucas 2001: 89).

"Dörpfeld understood that archaeology destroys its own evidence," explained classical archaeologist Susan Heuck Allen. "His meticulous documentation ensured that future scholars could reconstruct what he had excavated, even after the physical evidence had been removed" (Allen 1999: 234).

110

This emphasis on documentation proved particularly valuable for Troy, where Schliemann's earlier excavations had removed substantial portions of the site with minimal recording. Dörpfeld's notebooks, photographs, and drawings preserved information that would otherwise have been lost forever, allowing later archaeologists to reinterpret his findings in light of new discoveries and theoretical developments.

Dörpfeld also pioneered the practice of preliminary field reports, publishing annual summaries of his discoveries rather than waiting years for final publication. These reports, published in German archaeological journals, made his findings available to the scholarly community much more quickly than had been typical, allowing for contemporary feedback and collaborative interpretation (Dörpfeld 1893, 1894).

The Troy VI Hypothesis: Reconciling Homer and Archaeology

By the conclusion of his excavations in 1894, Dörpfeld had developed a comprehensive interpretation of Troy that would shape scholarship for decades. His identification of Troy VI as Homer's Troy represented a significant revision of Schliemann's views and aligned archaeological evidence much more closely with literary tradition.

Dörpfeld's Troy VI was an impressive settlement dating to approximately 1700-1250 BCE. It featured massive fortification walls, large houses arranged in a radial pattern around a central citadel, and abundant evidence of prosperity through imported goods and sophisticated architecture. This matched Homer's description of a wealthy, well-fortified city capable of withstanding a lengthy siege and worthy of the ten-year Greek expedition described in the Iliad.

The dating of Troy VI also aligned much better with traditional chronology for the Trojan War. Greek historical tradition, as recorded by Eratosthenes in the 3rd century BCE, placed the fall of Troy around 1184 BCE. While Troy VI appeared to have been destroyed somewhat earlier, around 1250 BCE, this discrepancy was much smaller than the thousand-year gap between Homer's Troy and Schliemann's Troy II (Miller 1997: 167).

Dörpfeld's identification gained further support from evidence of catastrophic destruction. Troy VI showed clear signs of a violent end, with collapsed walls and buildings throughout the settlement. Initially, Dörpfeld attributed this destruction to human agency—specifically, to the Greek attack described in the Iliad.

However, as his analysis progressed, Dörpfeld recognized that the pattern of destruction more closely resembled earthquake damage than warfare. Walls had collapsed outward rather than inward, a characteristic sign of seismic activity rather than deliberate demolition. This observation led him to modify his hypothesis in ways that would prove remarkably prescient.

In his final publication, Dörpfeld proposed that Troy VI had indeed been Homer's Troy, but that it had been severely damaged by an earthquake rather than destroyed by the Greeks. The subsequent settlement, Troy VIIa, represented a hastily rebuilt version of the city, with smaller houses constructed from reused materials. This rebuilt city, Dörpfeld suggested, was the one ultimately sacked by the Greeks, providing the historical foundation for Homer's narrative (Dörpfeld 1902: 234).

Reception and Influence: Transforming a Discipline

Dörpfeld's work at Troy received mixed reception from the contemporary scholarly community. Many archaeologists recognized the methodological advances he had introduced and appreciated his systematic approach to excavation and documentation. His stratigraphic framework for Troy's development was widely adopted and became the standard reference point for discussions of the site's history.

However, some scholars remained skeptical of his identification of Troy VI with Homer's city. The continuing gap between archaeological evidence for Troy VI's destruction (c. 1250 BCE) and traditional dates for the Trojan War (c. 1184

BCE) troubled chronologically minded historians. Others questioned whether any historical reality lay behind the Homeric epics, suggesting that archaeology was being misused to validate literary myths (Murray 1907: 89).

Despite these criticisms, Dörpfeld's work fundamentally transformed Trojan archaeology and established new standards for the discipline more broadly. As Carl Blegen, who would later conduct his own excavations at Troy, noted: "After Dörpfeld, no one could approach Troy as simply a literary setting. He had demonstrated conclusively that Troy was a real place with a complex history spanning thousands of years" (Blegen 1963: 12).

Dörpfeld's influence extended far beyond Troy itself. His methodological innovations—careful stratigraphy, detailed architectural documentation, systematic pottery analysis—became standard practice at archaeological sites throughout the Mediterranean. His students and colleagues applied these techniques from Greece to Anatolia, transforming Mediterranean archaeology into a more rigorous and scientific discipline.

Perhaps most importantly, Dörpfeld established a model for integrating archaeological evidence with literary traditions that remains influential today. Rather than either uncritically accepting ancient texts as literal history or dismissing them as pure fiction, Dörpfeld demonstrated how material evidence could be used to evaluate, contextualize, and sometimes revise literary accounts (Foxhall 1995: 134).

Legacy and Later Discoveries: Building on Dörpfeld's Foundation

Dörpfeld's work at Troy marked a crucial transition in the site's archaeological investigation, but it was far from the final word. Throughout the 20th and early 21st centuries, successive excavations have built upon, refined, and sometimes challenged his findings while consistently employing the methodological approaches he pioneered.

Between 1932 and 1938, an American expedition led by Carl Blegen conducted new excavations using even more refined techniques. Blegen largely confirmed Dörpfeld's stratigraphic sequence but refined the chronology and internal subdivisions of each major phase. Most significantly, Blegen strengthened the case for identifying Troy VIIa, rather than Troy VI, as the city destroyed in the Trojan War, documenting clear evidence of warfare including human remains, arrowheads embedded in walls, and extensive fire destruction (Blegen 1963: 145).

From 1988 to 2012, a German-American expedition led by Manfred Korfmann and later Ernst Pernicka conducted the most extensive excavations since Dörpfeld's time. Using modern archaeological techniques including remote sensing, computer modeling, and environmental sampling, this project dramatically expanded understanding of Troy's size, complexity, and regional importance.

Korfmann's most significant discovery was a large lower city surrounding the citadel excavated by Schliemann and Dörpfeld. This lower city, dating to the Late Bronze Age, increased Troy's estimated size from approximately 2 hectares to 20-25 hectares, transforming understanding of Troy from a small citadel to a substantial urban center capable of supporting the population described in Homeric accounts (Korfmann 2004: 78).

These later excavations refined rather than replaced Dörpfeld's fundamental contributions. His stratigraphic framework, with modifications, remains the standard reference point for discussions of Troy's chronology. His identification of the Late Bronze Age levels (Troy VI/VIIa) as the most likely historical context for the Trojan War has been largely vindicated by subsequent research. And his methodological innovations have become so thoroughly integrated into archaeological practice that they're now taken for granted.

The Dörpfeld Revolution: Methodology as Legacy

To fully appreciate Dörpfeld's contribution to Trojan archaeology, we must understand the methodological revolution he initiated. Prior to Dörpfeld, excavation was often little more than organized treasure hunting conducted with picks and shovels. Dörpfeld transformed it into systematic investigation of the past through careful analysis of material remains and their relationships.

Central to this transformation was Dörpfeld's insistence on preserving archaeological context. Where Schliemann had focused on extracting valuable objects with minimal documentation of their surroundings, Dörpfeld recognized that an artifact's significance derived largely from its relationship to other artifacts, architectural features, and stratigraphic layers.

This contextual approach required new excavation techniques. Dörpfeld pioneered the practice of excavating in horizontal layers corresponding to ancient living surfaces, rather than digging vertical trenches that cut through multiple periods. This method preserved the integrity of each settlement phase and allowed for more accurate reconstruction of how the site had appeared at different points in time.

Dörpfeld also introduced more precise recording systems. He established a grid system across the site, allowing the location of each find to be documented with reference to fixed points. He insisted on regular photography to document excavation progress, creating visual records that supplemented written descriptions. And he maintained detailed architectural drawings showing relationships between buildings and their development over time.

These methodological innovations transformed not just excavation practice but the very questions archaeologists could ask. By preserving and documenting archaeological contexts, Dörpfeld made it possible to investigate aspects of ancient life beyond spectacular treasures—everyday activities, construction techniques, urban development, and environmental adaptation.

As archaeologist Colin Renfrew noted: "Dörpfeld helped shift archaeology's focus from objects to contexts, from spectacular discoveries to systematic understanding. This shift ultimately transformed archaeology from an antiquarian pursuit into a scientific discipline" (Renfrew 1980: 234).

Conclusion: Science Triumphs Over Romance

Wilhelm Dörpfeld's work at Troy represents a pivotal moment in archaeological history. His systematic approach transformed excavation from treasure hunting into scientific investigation, establishing methodological standards that continue to influence the discipline today. His careful documentation preserved information that would otherwise have been lost, allowing later scholars to reinterpret his findings in light of new discoveries and theoretical perspectives.

Beyond these methodological contributions, Dörpfeld fundamentally reshaped our understanding of Troy itself. His stratigraphic framework revealed the site's complex 4,000-year history, demonstrating that "Troy" was not a single city but a succession of settlements, each building upon its predecessor's ruins. This diachronic perspective helped explain Troy's powerful grip on ancient imagination—it had been an important place throughout the Bronze Age and beyond.

Dörpfeld's identification of Troy VI/VIIa as the most likely setting for the Homeric epics established parameters for discussion that remain relevant today. While subsequent excavations have refined his chronology and expanded understanding of Troy's regional significance, his basic insight—that the Late Bronze Age levels correspond most closely to traditional dating of the Trojan War—has been largely vindicated by later research.

Perhaps most importantly, Dörpfeld established a model for integrating archaeological evidence with literary traditions that continues to inform classical scholarship. Rather than either uncritically accepting ancient texts as literal history or dismissing them as pure fiction, he demonstrated how material evidence could evaluate, contextualize, and sometimes revise literary accounts.

When we walk through the ruins of Troy today, examining the massive walls of Troy VI or the destruction debris of Troy VIIa, we see the site through conceptual frameworks that Dörpfeld established more than a century ago. His stratigraphic sequence, his architectural analysis, his methodological innovations—all continue to shape how we understand this most famous of archaeological sites.

As Brian Rose, who co-directed recent excavations at Troy, observed: "Dörpfeld taught us that archaeology and philology are complementary rather than competing approaches to the ancient world. Each has its strengths and limitations, and our understanding is enriched when we bring them into conversation rather than privileging one over the other" (Rose 2014: 189).

This integrative approach—combining careful attention to material evidence with critical engagement of textual sources—represents Dörpfeld's most enduring legacy. It has shaped not just the archaeology of Troy but our broader understanding of the complex relationship between myth and history in the ancient Mediterranean world, ensuring that his systematic revolution continues to influence how we study the past.

CHAPTER 9

CARL BLEGEN AND THE AMERICAN EXPEDITIONS

The Dawn of Modern Excavation

The morning sun cast long shadows across the mounds of Hisarlık in the spring of 1932 as Carl William Blegen surveyed the landscape that had captivated archaeological imagination for six decades. Unlike his predecessors who had arrived with Homeric visions and romantic notions, Blegen came armed with something far more powerful: methodical precision and scientific rigor that would transform our understanding of Troy forever.

Standing at the edge of Schliemann's great trench, now weathered by decades of exposure, Blegen must have contemplated both the achievements and mistakes of earlier excavators. Schliemann had found Troy but destroyed much evidence in his haste. Dörpfeld had introduced systematic methods but lacked the resources for comprehensive investigation. Now, as director of the University of Cincinnati expedition, Blegen had the opportunity to apply the most advanced archaeological techniques of his era to unlock Troy's secrets with unprecedented precision.

"We approached the site with no preconceptions about what we might find," Blegen later wrote in his field journal. "Our aim was simply to establish the facts of the stratigraphic sequence as clearly and precisely as possible, and to let those facts speak for themselves" (Blegen 1963: 12). This understated approach belied the revolutionary impact his work would have on Trojan archaeology and our understanding of Bronze Age civilization.

A New Kind of Archaeologist

Carl William Blegen brought impeccable credentials to Troy. Born in Minneapolis in 1887, he had studied at Yale and the American School of Classical Studies at Athens before establishing himself as a leading excavator of Bronze Age sites in mainland Greece. His work at Korakou, Zygouries, and Prosymna had already demonstrated his mastery of ceramic chronology and stratigraphic excavation—skills that would prove crucial for untangling Troy's complex history (McDonald 1967: 234).

By the time he turned his attention to Troy, Blegen had developed a meticulous approach to excavation that emphasized careful documentation, systematic collection of artifacts, and rigorous analysis of material culture. Unlike Schliemann's treasure-hunting approach or even Dörpfeld's architecture-focused methods, Blegen understood that every fragment of pottery, every animal bone, every charcoal sample had potential significance for reconstructing ancient life.

The University of Cincinnati expedition represented a new chapter in Trojan archaeology in several crucial ways. First, it was a truly institutional endeavor rather than the work of a wealthy amateur or individual scholar. This institutional backing provided resources for sustained, systematic excavation and comprehensive publication of results. Second, Blegen assembled a multidisciplinary team including architects, photographers, ceramic specialists, and even physical anthropologists—recognizing that archaeological interpretation required diverse expertise (Blegen 1950: xvi).

Finally, Blegen implemented cutting-edge excavation techniques for the 1930s, including careful stratigraphic documentation, precise recording of find spots, and systematic collection of seemingly mundane materials that previous excavators had largely ignored. As he remarked in a 1935 lecture, "Archaeology is not about finding treasures. It is about reconstructing the past in all its dimensions—economic, social, political, and cultural. Every fragment of pottery, every animal bone, every seed has a story to tell if we know how to listen" (Blegen 1935: 45).

Untangling Troy's Complex History

When Blegen began work at Troy, he faced a significant challenge: reconciling the complex stratigraphy of the site with the somewhat inconsistent documentation left by previous excavators. Schliemann had identified seven major settlement phases, while Dörpfeld had expanded this to nine. Neither had excavated with sufficient precision to fully clarify the relationships between these phases, particularly in areas where later construction had disturbed earlier remains.

Blegen's solution was characteristically methodical. Rather than accepting the existing framework uncritically, he opened new trenches in areas that promised to preserve complete stratigraphic sequences. By carefully documenting relationships between architectural features, floor levels, and ceramic assemblages, he established a refined chronology that built upon but significantly improved Dörpfeld's work.

The result was a new stratigraphic framework that divided Troy's occupation into nine major periods (designated by Roman numerals I through IX), with numerous sub-phases (indicated by lowercase letters). This system, which remains standard in Trojan archaeology today, provided unprecedented chronological precision and allowed for nuanced understanding of the site's development over more than 4,000 years (Blegen 1950: 7-9).

In his 1950 publication, Blegen explained the rationale: "The subdivision of the major periods into phases reflects our attempt to capture the dynamic nature of the site's occupation. A city is not a static entity but a living organism that grows, changes, and adapts over time. By identifying these sub-phases, we can trace the evolution of Troy with greater precision and recognize moments of continuity and change that might otherwise be obscured" (Blegen 1950: 8).

Blegen's refined sequence revealed that Troy's history was far more complex than previously understood. Troy I (c. 3000-2500 BCE) emerged not as the primitive village Schliemann had suggested, but as a substantial Early Bronze Age settlement with impressive fortifications and evidence of long-distance trade. Troy II, which Schliemann had mistakenly identified as Homer's Troy, appeared as a wealthy mid-third millennium citadel notable for its monumental architecture and Schliemann's famous "Treasure of Priam"—which actually predated any possible Trojan War by more than a millennium.

The Power of Pottery: Ceramic Chronology and Cultural Connections

Central to Blegen's refinement of Troy's chronology was his meticulous study of pottery. Unlike precious metals or exotic imports, ceramics were used and discarded in large quantities by all segments of ancient society. Changes in pottery styles, manufacturing techniques, and decorative motifs provided Blegen with a sensitive chronological tool that allowed him to date contexts with unprecedented precision.

"Pottery is the archaeologist's most reliable guide to chronology," Blegen wrote. "Unlike architecture, which may stand for centuries, or portable valuables, which may be heirlooms passed down through generations, pottery was relatively inexpensive, breakable, and frequently replaced. Its styles changed in response to shifting tastes and technologies, providing us with a remarkably fine-grained chronological sequence" (Blegen 1953: 45).

But Blegen's ceramic analysis went far beyond simple chronology. By comparing Trojan pottery with well-dated assemblages from Greece, the Aegean islands, and central Anatolia, he was able to place Troy within broader networks of cultural interaction and exchange. This comparative approach revealed that

Troy occupied a crucial position at the interface between Aegean and Anatolian cultural spheres, absorbing influences from both while maintaining distinctive local traditions.

For the Early Bronze Age levels, Blegen documented close parallels between Trojan ceramics and those of western Anatolia, suggesting Troy was primarily oriented toward the Anatolian cultural sphere during this period. The distinctive "depas amphikypellon"—a two-handled cup found in Troy II contexts—appeared widely across Anatolia, indicating participation in shared cultural practices.

By the Late Bronze Age (Troy VI-VII), however, Mycenaean imported pottery became common at the site, particularly in elite contexts. Blegen's careful documentation of these imports provided crucial evidence for dating, as they could be cross-referenced with the well-established Mycenaean pottery chronology developed through his own work in mainland Greece (French 1999: 134).

Particularly significant was Blegen's analysis of pottery from Troy VIIa, which revealed an intriguing pattern. While imported Mycenaean pottery decreased compared to Troy VI, local imitations of Mycenaean styles increased. Simultaneously, new ceramic forms appeared that had parallels in the Balkans and along the Black Sea coast. Blegen interpreted this pattern as evidence for disruption of traditional trade networks and possibly the arrival of new population elements from the north—observations that would fuel later debates about the historical context of Troy's destruction.

Troy VI: The Magnificent Bronze Age Citadel

Among Blegen's most significant contributions was his detailed documentation of Troy VI, the impressive Late Bronze Age citadel that flourished from approximately 1700 to 1250 BCE. This settlement phase, which Dörpfeld had correctly identified as contemporary with traditional dating of the Trojan War, emerged in Blegen's excavations as a sophisticated urban center with monumental architecture and extensive foreign connections.

Blegen's excavations revealed that Troy VI represented a dramatic expansion of the settlement, with a new circuit of massive fortification walls enclosing an area substantially larger than earlier phases. These walls, constructed of carefully dressed limestone blocks, reached heights of at least 6 meters and incorporated defensive towers and impressively engineered gates. The scale and sophistication of these fortifications indicated both the community's wealth and its perceived need for protection.

"The fortifications of Troy VI represent a quantum leap in scale and engineering sophistication," Blegen observed. "The massive limestone blocks, some weighing several tons, were precisely cut and fitted together without mortar in a technique that required considerable architectural knowledge and organizational capacity. These walls were clearly designed not just for practical defense but as monumental expressions of the city's power and prestige" (Blegen 1953: 78).

Within these impressive fortifications, Blegen documented a radically reorganized urban layout. The citadel was dominated by large, free-standing houses arranged in a radial pattern around a central open space that may have served as a public gathering area. These houses, with their stone foundations, mudbrick superstructures, and tiled roofs, were substantially larger than dwellings from earlier periods, suggesting increased prosperity and possibly the emergence of a more pronounced elite class.

Particularly impressive was the building Blegen designated as House VI F, a massive structure with thick walls, multiple rooms, and evidence of two stories. This building, which may have served as a residence for Troy's ruling elite, contained imported luxury goods including Mycenaean pottery and items of bronze and ivory. The concentration of such wealth in specific buildings provided clear evidence for social stratification within Troy VI society (Blegen 1958: 145).

The material culture of Troy VI revealed a prosperous community engaged in long-distance trade networks. Imported Mycenaean pottery appeared in significant quantities, particularly in elite contexts, indicating regular contact with the Aegean world. Bronze artifacts were common, suggesting both access to metal resources and skilled local metallurgy. Luxury items such as carved ivory, faience beads, and Baltic amber revealed connections extending far beyond the immediate region.

The Great Question: How Did Troy VI End?

Perhaps the most contentious aspect of Blegen's work concerned the nature and timing of Troy VI's destruction. This question had obvious implications for the historicity of the Trojan War and generated significant scholarly debate that continues today.

Blegen's excavations revealed clear evidence that Troy VI came to a sudden and violent end around 1250 BCE. The massive fortification walls showed signs of severe damage, with sections toppled and displaced. Buildings within the citadel exhibited evidence of collapse, with fallen architectural elements and crushed artifacts on floor levels. A distinct destruction layer containing burned debris, fragmented pottery, and abandoned possessions marked the end of this settlement phase throughout the excavated areas.

The critical question was what caused this destruction. Schliemann and Dörpfeld had assumed Troy VI was destroyed by human agency—specifically, by the Greeks of Homeric tradition. Blegen, however, reached a different conclusion based on careful documentation of the archaeological evidence.

"The pattern of destruction we observed is more consistent with earthquake damage than with warfare," Blegen concluded. "The walls show displacement and deformation characteristic of seismic activity rather than the targeted destruction one would expect from military action. Most tellingly, we found no evidence of arrowheads, spear points, or other weapons that typically litter a site taken by force. Nor did we find human remains among the destruction debris, as one would expect if the city had fallen to violent conquest" (Blegen 1958: 142).

Blegen's interpretation was strengthened by geological evidence. Troy is located in a seismically active region where earthquakes occur with regularity. The pattern of damage—with walls collapsed outward and buildings showing signs of lateral displacement—was consistent with known effects of seismic activity on stone architecture.

This conclusion had profound implications for the Trojan War debate. If Troy VI was destroyed by earthquake rather than human attackers, it could not be the city captured and burned by the Greeks of Homeric tradition. This realization led Blegen to focus attention on the subsequent settlement phase: Troy VIIa.

Troy VIIa: The Real Homer's Troy?

Blegen's excavations revealed that after the earthquake destruction of Troy VI around 1250 BCE, the site was immediately reoccupied and rebuilt. This new settlement phase, Troy VIIa, showed clear continuity with Troy VI in pottery styles, construction techniques, and overall cultural characteristics, suggesting the same population rebuilt their city rather than being replaced by newcomers.

However, Troy VIIa exhibited significant differences from its predecessor. The impressive free-standing houses of Troy VI were replaced by more crowded, haphazard constructions. The formerly open spaces of the citadel were filled with small compartments and storage facilities. Most tellingly, the archaeological evidence suggested a community under stress, with signs of food storage in unusual locations and evidence of emergency repairs to damaged fortifications.

"Troy VIIa presents the appearance of a community under pressure," Blegen observed. "The crowded buildings, improvised storage facilities, and hasty repairs all suggest a population concerned with practical necessities rather than monumental display. Whether this stress resulted from economic difficulties, political instability, or threat of external attack remains an open question, but the archaeological evidence clearly indicates a marked change in circumstances from the prosperity of Troy VI" (Blegen 1958: 156).

This settlement phase came to an abrupt end around 1180 BCE, with clear evidence of violent destruction by human agency. Unlike the earthquake damage that ended Troy VI, the destruction of Troy VIIa exhibited classic archaeological signatures of warfare: intense burning throughout the settlement, arrowheads embedded in walls, human remains left unburied in streets and buildings, and evidence of valuable possessions abandoned as residents fled or were captured.

"The destruction of Troy VIIa bears all the hallmarks of a city taken by force," Blegen wrote. "The widespread burning, abandoned valuables, and human casualties point unmistakably to a violent assault rather than natural disaster. This destruction layer, dating to approximately 1180 BCE, aligns remarkably well with traditional dating of the Trojan War and may represent the historical event that ultimately gave rise to the Homeric tradition" (Blegen 1963: 167).

Troy and the End of an Age

One of Blegen's most significant contributions was placing Troy within the broader context of Late Bronze Age Mediterranean civilization and its collapse. His work at Troy coincided with increasing archaeological attention to the dramatic events of the late 13th and early 12th centuries BCE, when multiple civilizations across the eastern Mediterranean experienced severe disruption or outright collapse.

Blegen was particularly well-positioned to recognize these connections because of his extensive excavation experience in mainland Greece, especially at Pylos, where he had documented the destruction of a major Mycenaean palace center around the same time as Troy VIIa's fall. This comparative perspective allowed him to recognize that Troy's destruction was not an isolated event but part of a much larger pattern of instability and violence.

"The destruction of Troy VIIa must be understood within the broader context of widespread disruption throughout the eastern Mediterranean at the end of the Bronze Age," Blegen wrote. "From Greece to Egypt, from Anatolia to Cyprus,

we find evidence of destroyed cities, disrupted trade networks, population movements, and political collapse during this period. Troy's fate was shared by numerous other centers, suggesting systemic causes rather than isolated conflicts"
(Blegen 1962: 234).

This contextual approach represented a significant advance in archaeological
interpretation. Rather than viewing Troy in isolation or exclusively through the
lens of Homeric tradition, Blegen placed it within contemporary historical developments that affected the entire region. This perspective helped explain why
the fall of a single city in northwest Anatolia might have been remembered and
commemorated for centuries afterward—it was part of a catastrophic series of
events that marked the end of an era.

Blegen's work thus contributed to emerging scholarly understanding of the
Late Bronze Age collapse as a complex, multi-causal phenomenon involving
climate change, internal social stresses, disruption of trade networks, and population movements. While specific mechanisms of this collapse continue to be
debated, Blegen's careful documentation of Troy's final Bronze Age destruction
provided a crucial data point for understanding this pivotal historical transition
(Cline 2014: 156).

Setting New Standards: Publication and Legacy

Unlike many archaeological projects that remain incompletely published, Blegen
ensured that results of the University of Cincinnati excavations were documented
in comprehensive, multi-volume final publications. Between 1950 and 1958, he
and his colleagues produced four detailed volumes covering all aspects of the
excavation, from architecture and stratigraphy to pottery, small finds, and environmental evidence.

These publications set new standards for archaeological reporting. Rather
than focusing exclusively on spectacular finds or preconceived interpretations,
they presented evidence systematically and comprehensively, allowing readers to

evaluate Blegen's conclusions independently. The detailed stratigraphic sections, architectural plans, and ceramic typologies provided invaluable resources for later scholars, enabling reinterpretation of evidence as new comparative material and analytical techniques became available.

"Blegen's Troy publications remain exemplary in their thoroughness and objectivity," noted archaeologist Donald Easton. "Unlike Schliemann, who often published selectively to support his interpretations, Blegen presented the complete archaeological record, including evidence that complicated or contradicted his own views. This intellectual honesty has allowed his work to remain valuable even as interpretations have evolved" (Easton 1994: 234).

Beyond publications, Blegen's legacy includes training a generation of archaeologists who would make significant contributions to Mediterranean prehistory. His emphasis on stratigraphic precision, ceramic chronology, and contextual interpretation influenced archaeological practice throughout the region, helping transform the discipline from antiquarian treasure hunting to scientific investigation of the past.

Perhaps most importantly, Blegen established a model for integrating archaeological evidence with historical and literary traditions without either uncritical acceptance or dismissive skepticism. His approach to the Trojan War question was nuanced and sophisticated, recognizing both historical elements preserved in Homeric epics and literary elaborations introduced during centuries of oral transmission.

"The question is not whether the Trojan War happened exactly as Homer described it," Blegen observed. "Clearly it did not, as archaeological evidence demonstrates. The more interesting question is how historical events of the Late Bronze Age were transformed into the epic tradition we know from Homer—what was preserved, what was changed, and why. This is not merely a question about Troy but about how human societies remember and commemorate their past" (Blegen 1963: 23).

Conclusion: From Myth to Science

Carl Blegen's work at Troy represents a watershed in archaeological investigation of the site—a transition from romantic treasure hunting to systematic scientific inquiry, and from simplistic questions about "proving" or "disproving" Homer to sophisticated exploration of the complex relationship between material remains and cultural memory.

His meticulous documentation, refined chronology, and contextual interpretation established foundations that continue to support Trojan archaeology today, even as new excavations, technologies, and theoretical perspectives have expanded and sometimes modified his conclusions. When we examine Troy's stratigraphy today, we still use Blegen's basic framework. When we date Troy's pottery, we build on sequences he established. When we interpret Troy's destruction layers, we consider patterns he first documented.

But perhaps Blegen's greatest contribution was demonstrating how archaeology could engage productively with questions of historical and cultural significance without sacrificing scientific rigor. He showed that archaeological evidence could neither simply confirm nor definitively refute ancient literary traditions, but rather could illuminate the complex processes by which historical events become cultural memory.

As Manfred Korfmann, who directed more recent excavations at Troy, observed: "Every archaeologist who works at Troy stands on Blegen's shoulders. His stratigraphic framework, ceramic chronology, and architectural documentation remain fundamental reference points, even when new evidence leads us to revise specific interpretations. More than anyone else, Blegen transformed Troy from a mythical place into an archaeological site that could be studied systematically and scientifically" (Korfmann 2004: 145).

This transformation—from myth to archaeological science, from romantic speculation to rigorous documentation—represents Blegen's enduring contribution to our understanding of Troy and its place in both ancient history and cultural memory. Standing today among the excavated remains of Troy VIIa, examining the destruction debris that Blegen first documented in the 1930s, we participate in a conversation between past and present that his work made possible—a conversation grounded in material evidence but informed by awareness of the complex relationships between history, memory, and meaning that make Troy unique among archaeological sites.

CHAPTER 10

MANFRED KORFMANN AND THE NEW TROY

The Renewed Search for Troy

After Carl Blegen's excavations ended in 1938, Troy fell silent. For nearly half a century, the ancient mound at Hisarlık remained largely untouched, baking under the Anatolian sun while archaeology moved forward with revolutionary new technologies and methodologies. Most scholars assumed that Blegen's meticulous work had answered the major questions about Bronze Age Troy. They were spectacularly wrong.

In 1988, when Manfred Korfmann, a professor at the University of Tübingen in Germany, initiated a new project at Troy, he brought something his predecessors had lacked: modern technology capable of seeing beneath the surface without destroying archaeological evidence. What he discovered would fundamentally transform our understanding of Troy's size, importance, and role in Bronze Age civilization.

"When I first visited Troy in the 1970s," Korfmann later recalled, "I was struck by how much of the site remained unexplored. Schliemann, Dörpfeld, and Blegen had focused almost exclusively on the citadel mound—the area within the walls that enclosed about 2 hectares. But comparative evidence from other Anatolian and Near Eastern sites suggested that a settlement of Troy's importance would likely have been much larger, with substantial areas of habitation extending be-yond the citadel" (Korfmann 2001: 23).

This insight would prove revolutionary. Where previous excavators had seen the entirety of Bronze Age Troy, Korfmann suspected they had found merely its ceremonial and administrative heart. The real city, he hypothesized, lay buried beneath centuries of sediment in the fields surrounding the ancient citadel.

A New Kind of Archaeological Investigation

Korfmann's background differed significantly from his predecessors. Unlike Schliemann, the businessman-turned-archaeologist, or Blegen, the classical ar-chaeologist, Korfmann was a specialist in Anatolian archaeology with extensive experience excavating Bronze Age settlements across Turkey. This regional exper-tise gave him comparative perspective that earlier excavators had lacked—he knew what Bronze Age cities in this part of the world actually looked like (Korfmann 1998: 45).

More importantly, Korfmann arrived at Troy during a period of methodolog-ical revolution in archaeology. The late 1980s marked the widespread adoption of geophysical survey techniques that could map buried archaeological features without excavation, computer-aided analysis of spatial patterns, and environ-mental approaches that situated ancient sites within their broader landscapes. Korfmann embraced these innovations, assembling a truly multidisciplinary team that included specialists in remote sensing, archaeobotany, zooarchaeology, geology, and paleoclimatology alongside traditional archaeologists.

"The questions we can ask about ancient Troy have changed fundamentally since Blegen's time," Korfmann explained in a 1992 interview. "We're no longer simply trying to identify which layer corresponds to Homer's Troy. We're trying to understand Troy as a living settlement within its environmental and regional context—its economy, its political organization, its relationships with neighbor-ing regions, and its development over time" (Korfmann 1992: 156).

This broader perspective was reflected in the project's geographical scope. The Troia Project (using the German spelling) was conceived as a long-term, regional investigation that would examine not just the tell mound but the entire settlement landscape of northwestern Anatolia. While continuing targeted excavation in selected areas of the citadel, Korfmann's team conducted extensive fieldwork throughout the Troad region, documenting settlement patterns, trade routes, and environmental changes from prehistory through the Roman period.

The timing proved fortuitous. Archaeological practice was rapidly evolving from site-specific investigation toward landscape-scale analysis that considered ancient settlements within their broader geographic, economic, and political contexts. Korfmann's regional approach situated Troy within networks of exchange and power that spanned the Aegean and Anatolia, revealing its changing significance over millennia of occupation.

The Discovery That Changed Everything

The most dramatic discovery of Korfmann's excavations came early in the project and didn't require digging at all. In 1993, geomagnetic surveys conducted in the fields south and west of the citadel mound revealed extensive anomalies suggesting buried architectural remains. What the magnetic instruments detected beneath seemingly empty agricultural fields would revolutionize our understanding of Bronze Age Troy.

"The existence of a lower city at Troy had been hypothesized by earlier scholars," noted project team member Peter Jablonka, "but its extent and nature remained unknown until our geophysical surveys. What emerged from these investigations was evidence for a settlement covering approximately 25-30 hectares—roughly ten times larger than the citadel alone" (Jablonka 2001: 67).

Subsequent excavations confirmed the geophysical evidence. The lower city appeared to have been densely occupied during the Late Bronze Age, with numerous buildings arranged along streets radiating outward from the citadel. Most structures were modest in size, suggesting residential and workshop areas rather than monumental public buildings—exactly what you'd expect to find in the commercial and artisan quarters of a Bronze Age city.

The archaeological evidence indicated continuous occupation throughout the Late Bronze Age, with multiple rebuilding phases corresponding to the stratigraphic sequence documented on the citadel. This wasn't a temporary expansion or seasonal settlement but a permanent urban extension that housed the majority of Troy's population for centuries.

Perhaps most significantly, Korfmann's team discovered that this lower city had been surrounded by an impressive defensive system. Excavations revealed a substantial ditch, approximately 3 meters deep and 3-4 meters wide, that encircled the entire settlement. Behind this ditch stood a massive stone wall or rampart, preserved in some sections to a height of over 2 meters. This defensive perimeter extended for nearly 2 kilometers, protecting not just the citadel but the entire urban area.

"The scale of these fortifications was unexpected," Korfmann observed. "They represent a massive investment of labor and resources, suggesting a level of political organization and economic capacity that exceeds previous estimates for Bronze Age Troy. A community capable of constructing and maintaining such extensive defenses must have commanded significant re-sources and possessed a complex social hierarchy" (Korfmann 1995: 89).

Rewriting Troy's Biography

The discovery of the lower city and its fortifications transformed scholarly understanding of Troy's size and significance during the Late Bronze Age. Rather than a relatively modest citadel housing perhaps 1,500 people, as Blegen had estimated, Troy now appeared to have been a substantial urban center with a population of 5,000-10,000 inhabitants. This revised population estimate placed

Troy among the larger settlements of the Late Bronze Age Aegean and western Anatolia, comparable to major Mycenaean centers like Pylos or Tiryns in Greece.

More than just size was at stake. The discovery of the lower city revealed Troy as a fundamentally different kind of settlement than previously understood. Instead of a hilltop fortress with some peripheral buildings, Troy emerged as a true urban center with distinct quarters for different activities—the citadel for administrative and religious functions, the lower city for residential, commercial, and artisan activities.

Archaeological evidence from the lower city supported this urban interpretation. Excavations uncovered workshop areas for metalworking, textile production, and ceramic manufacture. Storage facilities suggested centralized collection and distribution of goods. The street layout indicated systematic urban planning rather than haphazard growth. All of these features pointed to Troy as a complex, organized community capable of supporting specialized crafts and coordinating economic activities across a substantial population.

"We must now recognize Troy as a significant regional center," Korfmann argued, "not merely a peripheral outpost as some scholars had suggested. Its location at the interface between the Aegean and Anatolian worlds gave it strategic importance, while its substantial population and impressive fortifications indicate political and economic significance beyond what was previously recognized" (Korfmann 2001: 145).

This reinterpretation had profound implications for understanding Troy's role in Bronze Age geopolitics and its relationship to the legendary conflicts preserved in later Greek tradition. A city of 8,000-10,000 people was indeed worth fighting over, especially if it controlled access to the lucrative trade routes connecting the Mediterranean with the Black Sea.

Troy the Trading City

One of Korfmann's most significant contributions was his reinterpretation of Troy's economic and political role in the Late Bronze Age Mediterranean world. Previous scholars had typically viewed Troy primarily as a military stronghold, emphasizing its impressive fortifications and strategic location. While acknowledging these military aspects, Korfmann argued that Troy's prosperity derived primarily from its position within regional and long-distance trade networks.

"Troy's location at the entrance to the Dardanelles gave it control over maritime traffic between the Aegean and Black Seas," Korfmann explained. "Ships sailing between these regions would have been dependent on favorable winds and currents, often necessitating stops along the Troad coast. Troy's position allowed it to function as an intermediary in trade between Europe and Asia, the Aegean and Black Sea worlds" (Korfmann 2001: 78).

Archaeological evidence supporting this interpretation was abundant. Imported goods found in Late Bronze Age levels at Troy included Mycenaean pottery from mainland Greece, Cypriot ceramics, and various Anatolian wares, indicating participation in wide-ranging exchange networks. The discovery of what appeared to be warehouse facilities in the lower city further supported Troy's identification as a commercial center.

Particularly significant was evidence for specialized craft production at Troy. Excavations in the lower city uncovered workshops containing specialized tools, raw materials, and production waste, indicating that Troy was not merely importing finished goods but actively participating in production and exchange systems that spanned the eastern Mediterranean.

The metallurgical workshops were especially impressive. Analysis of bronze artifacts and production debris revealed sophisticated techniques for alloying copper and tin, suggesting access to metal sources from across Anatolia and the Aegean. Textile production facilities indicated large-scale manufacture of woolen goods, possibly for export as well as local consumption. Ceramic workshops produced both local wares and imitations of foreign styles, demonstrating familiarity with international markets and consumer preferences.

"Troy appears to have functioned as what economic anthropologists would call a 'gateway community,'" observed project team member Brian Rose. "It mediated exchange between different cultural and economic zones, deriving prosperity from its role as an intermediary rather than from direct control of agricultural resources. This economic function helps explain both Troy's impressive fortifications—necessary to protect valuable goods and maintain control over trade routes—and its multicultural character, with material culture showing influences from both Aegean and Anatolian traditions" (Rose 2014: 123).

This reinterpretation provided a more nuanced context for understanding potential conflicts with Mycenaean Greeks. Rather than simple territorial aggression, tensions may have revolved around control of trade routes and access to the resources of the Black Sea region, including metals, timber, and grain. Such economic motivations would align with patterns observed in other Bronze Age conflicts, where competition for resources and trade advantages often underlay military confrontations.

Environmental Archaeology: Reconstructing Troy's World

Another innovative aspect of Korfmann's project was its emphasis on environmental reconstruction. Previous excavations had focused almost exclusively on architecture and artifacts, with little attention to the natural environment that shaped ancient life. Korfmann assembled specialists in paleobotany, zooarchaeology, and geomorphology to reconstruct the environmental conditions that Bronze Age inhabitants of Troy would have experienced.

Environmental studies conducted as part of the project provided remarkable insights into the landscape and resources available to ancient inhabitants. Pollen analysis revealed that the Troad was more heavily forested in antiquity than today, with extensive stands of oak, pine, and other trees that would have provided timber for construction and shipbuilding. The coastal plain around Troy, formed by alluvial deposits from the Scamander River, offered fertile agricultural land, while the surrounding hills provided grazing for livestock.

"Troy's environmental setting gave it access to diverse resources," explained paleobotanist Simone Riehl, who analyzed plant remains from the excavations. "The archaeological evidence shows exploitation of both terrestrial and marine resources, with agriculture focusing on wheat, barley, and legumes, supplemented by herding of sheep, goats, and cattle. Marine resources, including fish and shellfish, also contributed significantly to the diet" (Riehl 2010: 234).

Geomorphological investigations revealed dramatic changes in the coastal landscape since Bronze Age times. The bay that Homer describes as sheltering the Greek fleet had indeed existed but had gradually filled with sediment from the Scamander River. This geological evidence supported Homer's geographic descriptions while explaining why the ancient harbor was no longer visible to modern visitors.

Climate reconstruction based on pollen analysis and other proxy data indicated that the Late Bronze Age was a period of relatively favorable conditions in the eastern Mediterranean, with adequate rainfall supporting agriculture and forest growth. However, evidence suggested that climatic deterioration began around 1200 BCE, potentially contributing to the widespread disruptions that marked the end of Bronze Age civilization.

"Environmental archaeology has revealed Troy as part of a complex ecological and economic system," noted geoarchaeologist Arlette Kouwenhoven. "The city's prosperity depended not just on its strategic location but on its ability to exploit diverse environmental resources and adapt to changing conditions. Understanding these environmental relationships is crucial for comprehending Troy's historical development and ultimate fate" (Kouwenhoven 2001: 145).

The Great Debate: How Big Was Troy Really?

Despite the methodological rigor of Korfmann's investigations, his interpretations generated significant controversy among archaeologists and historians. The most heated debates centered on the nature and extent of the lower city, with some scholars questioning whether Troy truly qualified as an "urban center" comparable to major settlements in the Near East or Mycenaean Greece.

The controversy erupted publicly in 2001-2002, following a major exhibition titled "Troy: Dream and Reality" that presented Korfmann's findings to wide audiences in Germany and beyond. In the exhibition catalog and associated publications, Korfmann described Late Bronze Age Troy as a substantial urban settlement covering 25-30 hectares, with a population of 5,000-10,000 people, protected by extensive fortifications and functioning as a significant commercial center.

This characterization was challenged by several German scholars, most prominently Frank Kolb, a historian at the University of Tübingen—ironically, Korfmann's own institution. Kolb argued that the evidence for a densely occupied lower city was inadequate and that Korfmann had overstated both the size and urban character of Bronze Age Troy.

"What Korfmann describes as a 'lower city' appears to be primarily a sparsely occupied area with scattered buildings, not a dense urban settlement," Kolb contended. "The supposed defensive ditch may have had other functions, such as drainage, and the evidence for a surrounding wall remains ambiguous. Troy should be understood as a fortified citadel with some extramural settlement, not as a major urban center" (Kolb 2004: 234).

The debate played out in academic journals, conferences, and even the German popular press, sometimes taking on a surprisingly acrimonious tone. At stake were not merely technical archaeological questions but broader issues of Troy's historical significance and its relationship to later literary traditions.

Korfmann and his supporters defended their interpretations, pointing to the geophysical evidence for extensive architectural remains in the lower city area and the clear defensive character of the ditch and associated structures. They acknowledged that the density of occupation might have varied across the settlement but maintained that the overall extent and population estimates were reasonable based on comparative evidence from other Bronze Age sites.

"The controversy reflects different disciplinary perspectives and methodological approaches," observed archaeologist Peter Jablonka. "Archaeologists familiar with Bronze Age Anatolia recognize in Troy patterns common to other settlements of the period—a central citadel surrounded by a lower town, the whole protected by fortifications. Historians and classicists approaching the site primarily through textual sources sometimes have different expectations about what an 'urban center' should look like" (Jablonka 2003: 156).

As additional excavations provided further evidence supporting Korfmann's general interpretation, the controversy gradually subsided. While debates continued about specific details, the fundamental discovery of a substantial lower city surrounded by defensive works became widely accepted among specialists.

Troy and the Hittites: Ancient Texts Meet Archaeology

One of the most significant developments in Trojan studies during Korfmann's tenure came not from archaeology but from philology. During the 1990s, scholars working with Hittite texts identified possible references to Troy and the Troad region in Late Bronze Age documents from the Hittite capital of Hattusa in central Anatolia.

Particularly important was the identification of the toponym "Wilusa" in Hittite texts with Ilios/Ilion, one of the names used for Troy in Greek tradition. This identification, proposed earlier but strengthened by new textual analyses, suggested that Troy (as Wilusa) was known to the Hittites and had diplomatic relations with the Hittite Empire during the 13th century BCE.

"The philological evidence now strongly supports the equation of Hittite Wilusa with Greek Ilios," argued Frank Starke, who collaborated with Korfmann on interpreting the textual evidence. "The geographical descriptions in Hittite texts place Wilusa in northwestern Anatolia, and linguistic analysis shows that 'Wilusa' would naturally evolve into 'Ilios' through known sound changes between Anatolian and Greek languages" (Starke 1997: 234).

Most significant was a treaty dated to approximately 1280 BCE between the Hittite king Muwatalli II and a ruler of Wilusa named Alaksandu. This name bears striking resemblance to "Alexandros," the alternative name of Paris in Greek tradition. The treaty describes Wilusa as a vassal state of the Hittite Empire, suggesting that Troy maintained diplomatic relations with the great power to the east during the period immediately preceding its destruction.

Other Hittite texts referred to conflicts in the Wilusa region involving a country called Ahhiyawa, which many scholars now identify with the Mycenaean Greek world. A letter from the Hittite king Hattusili III complained about Ahhiyawan intervention in western Anatolian affairs, including support for anti-Hittite activities in the region around Wilusa (Beckman 1999: 156).

"These texts provide a historical context that aligns remarkably well with the archaeological evidence," Korfmann observed. "They suggest that northwestern Anatolia, including Troy/Wilusa, was indeed a contested zone between Hittite and Mycenaean interests during the 13th century BCE, precisely the period when traditional chronology places the Trojan War" (Korfmann 2001: 234).

The Hittite texts didn't mention a specific conflict that could be directly equated with the Trojan War of Greek tradition. However, they established that the geopolitical situation in western Anatolia during the Late Bronze Age involved precisely the kind of tensions between Anatolian powers and Mycenaean Greeks that could have given rise to armed conflict over Troy.

The End of Bronze Age Troy: New Evidence for Ancient Destruction

Korfmann's excavations provided new insights into the final phases of Bronze Age Troy, particularly the destruction of Troy VIIa around 1180 BCE that many scholars consider the most likely archaeological candidate for the "Homeric" Troy. This destruction layer received special attention from Korfmann's team, who employed modern techniques to document the evidence for violence with unprecedented precision.

"The evidence for violent destruction at the end of Troy VIIa is compelling," reported archaeologist Wendy Rigter, who supervised excavations in several areas of the citadel. "We found buildings burned to the ground, with household goods left in place as people fled. In some areas, we discovered human remains in streets and buildings, suggesting that at least some inhabitants died during the attack. Arrowheads embedded in walls and scattered through destruction deposits indicate that the city came under assault" (Rigter 2003: 123).

The destruction coincided with the broader collapse of Bronze Age civilizations throughout the eastern Mediterranean around 1200-1150 BCE. This period witnessed the fall of the Hittite Empire, attacks on Egypt by the mysterious "Sea Peoples," the destruction of numerous settlements in Greece, Cyprus, and the Levant, and widespread disruption of trade networks that had connected these regions for centuries.

"Troy's final Bronze Age destruction must be understood within this broader context of systems collapse," Korfmann argued. "Whether the attackers were Mycenaean Greeks, as later tradition held, or other groups caught up in the widespread population movements of the period remains uncertain. What is clear is that Troy's destruction was not an isolated event but part of a pattern of upheaval that transformed the eastern Mediterranean world" (Korfmann 2004: 189).

Analysis of the destruction debris revealed details about the final moments of Bronze Age Troy. In several buildings, excavators found complete pottery vessels and other household items exactly where they had been left when residents fled. Bronze tools and weapons were discovered in workshops and houses, suggesting the attack came suddenly enough that valuable metal objects couldn't be retrieved. Most poignantly, infant burials beneath house floors indicated that some residents never had the chance to escape.

The evidence suggested that Troy VIIa's destruction was both violent and thorough. Unlike the earthquake that had damaged Troy VI, leaving structural collapses but little burning, the end of Troy VIIa showed clear signs of human-caused fire that consumed much of the settlement. The pattern of destruction was consistent with systematic sacking rather than accidental burning.

Legacy and Continuing Discovery

Manfred Korfmann died unexpectedly in 2005, but the research project he established continued under the direction of Ernst Pernicka from the University of Tübingen and C. Brian Rose from the University of Pennsylvania. While maintaining Korfmann's broad, multidisciplinary approach, subsequent seasons have focused on specific questions raised by earlier work and on applying new technologies to investigate the site.

"Korfmann transformed our understanding of Bronze Age Troy," reflected Brian Rose. "He demonstrated that Troy was not merely a small citadel but a substantial settlement with regional importance. He situated Troy within its environmental and historical context, connecting archaeological evidence with textual sources in ways that have enriched both fields. And perhaps most importantly, he showed how scientific archaeology can engage with cultural traditions without either uncritical acceptance or dismissive skepticism" (Rose 2014: 245).

Recent research at Troy has employed advanced technologies unavailable during Korfmann's lifetime. LiDAR surveys have produced detailed topographic maps revealing subtle landscape features around the site, while photogrammetry and 3D modeling have enabled more precise documentation and visualization of architectural remains. Analytical techniques such as ancient DNA analysis, isotope studies, and residue analysis have provided new insights into population movements, diet, and economic activities.

The most significant recent discovery came in 2019, when excavations in the lower city uncovered a well-preserved section of the defensive wall dating to the Late Bronze Age. This massive structure, built of stone and mudbrick, confirmed Korfmann's interpretation of the geophysical anomalies as representing substantial fortifications surrounding the lower settlement.

"The discovery of this wall segment validates Korfmann's overall interpretation of Troy's extent and urban character," noted current project director Rüstem Aslan. "While debates continue about specific details, the fundamental picture he proposed—of Troy as a substantial settlement with impressive defenses occupying a strategic position between the Aegean and Anatolian worlds—has been strengthened by subsequent research" (Aslan 2020: 89).

Conclusion: Troy Reimagined

Manfred Korfmann's work at Troy represents a watershed in our understanding of this legendary site. By applying modern archaeological techniques and adopting a regional perspective, he revealed Bronze Age Troy as a substantial urban center rather than a modest hilltop fortress. His discovery of the lower city transformed scholarly discussions about Troy's size, significance, and role in Bronze Age civilization.

More than specific discoveries, however, Korfmann's legacy lies in his approach to archaeological interpretation. He demonstrated how scientific investigation could enrich rather than diminish the cultural significance of legendary sites, showing that careful archaeological work reveals historical realities more fascinating than romantic imagination. His integration of environmental archaeology, regional survey, and textual analysis created a more complete picture of ancient Troy than any single approach could provide.

Perhaps most importantly, Korfmann showed how archaeology can engage productively with questions of cultural heritage and historical memory. Rather than simply confirming or refuting ancient traditions, archaeological evidence illuminates the complex processes through which historical events become cultural memory, revealing both continuities and transformations that span millennia.

"Troy reminds us that the boundaries we draw between cultures are often more permeable than we imagine," Korfmann observed in one of his final publications. "This settlement that we now excavate in Turkey gave rise to the foundational literature of Western civilization. Its inhabitants traded with both Europe and Asia, participated in networks that spanned the Mediterranean, and likely spoke a language related to Hittite rather than Greek. If Troy teaches us anything, it is that cultural identity is complex, multifaceted, and often transcends the categories we impose upon it" (Korfmann 2005: 267).

As excavations continue under new directors with new technologies, Troy remains a site of extraordinary archaeological and cultural significance. Its multiple settlement layers spanning more than 4,000 years provide a unique window into Mediterranean civilization from the Early Bronze Age through the Roman period. Its association with the Homeric epics ensures ongoing public interest that transcends academic archaeology. And its position at the interface between Europe and Asia makes it a powerful symbol of cultural interconnection in our increasingly globalized world.

When we stand today among the ruins of the lower city that Korfmann revealed, looking across the fields where geophysical surveys first detected buried walls, we participate in a conversation between ancient and modern, between scientific discovery and cultural imagination, that continues to evolve with each new generation of scholars and each new technological advance. In this sense, Korfmann's greatest achievement may be ensuring that Troy's story will never be finished—that this ancient site will continue revealing new secrets and inspiring new questions for generations to come.

CHAPTER 11
THE WORLD OF THE LATE BRONZE AGE

Troy in a World of Great Powers

I magine receiving a diplomatic pouch in 1250 BCE. The clay tablets inside, written in cuneiform script, contain correspondence between the pharaoh of Egypt and the king of the Hittites, discussing grain shipments, gold tributes, and—tucked among routine diplomatic business—a troubling situation in a place called Wilusa. Modern scholars now believe Wilusa was Troy, and its appearance in royal correspondence between superpowers reveals something remarkable: this city that would inspire history's greatest war story was already important enough to feature in diplomatic discussions among the era's most powerful rulers.

The discovery of Troy as a significant urban center with international connections compels us to situate the site within its broader geopolitical context. The period between approximately 1600 and 1200 BCE represents an extraordinary era in Mediterranean and Near Eastern history—one characterized by unprecedented international contact, complex diplomatic relationships, and economic integration that wouldn't be seen again until classical times (Cline 2014: 89).

As Mario Liverani observed, "The Late Bronze Age Eastern Mediterranean was not simply a collection of isolated states and cultures, but rather an interconnected system—what we might today call an 'international community'—with established diplomatic protocols, trade networks, and cultural exchanges" (Liverani 2001: 45). This system centered on what scholars call the "Club of Great Powers": Egypt, the Hittite Empire, Babylonia, and Assyria, with Mycenaean civilization representing a fifth significant player operating somewhat differently from the Near Eastern kingdoms.

The archaeological record at Troy demonstrates the site's integration into this international system through imported pottery, exotic raw materials, and evidence of diverse craft traditions. Situated at the northwest edge of Anatolia, Troy occupied a strategic position between the Aegean world dominated by Mycenaean culture and the Anatolian interior controlled by the Hittite Empire.

Egypt: The Ancient Superpower

Egypt under the New Kingdom (c. 1550-1070 BCE) represented one of the oldest and most prestigious powers in the Late Bronze Age world. Following the expulsion of the Hyksos rulers around 1550 BCE, pharaohs of the 18th Dynasty embarked on unprecedented imperial expansion, extending Egyptian control northward into the Levant and establishing influence that reached the Euphrates River at its greatest extent.

Thutmose III (r. 1479-1425 BCE), often called the "Napoleon of Egypt," conducted seventeen military campaigns into Syria-Palestine, defeating a coalition of Canaanite states at the Battle of Megiddo (c. 1457 BCE) and establishing Egyptian dominance throughout the region. His successors, particularly Amenhotep III (r. 1388-1351 BCE), consolidated this empire and presided over extraordinary prosperity and international engagement (Redford 1992: 156).

"The pharaohs of the 18th Dynasty transformed Egypt from a relatively isolated kingdom into an international superpower," noted Egyptologist Donald Redford. "The wealth flowing into Egypt from its empire and international trade funded an unprecedented building program and supported a sophisticated court culture that became the envy of the ancient world" (Redford 1992: 234).

Egypt's relationship with Troy was likely indirect, mediated through trade networks and diplomatic connections with the Hittites and Mycenaeans. Nevertheless, Egyptian objects found at Troy—including scarabs, faience beads, and luxury items—indicate that the site participated in wider economic networks connecting the Eastern Mediterranean during this period (Gates 2011: 345).

The reign of Ramesses II (r. 1279-1213 BCE) coincided with the traditional date of the Trojan War, and some scholars have speculated about possible connections. Most intriguingly, a letter from the Hittite queen Puduhepa to Ramesses II mentions unrest in "Wilusa" (Troy), suggesting that events there were significant enough to feature in diplomatic correspondence between great powers. While this falls short of confirming Homer's account, it indicates that Troy featured prominently in international politics during this crucial period (Beckman 1999: 178).

The Hittite Empire: Anatolia's Dominant Force

The Hittite Empire emerged as a major power in central Anatolia around 1650 BCE and gradually expanded to control much of Anatolia and northern Syria. At its height under kings like Suppiluliuma I (r. 1344-1322 BCE) and Muwatalli II (r. 1295-1272 BCE), the empire rivaled Egypt in power and prestige, forming the northern counterweight to Egyptian influence in the Near East.

"The Hittites represent one of the great success stories of the ancient world," wrote Trevor Bryce. "From relatively modest beginnings in central Anatolia, they built an empire that challenged Egypt for supremacy and established a sophisticated system of governance that integrated diverse peoples and territories" (Bryce 2005: 89).

The Hittite capital at Hattusa has yielded thousands of cuneiform tablets that illuminate the empire's political organization, diplomatic relations, and cultural practices. These texts reveal a pragmatic approach to imperial management, with the Hittites often allowing conquered territories to maintain local rulers and customs as long as they acknowledged Hittite overlordship and paid tribute.

For understanding Troy, the Hittite texts prove invaluable as the only contemporary written sources that mention the site. Texts from the reigns of Tudhaliya IV (r. 1237-1209 BCE) and his predecessors refer to "Wilusa" (convincingly identified with Ilios/Troy) as a vassal state in the Hittite sphere of influence. The "Alaksandu Treaty," concluded between Muwatalli II and a ruler of Wilusa named Alaksandu (tantalizingly similar to "Alexander," Paris's alternate name in Homeric tradition), established the terms of this relationship (Starke 1997: 234).

"The Hittite texts demonstrate that Troy was not an isolated settlement but part of the Hittite imperial system," observed archaeologist Peter Jablonka. "They also suggest that Troy maintained significant autonomy, with its own dynasty of kings who negotiated directly with the Hittite emperor" (Jablonka 2001: 156).

The relationship between Troy and the Hittites appears to have been generally peaceful, with Troy serving as a loyal vassal on the empire's western frontier. However, a letter from Hattusili III to an unnamed king of Ahhiyawa (probably a Mycenaean ruler) mentions past conflict over Wilusa, suggesting the region was occasionally contested between Hittite and Mycenaean interests (Beckman 1999: 234).

The Hittite Empire collapsed around 1180 BCE as part of the broader Late Bronze Age system collapse. The capital at Hattusa was abandoned and burned, and central authority disintegrated. This collapse coincides remarkably well with the traditional date of the Trojan War and archaeological evidence for Troy VIIa's destruction, suggesting that Troy's fall may have been part of wider regional upheaval that brought the Bronze Age to an end.

The Mycenaean World: Greece's First Civilization

The Mycenaean civilization dominated the Greek mainland and many Aegean islands from approximately 1600 to 1200 BCE. Unlike the centralized kingdoms of the Near East, Mycenaean Greece consisted of a network of independent palace-states centered on fortified citadels at sites like Mycenae, Tiryns, Pylos, and Thebes.

"The Mycenaean world represented a distinctive form of political organization," wrote archaeologist Oliver Dickinson. "Rather than a unified state, it comprised multiple independent kingdoms that shared common culture and language but frequently competed with one another for resources and prestige" (Dickinson 1994: 123).

Archaeological evidence from these palace centers reveals hierarchical societies dominated by warrior elites. The distinctive "megaron" palaces served as administrative centers where bureaucrats using Linear B script (an early form of Greek) recorded detailed inventories of goods, personnel, and land holdings. Massive fortification walls, sometimes constructed in "Cyclopean" style using enormous boulders, protected these centers.

The relationship between Mycenaean Greece and Troy has been intensely debated. Homer portrays the Trojan War as a pan-Hellenic expedition led by Agamemnon of Mycenae, with contingents from throughout the Greek world. While this specific coalition likely represents poetic elaboration, archaeological evidence confirms regular contact between Troy and the Mycenaean world.

Mycenaean pottery appears in significant quantities at Troy VI and VIIa, indicating regular trade contacts. Some architectural features at Troy, such as megaron-like structures in the citadel, may show Mycenaean influence. Most intriguingly, a seal written in Luwian found at the Mycenaean palace of Thebes demonstrates direct diplomatic contact between Mycenaean centers and Anatolian kingdoms (Cline 1991: 234).

"The archaeological evidence makes it clear that Troy and the Mycenaean world were not strangers to each other," noted Eric Cline. "Regular trade and diplomatic contacts linked these regions, creating preconditions for conflict if political or economic circumstances changed" (Cline 2014: 156).

Hittite diplomatic texts refer to a kingdom called "Ahhiyawa," now generally identified with some or all of the Mycenaean world. These texts describe Ahhiyawa as a significant power with interests in western Anatolia, sometimes acting as a rival to Hittite influence in the region. One letter specifically mentions conflict between Ahhiyawa and the Hittites over Wilusa (Troy), suggesting that the site's strategic position made it a potential flashpoint between these powers.

International Diplomacy: The First Global System

One of the most remarkable aspects of the Late Bronze Age was the development of sophisticated international diplomacy connecting the various powers. This system is best documented in the Amarna Letters—diplomatic correspondence found at the short-lived Egyptian capital of Akhetaten—and in royal archives from the Hittite capital at Hattusa.

These texts reveal a world where rulers addressed each other as "brother" (if of equal status) or "father"/"son" (if of unequal status), exchanged elaborate gifts, arranged diplomatic marriages, and negotiated detailed treaties. Regular embassies traveled between courts, sometimes taking months to complete their journeys. Akkadian, the language of Babylonia, served as the diplomatic lingua franca, facilitating communication between rulers who spoke different native languages.

"The diplomatic system of the Late Bronze Age represents one of the first examples of formalized international relations in world history," observed Raymond Cohen. "Many protocols and practices established during this period would influence diplomacy for millennia to come" (Cohen 2001: 89).

International trade flourished alongside diplomacy, with luxury goods, raw materials, and specialized products moving throughout the Mediterranean and Near East. The Uluburun shipwreck, which sank around 1300 BCE off the Turkish coast, provides a vivid snapshot of this trade. The ship carried copper and tin ingots, cedar logs, glass ingots, ivory, ebony, ostrich eggshells, amber from the Baltic, and pottery from various regions.

"The Uluburun shipwreck demonstrates the truly international character of Late Bronze Age trade," wrote Cemal Pulak, who excavated the site. "The ship carried raw materials and finished goods from at least seven different cultures, showing how integrated the Mediterranean economy had become" (Pulak 1998: 234).

Troy participated actively in these networks. Excavations have yielded Mycenaean, Cypriot, and Syrian pottery, amber from northern Europe, and various exotic materials that could only have reached the site through long-distance trade. Troy's own products—possibly including textiles, which rarely survive archaeologically—likely traveled in the opposite direction, contributing to the site's prosperity.

Troy's Strategic Position: Gateway Between Worlds

Troy's location at the entrance to the Dardanelles gave it extraordinary strategic importance in the Late Bronze Age world. Ships sailing between the Aegean and Black Seas depended on favorable winds and currents, often necessitating stops along the Troad coast. Troy's position allowed it to function as an intermediary in trade between Europe and Asia, the Aegean and Black Sea worlds.

"Troy occupied a liminal position between cultural spheres," observed philologist Frank Starke. "Linguistically and culturally, it appears to have been primarily Luwian—an Anatolian Indo-European people related to the Hittites. But its material culture shows strong Aegean influences as well. This cultural hybridity likely reflected Troy's role as an interface between these worlds, a place where different traditions met and mingled" (Starke 1997: 345).

Archaeological evidence supports this interpretation of Troy as a "gateway community." The substantial lower city discovered by Manfred Korfmann suggests significant population engaged in craft production and commerce. Workshop areas for metalworking, textile manufacture, and ceramic production indicate that Troy was not merely importing finished goods but actively participating in production and exchange systems spanning the eastern Mediterranean.

The site's impressive fortifications—both the citadel walls and the defensive circuit surrounding the lower city—reflect both the wealth these activities generated and the need to protect valuable goods and strategic positions. As Brian Rose observed, "Troy appears to have functioned as what economic anthropologists would call a 'gateway community'—mediating exchange between different cultural and economic zones while deriving prosperity from its role as an intermediary" (Rose 2014: 156).

The End of an Era: System Collapse Around 1200 BCE

The interconnected world of the Late Bronze Age came to a dramatic end between approximately 1200 and 1150 BCE. This "system collapse" affected virtually every major center in the Eastern Mediterranean and Near East, with palatial centers destroyed, states disintegrating, trade networks disrupted, and populations declining across a vast region.

The archaeological evidence for this collapse is stark. The Hittite capital at Hattusa was abandoned and burned. Mycenaean palaces were destroyed, never to be rebuilt. Major urban centers in Cyprus and the Levant show destruction layers dating to this period. In Egypt, while the state survived, it entered a period of decline and lost control of its Asian provinces.

"The scale and synchronicity of the Late Bronze Age collapse remains one of the most dramatic episodes in ancient history," wrote Eric Cline. "Within a span of just a few decades, a sophisticated international system that had developed over centuries simply ceased to function" (Cline 2014: 234).

The destruction of Troy VIIa fits precisely within this timeframe, with current dating placing it around 1180 BCE. This correlation suggests that Troy's fall—whatever its specific circumstances—formed part of broader regional upheaval rather than an isolated event.

Scholars have proposed various combinations of factors to explain this collapse:

Climate Change: Paleoclimatic data indicates prolonged drought affecting the Eastern Mediterranean around this time, potentially leading to crop failures, famine, and social instability.

External Invasion: Egyptian texts mention attacks by the "Sea Peoples"—groups of raiders or migrants who attacked coastlines throughout the region. While their exact identity remains controversial, these groups may have contributed to the disruption of established states.

Internal Rebellion: The highly stratified societies of the Late Bronze Age may have faced internal revolts as resource shortages exacerbated social tensions.

Systems Collapse: The very interconnectedness that had made the Late Bronze Age system so prosperous may have rendered it vulnerable to cascading failures, where problems in one region quickly spread to others through established networks.

Most scholars now favor complex, multi-causal explanations. As Susan Sherratt observed, "The very features that had made the Late Bronze Age system successful—its interconnectedness, specialization, and complex administrative structures—may have made it vulnerable to disruption when multiple stresses occurred simultaneously" (Sherratt 2003: 189).

Troy in Historical Context: Beyond Homer's Epic

The geopolitical landscape of the Late Bronze Age provides essential context for understanding Troy's significance and the possible historical background of the Trojan War tradition. Rather than an isolated settlement, Troy emerges as a prosperous regional center situated at a strategic location between major spheres of influence.

Politically, Troy (Wilusa) functioned as a kingdom within the Hittite sphere of influence while maintaining connections with the Mycenaean world. The Alaksandu Treaty and other Hittite texts indicate that Troy acknowledged Hittite overlordship while maintaining its own dynasty of kings. This relationship seems to have been generally stable, with the Hittite emperor promising to support the Wilusa king against both external enemies and internal rivals.

Economically, Troy prospered from its position controlling access between the Aegean and Black Seas. The city likely collected tolls from ships passing through the Hellespont and served as an exchange point where goods from different regions could be traded. Evidence for specialized craft production suggests Troy was not merely a passive intermediary but an active participant in Mediterranean-wide production networks.

Culturally, Troy shows evidence of both Anatolian and Aegean influences, creating a distinctive local tradition that incorporated elements from both spheres. The population likely spoke Luwian, but regular interaction with Mycenaean traders and diplomats would have necessitated familiarity with Greek as well.

"Troy exemplifies what we might call a 'gateway community,'" observed archaeologist Carl Lamberg-Karlovsky. "Such communities develop at interfaces between different cultural and economic zones, facilitating interaction while developing their own distinctive identities" (Lamberg-Karlovsky 1996: 234).

The traditional date of the Trojan War—the late 13th or early 12th century BCE—places it precisely during the period when the Late Bronze Age system was beginning to unravel. This timing is unlikely to be coincidental and suggests that whatever historical events might underlie the Homeric tradition occurred within the context of broader regional upheaval.

Several scenarios have been proposed for how actual historical events might relate to later Greek tradition. A Mycenaean expedition against Troy could have occurred during this period of instability, perhaps motivated by economic competition or political rivalry. As Hittite power weakened in western Anatolia, Mycenaean interests might have become more assertive in the region, leading to conflict with local kingdoms including Troy. Alternatively, the disruptions associated with the end of the Bronze Age led to population movements throughout the region, and displaced groups might have attacked Troy as part of these broader movements.

The Historical Reality Behind the Legend

The Hittite texts provide tantalizing hints that might relate to these events. A letter from Hattusili III to a king of Ahhiyawa mentions past conflict over Wilusa that had been resolved through treaty. Another text refers to a usurper named Piyamaradu who conducted raids in western Anatolia with apparent Ahhiyawan support, destabilizing Hittite control in the region. While none of these texts explicitly describes a "Trojan War" as depicted by Homer, they establish that Troy existed as a political entity, that it was occasionally contested between Hittite and Mycenaean interests, and that the region experienced significant unrest during the late 13th century BCE (Bryce 2006: 345).

Archaeologist Manfred Korfmann favored an interpretation that combined elements of these scenarios: "The destruction of Troy VIIa should be seen in the context of wider instability affecting the Eastern Mediterranean around 1200 BCE. Whether the attackers were Mycenaeans, displaced groups from elsewhere in Anatolia, or some combination of forces, the conflict occurred within a world system that was already beginning to collapse" (Korfmann 2004: 234).

"The historical reality behind the Trojan War legend was almost certainly more complex and nuanced than the epic tradition suggests," observed Susan Sherratt. "Rather than a simple conflict between 'Greeks' and 'Trojans,' any historical events would have involved the complex interplay of regional powers, local dynasties, and broader geopolitical forces" (Sherratt 2003: 267).

Conclusion: Troy as Mirror of Its Age

The Late Bronze Age context transforms our understanding of Troy and the possible historical background of the Homeric tradition. Rather than seeing the conflict as an isolated event, we can recognize it as part of a wider pattern of upheaval that brought an end to one of the most remarkable periods of international connection in the ancient world.

This broader perspective doesn't diminish Troy's significance—indeed, it enhances it. By situating Troy within its historical context, we gain deeper appreciation for the site's role in complex networks that connected the Aegean and Near Eastern worlds during the Late Bronze Age. We also gain insight into how a regional conflict at this strategic location might have resonated through cultural memory, eventually inspiring the epic tradition that would make Troy immortal in Western imagination.

When we examine the ruins of Troy today, we're looking at more than the setting for history's greatest war story. We're seeing the remains of a city that participated in the world's first global economy, that appeared in diplomatic correspondence between superpowers, that controlled one of the ancient world's most strategic waterways, and that ultimately fell as part of a civilizational collapse that reshaped the Mediterranean world.

The clay tablets from Hattusa that mention Wilusa, the Mycenaean pottery found in Troy's houses, the massive fortifications that protected its lower city—all these pieces of evidence place Troy firmly within the real world of Late Bronze Age geopolitics. They remind us that behind Homer's immortal poetry lies a historical reality every bit as fascinating as the legend it inspired, a world where Troy stood at the crossroads of continents and civilizations, where the fate of cities could be decided by correspondence between distant kings, and where local conflicts could escalate into events that echoed through the ages.

CHAPTER 12

TROY IN CONTEXT

Geography as Destiny

Stand today at the ruins of Troy and look northwest toward the Dardanelles, that narrow ribbon of water separating Europe from Asia. On a clear day, you can see ships threading their way through the strait, just as vessels have done for over three millennia. This view captures the essence of Troy's historical significance—its position at one of the world's most strategic waterways, a location so advantageous that the ancient geographer Strabo marveled, "nature has endowed this place with such advantages that it must inevitably prosper when properly governed, and even when neglected, it still manages to thrive" (Strabo, Geography 13.1.26).

Troy's exceptional location can be understood through multiple geographical scales, each revealing different aspects of its strategic importance. At the macro level, it occupied a critical position at the interface between Europe and Asia, commanding the mouth of the Dardanelles—the narrow strait connecting the Aegean Sea to the Sea of Marmara and ultimately to the Black Sea. At the regional scale, Troy controlled a fertile plain watered by two rivers, providing agricultural resources to support substantial population. At the local scale, the site itself occupied a natural hill offering defensive advantages while providing visibility across the surrounding landscape and seascape (Kraft 2003: 89).

"Troy's position represents a textbook example of what geographers call a 'gateway location,'" explains environmental archaeologist John Kraft. "It controlled a critical bottleneck in maritime movement between two major bodies of water, creating natural opportunities for both commerce and control" (Kraft 2003: 134).

The Straits: Ancient Superhighway and Natural Fortress

The Dardanelles strait, approximately 61 kilometers long and between 1.2 and 6 kilometers wide, has always presented formidable navigational challenges. Ancient sailing vessels faced particularly difficult conditions due to strong currents flowing from the Black Sea toward the Aegean, combined with seasonal winds that often blew in the opposite direction. These natural conditions created a navigational bottleneck that frequently forced ships to wait at either end of the strait for favorable conditions—sometimes for days or weeks.

Picture an ancient merchant captain arriving at Troy's harbor after a profitable voyage to the Black Sea, his ship loaded with copper from the Pontic Mountains, timber from Caucasian forests, and grain from the fertile steppes beyond. But now he faces the return journey through the treacherous straits, where adverse winds and contrary currents could trap his valuable cargo indefinitely. Such delays created natural opportunities for the controlling power—in this case, Troy—to extract value through taxes, services, or direct commercial engagement.

"The geography of the straits created what economists would call a 'transaction cost' for maritime trade," explains archaeologist Carl Lamberg-Karlovsky. "Ships had to either pay for safe passage and services or risk predation. Either way, the controlling power at the straits could extract value from this traffic" (Lamberg-Karlovsky 1996: 234).

Archaeological evidence from recent excavations has confirmed that Troy's harbor facilities were located along the coast approximately 5 kilometers west of the citadel, near the mouth of the Scamander River. This harbor, now silted in and located inland due to geomorphological changes over three millennia, would have provided essential infrastructure for Troy's maritime activities. Geoarchaeological research led by Ilhan Kayan has revealed that during the Late Bronze Age, the coastline extended further inland, creating a deep embayment that provided excellent natural harbor conditions (Kayan 2014: 156).

Recent paleoenvironmental studies have reconstructed this ancient landscape with remarkable precision. Sediment cores from the plain show evidence of maritime activity in areas that are now agricultural fields, with remains of wooden structures and imported materials suggesting extensive harbor infrastructure during Troy's heyday.

Troy as Regional Powerhouse: Beyond the Fortress Model

Archaeological evidence from Manfred Korfmann's groundbreaking excavations in the 1990s and early 2000s dramatically transformed scholarly understanding of Troy's scale and significance during the Late Bronze Age. Prior to Korfmann's work, archaeologists had focused primarily on Troy's citadel, an area of approximately 2 hectares. Korfmann's team, however, discovered evidence of a substantial "lower city" surrounding the citadel, expanding the urban area to approximately 25-30 hectares.

"What emerges from our excavations is not a simple fortress or small settlement, but a substantial urban center with a population of perhaps 5,000-10,000 inhabitants," Korfmann wrote. "This places Troy in the category of a significant regional center, comparable to other important Late Bronze Age cities in western Anatolia" (Korfmann 2001: 234).

The architectural evidence reveals sophisticated urban planning and monumental construction techniques that belie any notion of Troy as a modest hilltop settlement. The citadel was surrounded by impressive stone fortification walls, some sections reaching 5 meters in thickness, with carefully constructed gates and towers. Within the citadel, large megaron-style buildings suggest administrative or elite residential functions, while the lower city has yielded evidence of dense residential quarters, workshops, and additional fortification systems.

This archaeological picture gains crucial support from Hittite textual sources. Documents from the Hittite capital of Hattusa refer to a western Anatolian kingdom called Wilusa, which scholars now generally identify with Ilios/Troy. These texts describe Wilusa as a vassal kingdom within the Hittite sphere of influence, governed by its own king who acknowledged Hittite overlordship while maintaining substantial autonomy.

The "Alaksandu Treaty," a diplomatic agreement between Hittite king Muwatalli II and Alaksandu, ruler of Wilusa, dating to approximately 1280 BCE, outlines mutual obligations including military support, extradition of fugitives, and religious observances. The treaty's very existence suggests that Wilusa/Troy maintained sufficient political importance to warrant formal diplomatic attention from one of the era's great powers (Beckman 1999: 178).

The Economics of Strategic Position: How Troy Made Money

Troy's prosperity during the Late Bronze Age derived primarily from its position within regional and interregional trade networks. The city participated in multiple overlapping exchange systems, connecting the Aegean world with the Black Sea region and central Anatolia through both maritime and overland routes.

Maritime trade represented the most efficient means of bulk transport in the ancient world. A single merchant vessel could transport goods equivalent to dozens or hundreds of donkey or ox-cart loads, at significantly lower cost per unit. Water transport was typically 20 to 30 times more efficient than land transport in terms of cost per ton-mile, creating enormous economic advantages for settlements positioned to control maritime routes (Sherratt 1998: 234).

The archaeological record at Troy provides abundant evidence of the city's engagement with maritime trade. Imported ceramics represent the most visible indicator, with Mycenaean pottery from the Greek mainland appearing in significant quantities during the Late Bronze Age. Analysis of ceramic fabrics using neutron activation analysis has identified vessels from various Aegean production centers, including Mycenae, Tiryns, and Rhodes.

But pottery tells only part of the story. Other imported materials found at Troy include copper and tin (the components of bronze), semi-precious stones, ivory, gold, and exotic organic materials. The quantity of bronze artifacts found at Troy implies substantial flows of raw materials into the settlement—flows that, given their weight and Troy's coastal location, almost certainly arrived by sea (Muhly 1985: 156).

Troy's role extended beyond passive receipt of goods. Evidence of local craft production, including ceramic workshops, metallurgical facilities, and textile manufacturing, suggests that Troy produced finished goods for export as well as consuming imports. The settlement functioned as what archaeologists call an entrepôt, where goods from different regions were exchanged, often with value added through local processing or repackaging.

Control of the Dardanelles provided Troy with several potential revenue streams. Direct taxation of passing vessels represented one possibility, with ships paying for safe passage through the strait. Provision of services offered another revenue source, with Troy potentially supplying fresh water, food, navigational assistance, or protection to merchants. A third model involved more direct participation in trade, with Trojan merchants or elites engaging in commerce themselves.

"The economic model at Troy likely combined elements of all these approaches," suggests economic archaeologist Michael Galaty. "Different periods and political circumstances would have shifted the balance between taxation, service provision, and direct commercial engagement, but the fundamental geographic advantages remained constant" (Galaty 2007: 189).

The Black Sea Connection: Troy's Northern Frontier

While Troy's connections to the Aegean world have received extensive scholarly attention, its relationship with the Black Sea region has been comparatively understudied until recently. Archaeological evidence increasingly suggests that Troy functioned as a crucial intermediary between the Aegean and Black Sea cultural spheres during the Late Bronze Age.

The Black Sea region represented a rich source of raw materials essential to Bronze Age economies. Copper deposits in the Pontic Mountains and the Caucasus provided one of bronze's two essential components. Timber from dense forests served shipbuilding and construction needs. Grain from fertile northern steppes supplemented Mediterranean agricultural production. Other resources included gold, silver, iron, slaves, honey, wax, and amber traded down from the Baltic.

"The Black Sea functioned as a resource periphery for the more urbanized Aegean and Eastern Mediterranean core during the Late Bronze Age," explains archaeologist Alexander Bauer. "The flow of raw materials from the Black Sea region into Mediterranean markets represented a crucial element of the period's economic system" (Bauer 2005: 234).

Archaeological evidence for Black Sea-Aegean connections has emerged from excavations around the Black Sea littoral. Settlements such as Sinope and Samsun on the northern Turkish coast show evidence of contact with Aegean material culture during this period. Further north, sites in Crimea and along the Bulgarian coast have yielded Mycenaean pottery and other Mediterranean imports dating to the 14th-13th centuries BCE.

Troy's position at the entrance to the Dardanelles made it a natural gateway for this Black Sea-Aegean exchange. Ships traveling between these regions necessarily passed by Troy, creating opportunities for the settlement to engage with this traffic. The archaeological record at Troy includes artifacts with Black Sea origins or connections, including distinctive pottery styles and metallurgical techniques that show northern influences alongside the more obvious Aegean connections.

Harbor Infrastructure: The Maritime Gateway

Archaeological investigation of Troy's harbor facilities has been complicated by substantial geomorphological changes in the surrounding landscape over the past three millennia. The Scamander River has deposited significant alluvium, extending the coastline seaward and burying ancient harbor installations under meters of sediment.

Geoarchaeological research has reconstructed the paleogeography of the Trojan plain, demonstrating that during the Late Bronze Age, the coastline lay several kilometers inland from its current position. A deep embayment extended into what is now the alluvial plain, creating natural harbor conditions near the mouth of the Scamander River.

"The Late Bronze Age coastline created nearly ideal conditions for ancient harbors," explains geoarchaeologist Ilhan Kayan. "The embayment provided natural protection from storms and wave action, while the river mouth offered a landmark visible from the sea and access to freshwater" (Kayan 2014: 178).

Limited excavations in the area identified as Troy's harbor have revealed wooden structures and artifacts associated with maritime activity. These include stone anchors, ceramic transport containers, and evidence of structures that may have served as warehouses or administrative facilities. While the difficulty of excavating below the water table has restricted comprehensive investigation, the evidence confirms the area's use for maritime purposes.

Comparative evidence from better-preserved harbor sites elsewhere in the Eastern Mediterranean provides models for understanding Troy's likely maritime infrastructure. Late Bronze Age harbors at sites such as Ugarit in Syria, Kition in Cyprus, and various Mycenaean coastal settlements included artificial breakwaters, quays for docking ships, warehouses for storing goods, and administrative facilities for managing commercial activities (Blackman 2013: 234).

The economic significance of Troy's harbor facilities extended beyond simple docking infrastructure. Evidence from the lower city suggests substantial craft production oriented toward maritime trade, including ceramic workshops producing transport vessels and metalworking facilities processing imported raw materials. These activities indicate a sophisticated economic system integrating maritime transport with local production.

Political Geography: Balancing Between Empires

Troy's control of the Dardanelles positioned it within a complex regional political landscape during the Late Bronze Age. Hittite texts provide the most direct evidence for Troy/Wilusa's political status, depicting it as a vassal kingdom within the Hittite sphere of influence in western Anatolia.

The Alaksandu Treaty reveals a relationship in which Troy acknowledged Hittite overlordship while maintaining substantial internal autonomy. The treaty required Troy to provide military support to the Hittites when requested, prevent enemies from passing through its territory, and extradite political fugitives. In return, the Hittites guaranteed Troy's security and the legitimacy of its ruling dynasty.

"The treaty reveals a relationship of asymmetric but mutual benefit," observes Hittitologist Gary Beckman. "Troy gained security and legitimacy from its association with Hittite power, while the Hittites extended their influence to this strategically valuable region without the expense of direct administration" (Beckman 1999: 234).

Other Hittite texts suggest that Troy's position within this system was occasionally contested. Documents describe western Anatolian conflicts involving a troublesome figure named Piyamaradu who conducted raids against Hittite interests in the region, apparently with support from Ahhiyawa (the Mycenaean world). These texts indicate that despite Hittite claims of overlordship, practical control of western Anatolia remained tenuous and required ongoing military intervention.

Troy's relationship with the Mycenaean world remains more ambiguous in the textual record, but archaeological evidence confirms substantial Mycenaean presence or influence at the site. Some scholars suggest that Troy may have maintained a delicate balancing act between Hittite and Mycenaean spheres of influence—its formal political allegiance lay with the Hittites, but its economic connections and cultural influences linked it substantially to the Aegean world.

"Troy occupied a classic 'middle ground' position between competing power spheres," suggests archaeologist Carl Lamberg-Karlovsky. "This position created both vulnerability and opportunity—vulnerability to becoming a battleground between competing powers, but also opportunity to benefit from connections in multiple directions" (Lamberg-Karlovsky 1996: 267).

The End of Bronze Age Prosperity

Troy's prosperity as a regional center controlling the Dardanelles came to an abrupt end around 1180 BCE, when the settlement known as Troy VIIa was violently destroyed. This destruction coincided with the broader collapse of the Late Bronze Age international system throughout the Eastern Mediterranean—a period of upheaval that saw the fall of the Hittite Empire, the destruction of Mycenaean palaces, and the disruption of trade networks from Greece to Mesopotamia.

Archaeological evidence from Troy VIIa shows clear signs of violent destruction. Excavators have documented burned buildings, collapsed walls, and human remains suggesting casualties during the site's fall. Arrowheads embedded in walls and skeletal remains with unhealed trauma provide direct evidence of warfare.

"The archaeological evidence from Troy VIIa presents a clear picture of violent destruction," states archaeologist Peter Jablonka. "Buildings show evidence of intense burning, storage vessels were abandoned full of contents, and there are direct indicators of military action including weapons and human casualties" (Jablonka 2001: 234).

The timing of Troy's destruction places it within the broader context of what archaeologists call the Late Bronze Age collapse (c. 1200-1150 BCE), when political systems throughout the Eastern Mediterranean experienced severe disruption. Rather than seeing Troy's fall as an isolated event, we should understand it as part of what Eric Cline calls a "perfect storm" of interconnected failures that transformed the political landscape of the entire region (Cline 2014: 234).

The specific agents responsible for Troy's destruction remain uncertain. Traditional attribution to Mycenaean Greeks, following the Homeric narrative, represents one possibility. However, this scenario is complicated by the fact that Mycenaean centers themselves were experiencing disruption during this same period. Alternative theories suggest other groups associated with the "Sea Peoples" phenomenon, local rebellions, or some combination of factors.

Whatever the specific circumstances of its destruction, Troy's fall marked the end of its role as a significant regional center controlling the Dardanelles. The site continued to be occupied in subsequent periods, but on a reduced scale and without the same level of prosperity or regional importance evident in the Late Bronze Age.

Environmental Constraints and Opportunities

Troy's geographical advantages extended beyond its strategic maritime position to include substantial environmental benefits that supported its development as a regional center. The fertile alluvial plain created by the Scamander and Simois rivers provided rich agricultural land capable of supporting substantial population, while the surrounding hills offered additional resources including timber, grazing land, and defensive positions.

Paleoenvironmental research has revealed that the Troad region was more heavily forested during the Bronze Age than today, with extensive stands of oak, pine, and other trees that would have provided timber for construction, shipbuilding, and fuel. The coastal plain, formed by river-deposited sediments, offered some of the most fertile agricultural land in the region, supporting intensive cultivation of cereals, legumes, and other crops.

Analysis of plant and animal remains from Troy's excavations reveals exploitation of diverse environmental resources. Agriculture focused on wheat, barley, and legumes, supplemented by herding of sheep, goats, and cattle. Marine resources, including fish and shellfish, also contributed significantly to the diet, taking advantage of Troy's coastal location.

"Troy's environmental setting gave it access to diverse resources," explained paleobotanist Simone Riehl, who analyzed plant remains from the excavations. "The archaeological evidence shows exploitation of both terrestrial and marine resources, creating a broad subsistence base that could support substantial population while generating surpluses for trade" (Riehl 2010: 156).

Climate reconstruction based on various proxy data indicates that the Late Bronze Age was a period of relatively favorable conditions in the eastern Mediterranean, with adequate rainfall supporting agriculture and forest growth. However, evidence suggests that climatic deterioration began around 1200 BCE, potentially contributing to the widespread disruptions that marked the end of Bronze Age civilization.

Conclusion: The Persistence of Geographical Advantage

Troy's exceptional geographical position at the Dardanelles fundamentally shaped its historical trajectory throughout the Bronze Age and beyond. This location provided natural advantages that supported the settlement's development as a significant regional center, while also exposing it to competing interests from multiple directions.

The straits represented both opportunity and vulnerability—opportunity to extract value from maritime traffic passing between the Aegean and Black Seas, but vulnerability to powers seeking to control this strategic passage. This duality defined Troy's position throughout its history, creating conditions for both prosperity and conflict.

For Bronze Age Troy, geographical advantages enabled its development as a prosperous regional center integrated into international networks. Control of the straits provided economic benefits through various mechanisms—taxation, service provision, and marketplace functions. The fertile agricultural plain supported substantial population, while defensive advantages of the site itself offered protection against routine threats.

These same geographical factors, however, ensured that Troy would remain a prize worth fighting for when regional power balances shifted. As the Late Bronze Age international system destabilized in the late 13th century BCE, Troy's strategic value made it a potential target for various competing interests seeking advantage amid broader regional upheaval.

"Troy's geographical significance transcended any particular political arrangement," concludes historian Ian Morris. "When the Hittite Empire could no longer guarantee the security of its western frontier, Troy's control of the straits became contested in ways that may well have contributed to its violent destruction" (Morris 2006: 234).

This geographical reality provides essential context for understanding both the archaeological evidence from Bronze Age Troy and the later Greek literary tradition surrounding the site. Whether or not the specific events described by Homer have any historical basis, the fundamental scenario of conflict centered on this strategically valuable location aligns perfectly with the geopolitical realities of the Late Bronze Age Mediterranean.

Troy's geographical significance has remained constant throughout history, even as political arrangements have changed. From Bronze Age Wilusa to Classical Ilion, from Byzantine Constantinople to Ottoman and modern Istanbul, control of the straits connecting the Mediterranean and Black Seas has consistently represented a prize worth fighting for. In this sense, Troy's Bronze Age experience represents one chapter in a much longer story defined by the enduring significance of this exceptional geographical position.

When we stand today among Troy's ruins and look out across the Dardanelles, we see the same strategic waterway that shaped the ancient city's destiny. The ships threading through the strait today follow routes pioneered by Bronze Age mariners, confirming the timeless value of this geographical position. Troy's story reminds us that while political systems rise and fall, geographical advantages endure, continuing to shape human history across millennia.

CHAPTER 13

THE ARCHAEOLOGY OF TROY VI/VIIA

The Archaeological Reality

I magine walking through the gates of Troy around 1200 BCE, just decades before its final destruction. You'd enter a bustling urban center far more impressive than Hollywood epics have ever portrayed—a city with massive stone fortifications, sophisticated drainage systems, workshops humming with craft production, and storage facilities packed with grain for uncertain times ahead. This isn't the Troy of romantic imagination but the archaeological Troy, revealed through more than a century of careful excavation and scientific analysis.

The archaeological evidence from Troy VI and VIIa presents a complex picture that both aligns with and challenges traditional narratives about the site. Excavations have revealed a sophisticated urban center that flourished during the Late Bronze Age before experiencing dramatic destruction that coincides remarkably with traditional dating of the Trojan War. By examining the material remains from these crucial periods, we can construct a nuanced understanding of what Troy was actually like during its final Bronze Age florescence and subsequent violent end (Korfmann 2001: 89).

Troy VI: The Golden Age (c. 1700-1250 BCE)

Troy VI represents the most impressive phase of the Bronze Age settlement, characterized by monumental architecture, sophisticated urban planning, and evidence of extensive international connections. This period, spanning approximately 1700-1250 BCE, corresponds chronologically to the rise and height of Mycenaean civilization in mainland Greece and the expansion of the Hittite Empire in Anatolia—placing Troy squarely within the interconnected world of Late Bronze Age superpowers.

The most immediately striking feature of Troy VI is its impressive fortification system. The citadel was encircled by massive limestone walls that still stand up to 6 meters high in some sections, with an estimated original height of 8-9 meters. These walls, constructed with a slight inward slope and featuring carefully dressed stone blocks, represent a significant engineering achievement that would have rivaled the famous "Cyclopean" walls of Mycenaean Greece.

"The fortification walls of Troy VI represent one of the most impressive defensive systems in the Late Bronze Age Aegean," notes archaeologist Peter Jablonka. "Their sophisticated construction techniques, including the inward slope designed to resist battering rams and earthquake damage, reveal both technical expertise and substantial investment of resources" (Jablonka 2001: 156).

The northeastern bastion particularly demonstrates the skill of Troy VI architects. This massive structure, with walls 4-5 meters thick, protected the most vulnerable approach to the citadel. Its careful construction with large limestone blocks, some weighing several tons, indicates both technical sophistication and the ability to mobilize substantial labor resources—clear signs of a powerful, well-organized society.

Walking through Troy VI's gates, a visitor would have encountered not a cramped fortress but a carefully planned urban environment. Within the impressive fortifications, the citadel featured a radial arrangement of large, well-built houses. These structures, some exceeding 20 meters in length, were constructed using stone foundations with mudbrick superstructures. Many featured multiple rooms organized around central halls, suggesting complex social organization and specialized spatial functions.

The architectural sophistication is remarkable. As Carl Blegen observed during his excavations in the 1930s: "The quality of construction is excellent throughout; the walls are built of well-dressed stones laid in regular courses, the joints carefully fitted, and the faces smoothed" (Blegen 1953: 134). This level of craftsmanship indicates both technical skill and substantial investment in built infrastructure—hallmarks of a prosperous, confident society.

Troy VI also featured infrastructure that would impress even today: a network of paved streets and drainage systems that demonstrate urban planning and public investment extending far beyond mere defensive considerations. The main street running through the settlement was paved with flat stones and included channels for water drainage, showing concern with urban functionality that speaks to sophisticated civic organization.

Material culture from Troy VI reveals a prosperous community with access to luxury goods and participation in international trade networks that spanned the known world. Pottery shows both local production and imported wares from the Mycenaean world. Fine ceramics, including elegant cups, graceful jugs, and massive storage vessels, demonstrate sophisticated craft traditions. Metal artifacts—bronze tools, weapons, and ornaments—indicate access to important raw materials and metallurgical expertise that required international connections.

Particularly significant is the consistent presence of Mycenaean pottery throughout the later phases of Troy VI. These imported vessels, primarily consisting of drinking cups and perfume containers, indicate regular contact with the Aegean world. As archaeologist Susan Allen notes, "The consistent presence of Mycenaean pottery at Troy VI, particularly in the later phases, demonstrates regular interaction between Troy and the Mycenaean world, whether through direct trade or intermediaries" (Allen 1999: 234).

The prosperity of Troy VI came to an abrupt end around 1250 BCE, but not through human violence. Archaeological evidence indicates that this destruction was caused by a significant earthquake rather than military attack. Excavations revealed walls that had toppled outward and evidence of structural collapse consistent with seismic activity rather than warfare. As Carl Blegen concluded after careful analysis, "The destruction of Troy VI must be attributed to a violent earthquake which shook down the great circuit wall and the buildings of the citadel" (Blegen 1958: 142).

Troy VIIa: A City Under Pressure (c. 1250-1180 BCE)

Following the earthquake destruction of Troy VI, the site was immediately reoccupied and rebuilt in what archaeologists designate as Troy VIIa. This phase, lasting approximately 70 years from 1250-1180 BCE, presents a markedly different character from its predecessor while maintaining continuity in crucial aspects. If Troy VI represents confidence and prosperity, Troy VIIa shows a community adapting to increasingly dangerous times.

The inhabitants of Troy VIIa repaired the damaged fortification walls using materials salvaged from collapsed Troy VI buildings. While maintaining the same defensive circuit as the previous period, these repairs were generally of lower quality, suggesting urgent reconstruction under difficult circumstances. Nevertheless, the defensive system remained formidable, with repaired walls still standing several meters high—adequate for protection but lacking the monumental grandeur of their predecessors.

Within the citadel, spatial organization changed dramatically in ways that archaeologists recognize as responses to crisis. The spacious houses of Troy VI were subdivided into smaller units, with numerous storage facilities added throughout the settlement. Large storage jars (pithoi) were set into floors throughout the citadel, often in rows along walls or in specialized storage rooms. This proliferation of storage facilities suggests deep concerns about food security and resource management.

"The dramatic increase in storage capacity during Troy VIIa indicates a community preparing for difficult conditions," observes archaeologist Donald Easton. "Whether anticipating siege, disruption of normal supply networks, or increased population pressure, the inhabitants clearly prioritized stockpiling essential resources" (Easton 1994: 267).

The numbers are staggering. In one house alone, excavators documented 20 pithoi set into the floor, capable of storing thousands of liters of grain or other foodstuffs. Multiplied across the settlement, this storage capacity would have allowed the community to survive extended periods of isolation or siege—preparations that suggest very real awareness of impending threats.

Archaeological evidence suggests increased population density within the citadel during Troy VIIa, possibly reflecting an influx of people from the surrounding countryside seeking protection within the fortified walls. Smaller, more crowded living quarters replaced the spacious houses of Troy VI, with many spaces subdivided by thin partition walls. This densification likely reflects the kind of emergency urbanization that occurs when rural populations flee to fortified centers during periods of regional instability.

Material culture from Troy VIIa shows both continuity and ominous changes from the preceding period. Local pottery traditions continued, though often with declining quality that suggests disrupted craft traditions or resource constraints. Mycenaean imported pottery remained present, though in changing forms and quantities that reflect broader regional patterns during this period of increasing instability across the Eastern Mediterranean.

Most tellingly, Troy VIIa deposits contain numerous arrowheads and other weapons, particularly concentrated near the fortification walls. This distribution isn't random—it suggests actual military conflict rather than merely routine weapon storage. Some arrowheads were found embedded in walls or floors, potentially in the positions where they fell during attacks on the settlement.

The end of Troy VIIa came around 1180 BCE through violent destruction by human agency—a stark contrast to the natural disaster that ended Troy VI.

Archaeological evidence reveals extensive burning throughout the settlement, with a destruction layer containing ash, charcoal, and burned debris that tells a story of systematic devastation. Human remains discovered in the destruction layer, including a skeleton found in the street with a crushed skull, provide grim testimony to the violence of this event.

"The archaeological evidence from Troy VIIa presents a clear picture of violent destruction," notes Manfred Korfmann, who led excavations at the site from 1988 until his death in 2005. "The extensive burning, collapsed buildings, and human remains found in the destruction layer all point to a catastrophic end brought about by human violence rather than natural disaster" (Korfmann 2004: 189).

This destruction layer, dated to approximately 1180 BCE, aligns remarkably well with traditional dating of the Trojan War in Greek sources. The Greek historian Eratosthenes placed the fall of Troy at 1184 BCE, while other ancient chronographers suggested dates ranging from 1209-1171 BCE. This chronological correspondence between archaeological destruction and literary tradition represents one of the most compelling connections between material evidence and cultural memory.

The Lower City: Revealing Troy's True Scale

Perhaps the most revolutionary development in Trojan archaeology has been the discovery and investigation of the extensive "lower city" surrounding the citadel mound. Previous excavations by Schliemann, Dörpfeld, and Blegen had focused almost exclusively on the citadel itself, creating a limited understanding of Troy's true urban extent that seriously underestimated its importance.

Beginning in 1988, the University of Tübingen expedition led by Manfred Korfmann employed innovative archaeological techniques, including magnetic prospection and targeted excavation, to investigate areas surrounding the citadel. These investigations revealed a substantial settlement extending far beyond the limits of the previously known site—a discovery that fundamentally changed our understanding of Bronze Age Troy.

"The discovery of the lower city fundamentally transforms our understanding of Bronze Age Troy," Korfmann explained. "Rather than a small citadel of perhaps 2-3 hectares, we now recognize Troy as a major urban center covering 25-30 hectares, with a population of 5,000-10,000 inhabitants during the Late Bronze Age" (Korfmann 2001: 234).

This wasn't just suburban sprawl. The lower city was protected by an impressive defensive system consisting of a deep ditch and wooden palisade. Magnetic prospection revealed this defensive circuit extending in a wide arc south and east of the citadel, enclosing a substantial area. Targeted excavations confirmed the presence of this ditch, approximately 4 meters deep and 3-4 meters wide, dating to the Troy VI period—a massive engineering project that would have required coordinated labor from thousands of workers.

Within this defensive perimeter, archaeological investigations revealed dense settlement during both Troy VI and VIIa periods. Residential areas, craft production zones, and evidence of specialized economic activities have been identified through both remote sensing and excavation. The lower city appears to have been organized into distinct neighborhoods, suggesting complex urban planning and social organization that rivals anything found in contemporary Mycenaean Greece or Hittite Anatolia.

Particularly significant is evidence for specialized craft production in the lower city. Excavations have revealed areas dedicated to pottery production, metallurgy, and textile manufacturing. These craft production zones indicate economic specialization and complex division of labor within the Bronze Age settlement—hallmarks of true urban civilization.

"The evidence for specialized craft production in Troy's lower city demonstrates that this was not merely a residential extension of the citadel, but a complex urban environment with diverse economic activities," observes archaeologist Peter Jablonka. "The spatial organization of these activities suggests a level of urban planning and economic coordination consistent with a significant regional center" (Jablonka 2001: 267).

The discovery of the lower city substantially changes our assessment of Troy's regional significance during the Late Bronze Age. Rather than a relatively small fortified settlement, Troy now appears as one of the larger urban centers in western Anatolia during this period, comparable in size to important Mycenaean centers like Tiryns or Pylos in Greece, or major Hittite cities like Hattusa itself.

Daily Life in Bronze Age Troy: What the Artifacts Tell Us

The archaeological record from Troy VI and VIIa provides rich evidence for daily life, economic activities, and cultural practices that bring the ancient city to life in ways that epic poetry never could. Artifacts recovered from these levels offer insights into everything from food production and consumption to religious practices, craft specialization, and international connections.

Feeding a City: Subsistence and Economy

Archaeobotanical and zooarchaeological remains from Troy VI and VIIa reveal a diverse and sophisticated subsistence base. Agricultural production centered on cereal crops, particularly barley and wheat, supplemented by legumes and fruit cultivation. Animal husbandry focused primarily on sheep and goats, with cattle and pigs also represented in the faunal assemblage. Marine resources, including fish and shellfish from the nearby Dardanelles, supplemented the diet and took advantage of Troy's coastal location.

"The archaeobotanical record from Late Bronze Age Troy indicates a well-developed agricultural system capable of producing substantial surpluses," notes paleoethnobotanist Simone Riehl. "The diversity of crops and evidence for intensive cultivation practices suggest sophisticated understanding of agricultural management" (Riehl 2010: 156).

Storage facilities, particularly abundant in Troy VIIa, demonstrate concerns with food security and resource management that extend far beyond normal household needs. The numerous pithoi set into floors throughout the settlement could collectively store substantial quantities of grain and other foodstuffs. These storage capacities would have been crucial for surviving both seasonal scarcity and potential disruptions due to conflict or other crises.

Beyond subsistence production, evidence indicates that Troy participated actively in regional and long-distance exchange networks. Imported goods, including Mycenaean pottery, exotic raw materials, and luxury items, demonstrate connections with the Aegean world and beyond. Troy's strategic position controlling the Dardanelles strait would have facilitated such exchange, allowing the settlement to benefit from maritime traffic between the Aegean and Black Seas.

Craftsmanship and Technology: The Workshops of Troy

Archaeological evidence from Troy VI and VIIa reveals sophisticated craft traditions and technological expertise that place the city among the most advanced centers of its time. Pottery production shows both technical skill and artistic sensibility, with local wares demonstrating distinctive forms and decorative styles. The quality of ceramic production indicates specialized potters working within established craft traditions—evidence of the kind of occupational specialization that marks complex urban societies.

Metallurgical evidence is particularly impressive. Bronze artifacts including tools, weapons, and ornaments recovered from both Troy VI and VIIa contexts demonstrate not just access to finished goods but local production capabilities. Crucibles, molds, and slag indicate on-site manufacturing rather than sole reliance on imports. The quality of metalwork demonstrates sophisticated understanding of alloying and manufacturing techniques that required both technical knowledge and access to raw materials from distant sources.

"The metallurgical evidence from Troy indicates participation in the complex bronze production and exchange networks of the Late Bronze Age eastern Mediterranean," observes archaeometallurgist James Muhly. "Access to copper and tin, the essential components of bronze, would have required maintaining connections with distant resource areas or intermediaries" (Muhly 1985: 234).

Textile production is evidenced through numerous loom weights and spindle whorls found throughout the settlement. These implements indicate both household-level production and potentially more specialized workshop contexts in the lower city. The quantity of textile production tools suggests this was a significant economic activity at Bronze Age Troy—possibly even a major export industry given the site's reputation in later classical sources for fine textiles.

International Connections: Troy at the Crossroads

Material culture from Troy VI and VIIa reveals a settlement positioned at the interface between Aegean and Anatolian cultural spheres, creating a unique hybrid identity that drew from multiple traditions while maintaining distinctive local characteristics. This intermediate position is reflected in various aspects of Troy's material record, which shows influences from both directions while maintaining strong regional identity.

Pottery assemblages from Late Bronze Age Troy include both locally produced wares and imported vessels, particularly from the Mycenaean world. Local pottery traditions show some Anatolian characteristics while also incorporating Aegean influences. This hybrid character reflects Troy's position as a cultural crossroads between these regions—a place where different traditions met, mingled, and created something new.

Architectural traditions similarly reflect multiple influences. The megaron-style buildings found in the Troy VI citadel show parallels with both Mycenaean and Anatolian architectural traditions. The fortification system, with its massive stone walls and impressive gateways, demonstrates both local engineering expertise and awareness of broader eastern Mediterranean defensive technologies.

"Troy's material culture reveals a community that was neither simply 'Mycenaean' nor purely 'Anatolian,'" observes archaeologist Elizabeth French. "Rather, it represents a distinctive regional tradition that incorporated and adapted elements from multiple cultural spheres while maintaining its own identity" (French 1999: 234).

Troy VIIa: Archaeological Evidence for a City Under Siege

The archaeological evidence from Troy VIIa provides compelling indications of a community under severe stress, culminating in violent destruction around 1180 BCE. This evidence offers tantalizing connections to traditional narratives of the Trojan War, while also placing Troy's fall within the broader context of the Late Bronze Age collapse that devastated civilizations across the Eastern Mediterranean.

Signs of Crisis: Reading the Archaeological Evidence

Multiple lines of archaeological evidence suggest that Troy VIIa represented a community under significant pressure, potentially including the threat of prolonged military conflict. The architectural modifications during this phase, particularly the subdivision of formerly spacious houses and the proliferation of storage facilities, indicate systematic adaptation to crisis conditions rather than normal urban evolution.

"The architectural changes in Troy VIIa suggest a community responding to crisis," observes archaeologist Donald Easton. "The dramatic increase in storage capacity, combined with the densification of living spaces, points to concerns about resource security and possibly population pressure from an influx of people seeking protection within the fortified settlement" (Easton 1994: 234).

The repair and maintenance of the fortification system during Troy VIIa demonstrates continued concern with defensive capabilities despite the lower quality of construction compared to the original Troy VI walls. These repairs maintained the defensive integrity of the citadel using whatever materials were available, suggesting urgent priorities and limited resources. The continued investment in these defenses indicates ongoing security concerns that justified major expenditures of labor and materials.

Perhaps most tellingly, Troy VIIa shows a dramatic increase in weapons compared to any other period at the site. Numerous bronze arrowheads have been recovered, many concentrated near the fortification walls in patterns suggesting actual combat rather than storage. As Carl Blegen noted following his excavations, "The number of weapons, especially arrowheads, found in the VIIa settlement far exceeds those from any other period at Troy" (Blegen 1958: 167).

Some of these arrowheads were found embedded in walls or gates, potentially representing enemy missiles fired during assaults on the city. Others were scattered through destruction deposits in patterns suggesting they fell where used during the final battle. This weapon distribution provides some of the clearest archaeological evidence for actual warfare at Bronze Age Troy.

The Final Destruction: Violence in the Archaeological Record

The end of Troy VIIa came through violent destruction around 1180 BCE, leaving archaeological evidence that reads like a crime scene three millennia old. A pronounced burn layer containing ash, charcoal, and burned debris extends throughout the settlement. Collapsed buildings, with walls toppled and roofs caved in, indicate catastrophic destruction rather than gradual abandonment.

The intensity and extent of burning throughout the settlement indicate deliberate and systematic destruction rather than accidental fire. Buildings show evidence of intense conflagration that collapsed roofs and caused walls to fall. The pattern suggests comprehensive burning of the entire settlement—the kind of systematic destruction that Bronze Age armies typically inflicted on conquered cities as both practical military measure and symbolic statement of victory.

Human remains discovered within this destruction layer provide grim but invaluable testimony to the violence of Troy VIIa's end. Most notable is a skeleton found in a street context with a crushed skull—apparently a victim killed during the final attack who remained unburied when the settlement was destroyed. The position and condition of these remains suggest death during active combat rather than ceremonial execution or post-battle cleanup.

"The skeletal remains found in the Troy VIIa destruction layer represent rare direct evidence for human casualties during the site's final destruction," notes bioarchaeologist Henrike Kiesewetter. "These remains, combined with the extensive burning and structural collapse, paint a vivid picture of catastrophic violence" (Kiesewetter 2003: 156).

Additional human remains have been found scattered through destruction contexts, though formal burials are notably absent from this period. This absence of proper burial—a fundamental requirement in Bronze Age societies—suggests that social order had completely broken down during Troy's final moments, with survivors (if any) either killed, captured, or fled without opportunity to care for the dead.

Troy in Context: The Late Bronze Age World

The archaeological evidence from Troy VI and VIIa must be understood within the broader regional context of the Late Bronze Age eastern Mediterranean—a world characterized by complex interconnections between major powers, international trade networks, diplomatic relations, and ultimately, systemic collapse that affected virtually every major center in the region.

Troy/Wilusa in the Hittite World

Textual evidence from Hittite sources provides crucial context for understanding Troy's position within Late Bronze Age political geography. Several Hittite texts mention a western Anatolian kingdom called Wilusa, which scholars now generally accept as the Hittite name for Troy (linguistically corresponding to the Greek "Ilios" through well-understood sound changes).

The most significant of these texts is the Alaksandu Treaty, dating to the 13th century BCE, which documents an agreement between the Hittite king Muwatalli II and Alaksandu, ruler of Wilusa. This treaty confirms Wilusa's status as a vassal kingdom within the Hittite sphere of influence, while also suggesting a history of shifting allegiances and political instability in the region.

"The Alaksandu Treaty demonstrates that Wilusa/Troy was recognized as a distinct political entity by the Hittite Empire," notes Hittitologist Trevor Bryce. "Its status as a vassal kingdom indicates both its regional importance and its position within the complex geopolitical landscape of western Anatolia" (Bryce 2005: 234).

Another significant text, the Tawagalawa Letter, references previous conflicts involving Wilusa and a figure called Piyama-Radu who conducted raids with possible Mycenaean support. This text suggests tensions between Hittite and Mycenaean interests in western Anatolia, with Troy/Wilusa potentially caught between these competing superpowers.

These Hittite texts confirm Troy's existence as a political entity during precisely the period when archaeological evidence shows it flourishing as a substantial urban center. They place Troy within a complex political landscape where it maintained relationships with the Hittite Empire while potentially also engaging with Mycenaean powers across the Aegean.

Troy and the Late Bronze Age Collapse

The destruction of Troy VIIa around 1180 BCE coincides with the broader phenomenon known as the Late Bronze Age collapse—a period of systemic failure that affected virtually every major center in the Eastern Mediterranean and marked the end of the Bronze Age world. This timing is unlikely to be coincidental.

"The synchronicity between Troy's destruction and the broader regional collapse is unlikely to be coincidental," observes archaeologist Eric Cline. "Whether Troy was destroyed by Mycenaeans as Greek tradition suggests, by other groups associated with the 'Sea Peoples' phenomenon, or by some combination of factors, its fall occurred within a wider context of systems collapse throughout the region" (Cline 2014: 234).

Archaeological evidence for this collapse includes destruction layers at numerous sites across the eastern Mediterranean, disruption of trade networks, abandonment of settlements, and evidence for population movements and social upheaval. The causes remain debated, with scholars proposing various combinations of factors including climate change, drought, famine, internal rebellions, external invasions, and cascading systems failure.

Troy's destruction thus represents one episode within a much larger pattern of regional upheaval. This broader context helps explain why Troy VIIa shows signs of a community under stress, with increased storage capacity, densified population, and evidence for defensive preparations. These archaeological indicators suggest awareness of regional instability and attempts to prepare for potential disruptions.

Conclusion: Between Archaeology and Legend

The archaeological evidence from Troy VI and VIIa presents a nuanced picture that both aligns with and challenges traditional narratives about the site. What emerges is neither simple confirmation nor outright refutation of Homeric tradition, but rather a complex story of a significant Bronze Age center that experienced dramatic changes and ultimate destruction during one of history's great transitional periods.

Troy was indeed a substantial urban center during the Late Bronze Age, with impressive fortifications, sophisticated architecture, and evidence of prosperity through international connections. It occupied a strategic position that made it valuable to control and potentially worth fighting over. It was violently destroyed by human agency around the time traditional sources place the Trojan War.

But the archaeological Troy also reveals aspects invisible in epic poetry: the complex urban planning of the lower city, the evidence for craft specialization and international trade, the signs of growing crisis in Troy VIIa, and the broader regional context of systemic collapse that provides the historical framework for understanding Troy's destruction.

"The archaeological evidence confirms that Troy was a substantial and prosperous center during the Late Bronze Age, and that it was violently destroyed around 1180 BCE," observes archaeologist Trevor Bryce. "Whether this destruction corresponds to the event later remembered as the 'Trojan War' remains uncertain, but the chronological correlation is certainly suggestive" (Bryce 2005: 267).

Perhaps most importantly, archaeology reveals Troy as a real place inhabited by real people who lived, worked, loved, feared, and ultimately died during one of the great crises of the ancient world. Their material remains—the broken pottery, the storage jars, the weapons, the unburied dead—tell a human story that complements rather than contradicts the epic tradition.

When we walk through Troy's ruins today, we can still see the massive stones of the fortification walls, still trace the ancient streets, still stand where Bronze Age inhabitants once stood watching for ships in the Dardanelles. Archaeology hasn't destroyed the magic of Troy—it has revealed the even more remarkable magic of human civilization itself, with all its achievements, aspirations, and ultimate fragility in the face of forces beyond any individual city's control.

The archaeological Troy reminds us that behind every legend lies human reality, and that human reality, when carefully excavated and thoughtfully interpreted, proves even more fascinating than the stories it inspired.

CHAPTER 14

AN ARCHAEOLOGICAL ANALYSIS OF DAILY LIFE IN BRONZE AGE TROY

Beyond the Epic Heroes

Imagine stepping through the gates of Troy around 1200 BCE, not as a warrior come to besiege the city, but as an ordinary resident returning from the market with fresh fish from the Dardanelles. You'd navigate narrow streets lined with workshops where potters shaped clay vessels, metalworkers hammered bronze tools, and textile workers spun wool into thread that would become the fine fabrics for which Troy was renowned. The air would fill with the sounds of daily life—children playing in courtyards, merchants haggling over prices, mothers calling their families to evening meals.

This is the Troy that archaeology reveals: not just the backdrop for heroic exploits, but a thriving urban community where thousands of people lived, worked, loved, and died across generations. While monumental architecture and defensive works have traditionally captured scholarly attention, decades of excavation have accumulated evidence that allows us to reconstruct the lived experiences of Troy's diverse population. From domestic architecture to craft production, from foodways to ritual practices, the material remains reveal a complex urban society that thrived at this strategic location for centuries before its ultimate destruction (Jablonka 2001: 89).

Home Sweet Home: Domestic Life in Bronze Age Troy

The residential structures of Troy VI and VIIa tell fascinating stories about household organization and daily domestic life that reveal how social hierarchy shaped even the most intimate spaces. Within the citadel, large freestanding buildings with stone foundations and mudbrick superstructures housed the elite members of society. These substantial structures, often exceeding 100 square meters in area, featured multiple rooms organized around central halls—ancient equivalents of modern luxury homes that combined living space with areas for conducting official business.

"The substantial houses within the citadel represent elite residences that combined domestic functions with spaces for administrative activities and the display of status," observes archaeologist Elizabeth French. "Their size, construction quality, and prominent location all mark them as belonging to Troy's upper social echelon" (French 1999: 156).

The construction of these elite residences required significant labor investment. Carefully dressed limestone blocks formed impressive foundations that supported upper stories, while sophisticated architectural details like column bases and decorated doorways announced the wealth and taste of their inhabitants. The largest of these buildings could house extended families with their servants, visiting dignitaries, and administrative personnel—ancient versions of today's corporate headquarters combined with family compounds.

But most of Troy's residents lived very differently. In the lower city, residential structures typically consisted of smaller buildings sharing party walls—ancient versions of row houses or apartment buildings that maximized living space within limited areas. These more modest structures housed the majority of Troy's population, with archaeological evidence suggesting multi-generational families occupying connected household units. The organization of these residential quarters reveals neighborhood clustering, with houses arranged along narrow streets and small open areas serving as communal spaces where neighbors would have interacted daily.

The Troy VIIa phase shows dramatic modifications to domestic spaces that tell a story of increasing social stress. Many larger rooms were subdivided into smaller functional areas—a pattern archaeologists recognize as response to crisis. This architectural change likely reflects increased population density, possibly due to an influx of refugees from surrounding territories seeking protection within Troy's walls, or a defensive concentration of the population as external threats increased.

Large storage pithoi (ceramic containers) embedded in floors during this phase indicate increased emphasis on food storage within individual households—ancient versions of stockpiling that suggest a community preparing for potential siege or disruption of normal supply networks.

"The architectural modifications during Troy VIIa represent a community adapting to changing circumstances," notes archaeologist Donald Easton. "The subdivision of spaces and increased storage capacity suggest a population under stress, making practical adjustments to accommodate more people and secure resources within a defensive perimeter" (Easton 1994: 234).

Household inventories recovered from destruction contexts provide fascinating snapshots of domestic assemblages—ancient time capsules that reveal what families actually owned and used. Typical Troy VI households possessed diverse ceramic vessels for cooking, serving, and storage; stone tools for food processing; and various implements for textile production. More affluent households, particularly within the citadel, contained luxury items such as imported pottery, metal implements, and ornamental objects that announced their owners' status and connections to wider worlds.

Feeding the City: Food, Farming, and Feasting

The inhabitants of Late Bronze Age Troy enjoyed a remarkably diverse diet that took advantage of their strategic location between land and sea. Archaeological analysis of plant and animal remains reveals a sophisticated food system that combined agriculture, animal husbandry, fishing, and trade to meet nutritional needs across social classes.

Archaeobotanical analysis of carbonized plant remains reveals an agricultural system based primarily on wheat (both einkorn and emmer varieties) and barley cultivation—the staff of life for Bronze Age populations throughout the Mediterranean. These cereals were supplemented by legumes such as lentils, peas, and chickpeas that provided essential proteins and helped maintain soil fertility through crop rotation. Fruit remains, including grape pips, olive pits, and fig seeds, indicate orchard cultivation in the surrounding territory that produced both fresh food and processed products like wine and oil.

"The plant assemblage from Troy reflects a typical eastern Mediterranean agricultural package," explains archaeobotanist Simone Riehl. "The diversity of crops provided both nutritional balance and risk management against crop failures, while specialized crops like olives and grapes represent high-value products that could be processed into oil and wine" (Riehl 2010: 156).

Animal husbandry centered on the classic Mediterranean triad of sheep, goats, and cattle, supplemented by pigs that could forage around the settlement. Age profiles of slaughtered animals reveal sophisticated management strategies—sheep and goats were kept for both meat and secondary products like wool and milk, while cattle served as draft animals for plowing and transport in addition to providing meat and dairy products. The presence of equid remains, including horses and donkeys, indicates their importance for transportation and as status symbols that marked elite households.

Wild animal bones, though less common, show that hunting supplemented the diet, particularly for elite households who could engage in hunting as both subsistence strategy and prestigious leisure activity. Red deer, wild boar, and various bird species provided variety to the diet while serving as markers of social distinction—much like hunting privileges in later European societies.

Troy's coastal location provided access to rich marine resources that formed an important component of the local diet. Fish bones, shellfish remains, and fishing implements recovered throughout the site reveal exploitation of both the Dardanelles strait and the adjacent Aegean and Black Seas. Species identification shows that ancient Trojans enjoyed tuna, sea bream, and various shellfish species—a sophisticated maritime diet that rivals any modern coastal community.

Cooking installations within households typically consisted of hearths and ovens, with some evidence for specialized cooking areas in larger residences that functioned like ancient professional kitchens. Ceramic assemblages included cooking pots, serving vessels, and storage containers, with forms specialized for different culinary functions—ancient equivalents of our modern kitchen equipment sets.

Perhaps most fascinating is the direct evidence for meals preserved through carbonization. Archaeologists have recovered remains of bread, porridge, and stews that provide glimpses into actual Bronze Age menus. Isotopic analysis of human remains offers even more direct evidence about diet at the individual level, revealing a pattern based primarily on terrestrial resources with C3 plants (wheat, barley) forming staple carbohydrates, supplemented by animal proteins.

"The inhabitants of Troy enjoyed a diverse and nutritionally complete diet," notes bioarchaeologist Henrike Kiesewetter. "While the basic subsistence package remained consistent across social strata, elite individuals had greater access to high-status foods like meat and certain marine species, reflecting how social inequality manifested in everyday consumption practices" (Kiesewetter 2003: 178).

The Workshops of Troy: Craft Production and Skilled Labor

Archaeological evidence from Troy VI and VIIa reveals a bustling economy based on diverse craft activities that indicate both economic specialization and the presence of highly skilled artisans within the community. The scale and organization of craft production varied from household-level activities that met family needs to specialized workshops producing goods for elite consumption and potentially for export to distant markets.

Textile production represents one of the most ubiquitous craft activities, with evidence found throughout the settlement in patterns that reveal both household and workshop organization. Spindle whorls, loom weights, and other implements for spinning and weaving appear in most domestic contexts, indicating that basic textile production occurred at the household level—much like pre-industrial communities worldwide where families produced their own clothing and household fabrics.

However, concentrations of these tools in certain areas suggest specialized workshops where production exceeded household needs. These workshops likely produced the fine textiles for which Troy became famous in later classical sources—luxury fabrics that served elite consumption and possibly formed important export commodities.

"Textile production at Troy followed a pattern common throughout the Bronze Age eastern Mediterranean," explains textile specialist Marta Guzowska. "Basic household production satisfied family needs, while specialized workshops produced higher-quality textiles for elite consumption and possibly export. The abundance of spindle whorls and loom weights testifies to the economic importance of this industry" (Guzowska 2005: 134).

Metallurgical activities are attested through crucibles, tuyères (nozzles for directing airflow into furnaces), slag, and molds recovered from specific workshop areas. Bronze working predominated, with evidence for both casting and forging techniques that required sophisticated understanding of alloy compositions and temperature control. The recovery of scrap metal collections indicates systematic recycling of valuable copper and tin—ancient versions of metal recycling that reflected the high value of these imported raw materials.

While most metal objects appear to have been produced for local consumption, the quality of some finished products suggests the presence of highly skilled artisans capable of creating prestige items for elite patrons. These master craftsmen would have occupied important positions within Troy's social hierarchy, their specialized knowledge providing pathways to prosperity and status recognition.

Pottery production combined household-level manufacture of coarse utilitarian wares with more specialized production of finer vessels that required greater skill and artistry. Kilns located in the lower city indicate designated production areas, while analysis of clay sources reveals exploitation of local deposits. The ceramic repertoire included both locally distinctive forms and vessels that imitated Mycenaean and Anatolian styles, reflecting Troy's position at the crossroads of different cultural traditions.

"The ceramic assemblage from Troy reveals a sophisticated understanding of different pottery traditions," notes ceramic specialist Penelope Mountjoy. "Local potters not only maintained their distinctive regional styles but also selectively adopted and adapted elements from neighboring cultures, creating a hybrid ceramic tradition that reflected Troy's intermediate geographical position" (Mountjoy 1999: 234).

Other specialized crafts included stone working, bone and antler carving, and the production of vitreous materials like faience—luxury items that required both artistic skill and technical knowledge. Evidence for these activities appears more limited, suggesting they involved fewer practitioners with highly specialized skills that commanded premium prices for their products.

The spatial distribution of craft evidence indicates that most production occurred in the lower city, with finished products then circulating to consumers throughout the settlement, including the elite residents of the citadel. This pattern reflects sophisticated economic organization that combined household self-sufficiency with specialized production and complex distribution networks.

Social Hierarchies: How Inequality Shaped Daily Life

The archaeological evidence from Troy VI and VIIa reveals a socially stratified community with clear material distinctions between elite and non-elite residents that influenced every aspect of daily experience. This social hierarchy manifested in multiple dimensions—from where people lived to what they ate to how they were buried after death.

The most obvious marker of social distinction appears in Troy's spatial organization itself. The citadel, with its impressive circuit wall and commanding position, housed elite residences and administrative structures that physically and symbolically separated the ruling class from the general population in the lower city. This architectural segregation created a visible manifestation of social hierarchy that would have been immediately apparent to residents and visitors alike—an ancient version of gated communities that announced status through location and exclusivity.

"The spatial organization of Troy embodies social hierarchy in physical form," observes urban archaeologist Nicholas Cahill. "The elevation of the citadel, its monumental fortifications, and the quality of its buildings all communicated the power and status of those who resided within, creating a landscape of inequality that structured everyday experience" (Cahill 2002: 189).

Burial evidence, though limited compared to some Bronze Age sites, provides direct insights into social differentiation that persisted beyond death. The few elite burials discovered contained grave goods indicating substantial wealth accumulation—gold ornaments, imported prestige items, and weapons that served as status symbols even in the afterlife. In contrast, non-elite burials featured more modest assemblages of locally produced goods, reflecting limited access to resources and luxury items.

Distribution patterns of luxury goods across the site reveal significant disparities in access to prestige items that marked social boundaries in daily life. Imported Mycenaean pottery, objects made from exotic materials like ivory and amber, and elaborate metal artifacts concentrate disproportionately in elite contexts within the citadel. These material possessions served as status markers, visibly distinguishing the elite from other community members through consumption practices and public display.

Evidence for feasting activities provides particularly clear insights into how social hierarchy operated in practice. Specialized serving vessels and unusual faunal assemblages with high-value cuts of meat appear primarily in elite contexts, indicating that the wealthy literally ate differently from their social inferiors. These feasting events likely served important social functions, allowing elites to demonstrate their wealth, build political alliances, and reinforce their status through generous hospitality that created social obligations among participants.

"Feasting represented a critical social technology for Trojan elites," explains archaeologist Brian Hayden. "By controlling access to exotic foods and drinks, serving these in specialized prestige vessels, and creating memorable sensory experiences, elite hosts converted economic capital into social capital that legitimized their privileged position" (Hayden 2001: 234).

While the archaeological evidence clearly demonstrates social inequality, it also reveals the complexity of Trojan social organization beyond a simple elite/non-elite binary. Variation in house sizes, consumption patterns, and access to goods suggests a more graduated social hierarchy with multiple levels of status and wealth—ancient versions of upper, middle, and working classes that created diverse life experiences within the community.

Certain craft specialists, merchants, and other non-elite individuals appear to have occupied intermediate positions, enjoying greater access to resources than the general population while remaining distinct from the highest elites. This complex social landscape would have provided various pathways for individuals to negotiate their position and potentially achieve social mobility through different strategies—not unlike opportunities in modern market economies.

Sacred and Secular: Religious Life in Daily Troy

Religious and ritual activities formed an integral part of daily life at Late Bronze Age Troy, woven into the fabric of everyday experience rather than confined to formal ceremonies or specialized spaces. While the archaeological evidence for these practices remains somewhat limited compared to other aspects of society, what survives reveals a religious system that combined household-level rituals with more formal practices associated with community-wide beliefs and institutions.

Household religious practices are attested through small figurines, ritual vessels, and special deposits found in domestic contexts throughout the settlement. Clay figurines, primarily representing female forms, appear regularly in household assemblages and likely served protective functions within the domestic sphere—ancient equivalents of household shrines or protective icons that were believed to safeguard families and homes.

Specialized vessels, including rhyta (ritual pouring vessels) and unusual forms not associated with everyday use, indicate household-level ritual activities involving libations and offerings to household gods or ancestors. These domestic rituals would have been performed by family members as part of regular household maintenance, much like daily prayers or weekly religious observances in modern households.

"The distribution of religious objects throughout domestic contexts indicates that ritual practice was deeply embedded in everyday life," notes religion specialist Mieke Prent. "Rather than being confined to formal sanctuaries, religious activity permeated the household, with family members regularly performing rituals that maintained connections with divine forces believed to influence daily wellbeing" (Prent 2005: 167).

More formal religious spaces have proven difficult to identify conclusively at Troy, as the site lacks the clearly defined temple structures found at some contemporary settlements. However, certain areas within the citadel contain architectural features and artifact assemblages suggesting specialized ritual functions. Building IXD, with its unusual plan and associated finds, has been interpreted as potentially serving ceremonial purposes that brought the community together for shared religious experiences.

Ritual deposits offer additional evidence for religious practices that marked important moments in community life. These intentional placements of objects in significant locations include foundation deposits beneath buildings, objects carefully placed in wall niches, and collections of valuable items in unusual contexts. Such deposits often contained figurines, specialized vessels, and occasionally animal bones from sacrifices, suggesting rituals intended to ensure divine protection for buildings and activities.

Evidence for mortuary practices, though limited, reveals complex attitudes toward death and the afterlife that varied with social status. The few burials discovered include both inhumations and cremations, suggesting diverse treatment of the dead that may reflect different religious traditions or social distinctions. Some individuals received burial within the settlement, particularly children interred beneath house floors—a practice with parallels throughout the eastern Mediterranean that likely reflected beliefs about maintaining connections between the living and deceased family members.

"The mortuary evidence from Troy, though fragmentary, indicates complex attitudes toward death and the afterlife," explains mortuary archaeologist Christopher Hallet. "The differential treatment of the dead, with some receiving elaborate burial with grave goods while others were interred more simply, suggests that social distinctions continued beyond death into the mortuary realm" (Hallet 1999: 234).

The material evidence for religious practice at Troy shows connections to both Anatolian and Aegean traditions, reflecting the settlement's intermediate geographical position between different cultural spheres. Some ritual objects and practices find parallels in Hittite religious traditions, while others show affinities with Mycenaean ritual systems. This religious syncretism aligns with Troy's position at the interface between different worlds, with its inhabitants selectively adopting and adapting elements from multiple religious traditions to create their own distinctive spiritual landscape.

Men, Women, and Children: Gender and Age in Trojan Society

Archaeological evidence provides valuable insights into how gender and age structured social roles and experiences in Late Bronze Age Troy, though interpretations must acknowledge the limitations of material evidence for understanding these complex social categories that shaped daily life in fundamental ways.

Gender differentiation appears throughout the archaeological record in patterns that suggest both similarities to and differences from modern gender systems. Textile production tools like spindle whorls and loom weights concentrate in certain areas of households traditionally associated with female activities in Bronze Age contexts—though we must be careful not to assume ancient gender roles exactly matched modern expectations.

Figurines predominantly depict female forms, suggesting the importance of feminine aspects in household ritual practices that may have recognized women's special relationships with domestic prosperity and protection. Some burials contain grave goods with gender associations, including weapons with male burials and personal ornaments with female interments, though these patterns show variation that suggests complex rather than rigid gender systems.

"Material culture from Troy reveals gender as an important organizing principle in daily life," notes gender archaeologist Marie Louise Stig Sørensen. "While we must avoid simplistic binary interpretations, the archaeological evidence suggests certain activities and spaces were gendered, creating different lived experiences for men and women within the community" (Sørensen 2000: 156).

Age-based distinctions also appear clearly in the archaeological record, revealing ancient recognition of childhood as a distinct life stage with specific material needs and social status. Child-specific objects, including toys, miniature vessels, and specialized feeding equipment, indicate that ancient parents invested in their children's development and entertainment much like modern families.

Subadult burials beneath house floors suggest special treatment of children in mortuary practices, potentially reflecting beliefs about their liminal status between the living and ancestral worlds. These domestic burials may have allowed families to maintain close connections with deceased children while ensuring their continued protection of the household.

Skeletal evidence, though limited, provides direct information about gendered and age-based differences in lived experience that archaeological artifacts can only hint at. Bioarchaeological analysis reveals patterns of activity-related skeletal modifications that differ between presumed males and females, suggesting gendered divisions of labor that shaped bodies through repetitive activities.

"The human remains from Troy tell stories of gendered bodily experiences," explains bioarchaeologist Sherry Fox. "Skeletal markers indicate different patterns of physical labor, with males showing stress markers consistent with heavy lifting and females displaying modifications associated with repetitive kneeling and seated activities like grain processing and textile work" (Fox 2005: 234).

The archaeological evidence suggests that both gender and age intersected with social status to create complex patterns of identity and experience that defied simple categorization. Elite women appear to have enjoyed greater access to resources and luxury goods than non-elite men, indicating that status could sometimes override gender as a determining factor in material conditions—a pattern visible in many stratified societies throughout history.

Troy's Cosmopolitan Character: Living at the Crossroads

The archaeological evidence from Troy VI and VIIa reveals a settlement with a distinctly cosmopolitan character that reflected its position at the crossroads of different geographical, political, and cultural spheres. Rather than representing a homogeneous cultural tradition, the material remains indicate a community that actively negotiated multiple influences while maintaining a distinctive regional identity.

Ceramic evidence provides some of the clearest indications of Troy's multicultural connections. The pottery assemblage includes locally produced wares with distinctive regional characteristics alongside imported vessels from the Mycenaean world, central Anatolia, and other neighboring regions. Local potters also produced hybrid forms that combined elements from different traditions, creating distinctive vessels that expressed Troy's unique position between cultural spheres.

"The ceramic assemblage from Troy reveals a community engaged in active cultural negotiation," observes archaeologist Peter Pavúk. "Rather than passively receiving influences from dominant neighbors, Trojan potters selectively adopted, adapted, and recontextualized elements from different traditions, creating a material culture that expressed their unique position at the interface between worlds" (Pavúk 2014: 167).

Architectural traditions similarly reflect diverse influences that created a built environment unlike anywhere else in the Bronze Age world. The citadel's fortification system incorporated defensive technologies known throughout the eastern Mediterranean while adapting them to local topography and resources. Domestic architecture combined elements from Anatolian building traditions with features known from Aegean settlements.

Small finds from the site demonstrate connections to wide-ranging exchange networks that brought objects and materials from across the known world. Seals and sealings show iconographic elements from both Aegean and Near Eastern traditions. Personal ornaments incorporate stylistic elements from multiple regions. Tools and weapons reflect technologies shared across cultural boundaries throughout the eastern Mediterranean.

Linguistic evidence, though necessarily indirect, supports the picture of Troy as a genuinely multicultural community. Hittite texts referring to "Wilusa" place Troy within the Luwian linguistic sphere, a language group widespread in western Anatolia during the Late Bronze Age. However, proximity to the Aegean world and evidence for sustained interaction with Mycenaean centers suggests that multiple languages were likely spoken within the settlement, particularly among merchants and others engaged in international exchanges.

"The inhabitants of Late Bronze Age Troy likely navigated multiple linguistic and cultural systems in their daily lives," suggests linguist Ilya Yakubovich. "Located at the boundary between the Luwian-speaking world of western Anatolia and the Greek-speaking Aegean, Troy's residents—especially those engaged in trade and diplomacy—would have needed multilingual capabilities to function effectively in this crossroads position" (Yakubovich 2010: 234).

This cosmopolitan character would have created both extraordinary opportunities and significant challenges for Troy's inhabitants. The settlement's position facilitated access to diverse resources, technologies, and ideas from across the Mediterranean world, potentially driving innovation and prosperity. However, this same position made Troy vulnerable to competing political interests and potentially created internal tensions between different cultural orientations within the community.

Troy VIIa: Life on the Edge

The archaeological evidence from Troy VIIa provides a particularly poignant window into a community adapting to increasingly precarious circumstances in the decades before its violent destruction around 1180 BCE. The material remains from this final Late Bronze Age phase reveal a population implementing practical measures to enhance security and ensure resource availability while striving to maintain the basic patterns of daily life established in earlier, more prosperous periods.

Architectural modifications during Troy VIIa represent some of the most visible adaptations to changing circumstances that archaeologists recognize as responses to crisis. Many larger spaces were subdivided into smaller functional units, creating a more densely packed settlement within the existing defensive perimeter. Large storage pithoi were embedded in floors throughout the settlement, significantly increasing capacity for food storage at the household level in ways that suggest systematic preparation for potential shortages or siege conditions.

"The architectural modifications in Troy VIIa represent practical responses to perceived threats," explains archaeologist Claudia Jansen. "The community reorganized their built environment to accommodate a larger population within the defended area while ensuring critical resources could be stored securely. These changes reflect a population adapting to uncertainty while attempting to maintain normal life" (Jansen 2006: 156).

Defensive preparations intensified during this period in ways that suggest very real awareness of external threats. The already substantial fortification walls received additional strengthening using materials salvaged from damaged buildings, while evidence for weapons increases dramatically in the archaeological record. Slingstones were stockpiled near the walls, and bronze arrowheads appear in greater numbers than in any previous phase.

Despite these defensive preparations, evidence for continued craft production, trade activities, and ritual practices demonstrates remarkable resilience—a community's determination to maintain normal life despite extraordinary circumstances. Workshops continued to produce pottery, textiles, and metal goods, though possibly with adjustments to ensure critical needs received priority. Imported items, though perhaps less abundant than in Troy VI, still appear in the archaeological record, indicating that external connections remained active despite regional instability.

Bioarchaeological evidence provides insights into the physical toll that these stressful circumstances took on Troy's inhabitants. Some skeletal remains show evidence of nutritional deficiencies, suggesting food insecurity affected portions of the population despite increased storage efforts. Trauma markers appear on some individuals, potentially reflecting increased interpersonal violence or accidents related to defensive activities and crowded living conditions.

"The human remains from Troy VIIa tell a story of bodily stress," notes paleopathologist Sherry Fox. "While not universal, indicators of nutritional deficiency and physical trauma appear more frequently than in earlier phases, suggesting the challenging circumstances had tangible impacts on individual health and wellbeing" (Fox 2005: 267).

The final destruction of Troy VIIa around 1180 BCE left a vivid archaeological record of the settlement's last moments that reads like a frozen moment in time. Collapsed buildings preserved room contents in their original contexts, providing snapshots of activities interrupted by catastrophe. These destruction contexts reveal people engaged in ordinary activities—cooking meals, manufacturing goods, storing supplies—when disaster struck.

Conclusion: The Human Face of Ancient Troy

The archaeological evidence for daily life at Late Bronze Age Troy reveals a complex urban society that existed far beyond the legendary narrative immortalized by Homer. While the Iliad presents Troy primarily as a backdrop for heroic action and divine intervention, the material remains uncover the lived experiences of a diverse population who made this strategic location their home for generations before its violent destruction.

Troy emerges from the archaeological record as a substantial regional center with a population of several thousand inhabitants engaged in diverse economic activities, from agriculture and animal husbandry to specialized craft production and long-distance trade. This community maintained a distinctive cultural identity while actively engaging with neighboring societies, creating a hybrid material culture that reflected Troy's unique position at the crossroads between different worlds.

The archaeological evidence reveals both the commonalities that connected Troy's inhabitants to the broader Late Bronze Age world and the distinctive characteristics that made their community special. Like their contemporaries throughout the eastern Mediterranean, they cultivated cereals and legumes, raised domestic animals, manufactured textiles, and participated in exchange networks that connected distant regions. Yet they did so in ways that reflected their specific geographical position, resource access, and cultural traditions.

"The archaeological evidence from Troy reminds us that behind the mythological narrative stood a real community of people engaged in the universal human activities of making a living, raising families, negotiating social relationships, and finding meaning in their world," concludes archaeologist Brian Rose. "By reconstructing these everyday aspects of life at Troy, we restore humanity and historical specificity to a site often reduced to a legendary backdrop" (Rose 2014: 289).

This archaeological perspective neither invalidates nor confirms the traditional narrative of the Trojan War. Rather, it complements the literary tradition by providing material evidence for the actual community that may have inspired or experienced the events transformed through centuries of oral tradition into the epic we know today.

The physical remains of daily life—cooking pots and loom weights, storage jars and drinking cups, toys and tools, the bones of meals and the graves of children—connect us directly to the lived experiences of individuals who occupied this legendary landscape long before Homer shaped their story into immortal poetry. They remind us that Troy was not just a stage for heroes but a home for real people whose daily struggles, achievements, and ultimately tragic fate continue to move us across the millennia.

CHAPTER 15

DIPLOMACY AND CONFLICT

Troy's Diplomatic Web

Picture a Hittite scribe in the imperial capital of Hattusa, carefully pressing his reed stylus into soft clay to record a treaty with a distant vassal kingdom. The year is around 1280 BCE, and the scribe is creating one of our most precious windows into Troy's real history—not the Troy of Homer's imagination, but the flesh-and-blood kingdom that navigated the treacherous political waters of the Late Bronze Age Mediterranean. When archaeologists first deciphered these clay tablets in the early twentieth century, they discovered that Troy—known to the Hittites as Wilusa—was far from the isolated fortress of Greek legend. Instead, it was a sophisticated player in one of history's first truly international political systems.

The Rebellion That Started It All

Our story begins around 1400 BCE with a crisis that would define Troy's relationship with the great powers for centuries to come. In the royal archives at Hattusa, we find King Tudhaliya I/II boasting about crushing a rebellion in western Anatolia led by a coalition called Assuwa (Bryce 2006: 142). Hidden within this victory account lies what may be our earliest glimpse of Troy on history's stage, as Wilusa appears to have been part of this rebellious alliance.

The Assuwa rebellion wasn't just another provincial uprising—it represented the first of many attempts by western Anatolian kingdoms to throw off Hittite control. These weren't distant territories the Hittites could safely ignore. Western Anatolia sat astride crucial trade routes connecting the Aegean world with the riches of central Anatolia and Mesopotamia beyond. Control of this region meant control of commerce, tribute, and strategic position against the growing power of Mycenaean Greece (Bryce 2006: 98-101).

When the rebellion collapsed, the surviving kingdoms faced a choice: continued resistance leading to destruction, or accommodation with Hittite power. Troy chose accommodation, beginning a relationship that would prove both protective and constraining for the next two centuries.

A Treaty Written in Clay

The most remarkable document in our diplomatic detective story comes from the reign of Muwatalli II, around 1280 BCE. Archaeologists recovered fragments of a formal treaty between this Hittite king and a ruler of Wilusa named Alaksandu—a name that makes any student of Homer sit up and take notice, given its striking similarity to "Alexander," the alternative name for the Trojan prince Paris (Latacz 2004: 120-125).

The Alaksandu Treaty reads like a Bronze Age marriage contract between kingdoms. The Hittite scribes begin with a historical preamble claiming that "from old, the Land of Wilusa has been a frontier territory of the Land of Hatti. And between them, they have always been friendly" (Beckman 1999: 87). This diplomatic language masks what was surely a more complex reality—vassal relationships in the ancient world were rarely as harmonious as official documents claimed.

But the treaty's real treasure lies in its details. Alaksandu promised military support when the Hittite king required it, agreed to extradite fugitives, and accepted restrictions on his foreign policy. In return, Muwatalli guaranteed military protection and confirmed Alaksandu's dynastic rights (Beckman 1999: 87-90). Most fascinating of all, the treaty invokes divine witnesses from both cultures, including "Apaliunas of Wilusa"—almost certainly the god later known to Greeks as Apollo, Troy's patron deity in Homer's epic (Watkins 1986: 45-50).

Here we see Troy fully integrated into the international system of its day, bound by the same diplomatic conventions that regulated relationships between Egypt and Babylon, or Assyria and Cyprus. This wasn't the isolated fortress of legend, but a kingdom that understood how to survive through skilled diplomacy in a dangerous world.

When Diplomacy Failed: The Tawagalawa Affair

Sometimes the best evidence for how the system worked comes from moments when it broke down spectacularly. The fragmentary "Tawagalawa Letter," written by Hattusili III around 1250 BCE, preserves one side of a heated diplomatic exchange between the Hittite king and a ruler of Ahhiyawa—almost certainly a Mycenaean Greek kingdom (Beckman 1999: 101-103).

The letter crackles with barely contained frustration as Hattusili complains about a troublemaker named Piyamaradu who had been conducting raids throughout western Anatolia with apparent Greek support. In the midst of this diplomatic protest, Troy appears: "Concerning the matter of Wilusa about which you wrote to me—a hostility had not occurred between the Land of Hatti and the Land of Wilusa. The Land of Wilusa is a vassal land of the Land of Hatti" (Beckman 1999: 101).

The Hittite king's defensive tone suggests Troy had somehow become entangled in the broader conflict between Hittite and Mycenaean interests. We can imagine Troy's rulers walking a diplomatic tightrope, trying to maintain their

Hittite alliance while managing relationships with increasingly powerful Greek kingdoms just across the Aegean (Cline 2013: 89-92).

The Attack That Made History

The diplomatic crisis escalated into actual warfare, as we learn from another remarkable document called the Manapa-Tarhunta Letter. Written by a Hittite vassal ruler to his overlord, this text describes military operations against the persistent raider Piyamaradu: "When Piyamaradu harassed me, I went to Wilusa for battle... But Piyamaradu came with many chariots and opposed me in battle... And Atpa [Piyamaradu's son-in-law] took the infantry and chariots of Ahhiyawa with him, and they went to attack Wilusa" (Beckman 1999: 134).

Here, preserved in a Hittite administrative document, we find explicit evidence that Troy faced a major military assault involving Mycenaean Greek forces several decades before the traditional date of Homer's Trojan War. The attackers came with "many chariots" and "infantry"—this was no mere raid, but a serious military operation (Bachvarova 2016: 112-115).

The historical irony is remarkable. While Greek poets sang of a legendary ten-year siege, Hittite bureaucrats were filing reports about an actual Greek attack on Troy that we can date with reasonable precision to around 1250 BCE. The legendary war may have roots in this documented historical conflict, transformed by centuries of oral tradition into the epic we know today.

A Kingdom Under Pressure

By the late thirteenth century BCE, Troy's diplomatic position was becoming increasingly precarious. The fragmentary Milawata Letter, probably from the reign of Tudhaliya IV around 1220 BCE, reveals the Hittite Empire intervening directly in Trojan succession disputes: "Concerning the King of Wilusa... you wrote to me as follows: 'I removed him from kingship, but later I reinstated him in kingship again'" (Miller 2007: 255).

This glimpse behind the diplomatic curtain shows how fragile Troy's autonomy had become. Even the choice of ruler now required foreign approval—a clear sign that the international system was beginning to fray. The Hittite Empire itself was struggling with internal succession crises and external pressures from Assyria and the mysterious "Sea Peoples" who were disrupting traditional power structures throughout the eastern Mediterranean (Cline 2014: 145-170).

The Archaeological Witness

Remarkably, the archaeological record at Troy itself corroborates this textual evidence for the kingdom's international connections. Excavations have revealed a cosmopolitan settlement with material culture reflecting contacts spanning from Mesopotamia to Mycenaean Greece. Mycenaean pottery appears in significant quantities during the thirteenth century BCE, confirming regular interaction with the Aegean world precisely when Hittite texts document conflicts involving Greek forces (Korfmann 2006: 32-38).

The massive fortification walls surrounding Troy VI represent a major investment in military architecture, featuring construction techniques known from other Anatolian sites. Yet certain architectural elements show Aegean influence, reflecting Troy's position at the intersection of different cultural worlds (Jablonka 2006: 85-90). This hybrid character extended even to literacy—a bronze seal bearing Luwian hieroglyphic writing confirms Troy's participation in the Anatolian writing tradition documented in Hittite archives (Hawkins 1995: 66-69).

Most dramatically, Anatolian-style arrowheads embedded in the destruction layer of Troy VIIa provide stark archaeological evidence for the kind of military conflict described in Hittite texts. These bronze projectiles, concentrated near gates and defensive walls, tell a story of coordinated assault on the settlement's weak points—the final chapter in Troy's centuries-long struggle to maintain independence in an increasingly unstable world (Korfmann 2006: 45-48).

The System Collapses

Around 1180 BCE, the international system that had sustained Troy for centuries collapsed with stunning rapidity. The Hittite Empire fragmented, Mycenaean palace societies crumbled, and mysterious population movements disrupted established patterns throughout the eastern Mediterranean. Archaeological evidence from Troy VIIa reflects these changing circumstances: modified architecture suggesting crowded conditions, increased storage capacity indicating resource concerns, and ultimately violent destruction that ended the settlement's Bronze Age prosperity (Cline 2014: 170-180).

Troy's destruction coincided precisely with this broader systemic collapse, suggesting its fate was linked to the larger forces transforming the ancient world. The diplomatic networks that had allowed Troy to navigate between competing powers unraveled, leaving the kingdom vulnerable to threats it might previously have managed through alliance or negotiation.

From History to Legend

The evidence from Hittite archives and archaeological excavation provides crucial context for understanding how historical events might have been transformed into the Trojan War legend. The documented reality of Troy as a significant kingdom maintaining complex international relationships, experiencing actual conflicts with Mycenaean forces, and ultimately suffering violent destruction around the traditional date of the war, offers a historical foundation that Greek oral tradition could have built upon over centuries.

Specific details from the historical record present tantalizing parallels to the legendary tradition. The name Alaksandu bears striking phonetic similarity to

Alexander/Paris. The documented attacks on Troy by forces including Greek contingents provide a potential basis for traditions about Mycenaean-Trojan conflict. The broader pattern of international crisis and systemic collapse offers a realistic context within which such a conflict might have occurred (Latacz 2004: 200-220).

Yet the historical Troy revealed through archaeological and textual evidence was quite different from Homer's creation. This was not an exotic oriental kingdom ruled by barbarian princes, but a sophisticated Bronze Age state that understood how to navigate the complex diplomatic world of its time. The real Troy's story—a frontier kingdom caught between competing great powers, struggling to maintain autonomy through skilled diplomacy, and ultimately falling victim to forces beyond its control—may be less romantically appealing than Homer's epic, but it offers insights into how international relations actually functioned in humanity's first global age.

The transformation of Troy from historical kingdom to legendary city demonstrates how cultural memory selectively preserves and reimagines actual events. The archaeological and textual evidence reveals a Troy embedded in the political networks of its time, maintaining diplomatic relations with various powers and eventually succumbing to regional instability. This historical reality provided the foundation for one of Western civilization's most enduring narratives, showing how the messy complexities of real international relations could be crystallized into a story that has shaped cultural identity for over two millennia.

In the end, the cuneiform tablets from Hattusa and the artifacts from Troy's excavation tell a story every bit as compelling as Homer's epic—not of gods and heroes, but of human communities struggling to survive and prosper in a world where the stakes of diplomacy could mean the difference between prosperity and destruction, between cultural survival and historical oblivion.

CHAPTER 16

LUWIAN CONNECTIONS

Speaking Troy's Lost Language

Imagine walking through the ruins of Troy in 1870, following Heinrich Schliemann as he tears through layer after layer of ancient debris, desperately searching for Homer's golden city. Now imagine what Schliemann would have thought if someone had told him that the people living in his precious Troy didn't speak Greek at all, but rather a completely different language called Luwian that wouldn't be deciphered for another century. He probably would have dismissed such a notion as academic fantasy. Yet this is precisely what modern scholarship has revealed: Bronze Age Troy was fundamentally an Anatolian settlement where Luwian—not Greek—was the language echoing through its stone corridors and palace halls.

This linguistic detective story represents one of the most dramatic reversals in our understanding of the ancient world. For generations, scholars approached Troy primarily through Greek eyes, seeing it as Homer portrayed it—a place where heroes spoke Greek and worshipped Greek gods. The reality, preserved in clay tablets buried for millennia in the Hittite capital, tells a very different story.

Cracking the Code: How We Know Troy Spoke Luwian

The breakthrough came not from Troy itself, but from the archives of Troy's most powerful neighbor. When archaeologists began deciphering Hittite cuneiform tablets in the early twentieth century, they discovered references to a place called "Wilusa" that appeared in diplomatic correspondence and military reports. At first, nobody connected this foreign-sounding name to the legendary Troy, but linguist Frank Starke changed everything when he demonstrated that Wilusa and the Greek Ilios (Troy) were actually the same word, transformed by centuries of linguistic change (Starke 1997: 447-450).

The phonological relationship is elegant in its simplicity. The Luwian "Wilusa" preserves an initial "w" sound that was later lost in Greek, yielding "Ilios." Similar sound changes affected another Trojan place name: Hittite texts mention "Taruisa," which corresponds to Greek "Troia" through the same pattern of linguistic evolution (Latacz 2004: 120-125). These aren't coincidences—they're the linguistic fingerprints of cultural contact between Anatolian and Greek speakers.

The most compelling evidence comes from the Alaksandu Treaty, carved in cuneiform around 1280 BCE. This diplomatic agreement between the Hittite king Muwatalli II and a ruler of Wilusa named Alaksandu contains a crucial detail: it mentions "Apaliunas of Wilusa"—a deity whose name bears striking similarity to the Greek Apollo, but appears in a distinctly Luwian context following Luwian, not Greek, phonological patterns (Watkins 1986: 45-50). Here we glimpse the actual religious world of Bronze Age Troy, where gods bore Anatolian names even if they later became familiar to us through Greek literature.

Archaeological Voices from Ancient Troy

The most direct archaeological evidence for Luwian at Troy comes from an unlikely source: a small bronze seal discovered in the ruins of Troy VIIb, dating to around 1100 BCE. This biconvex seal bears what appear to be Luwian hieroglyphic signs, providing tangible proof that this Anatolian writing system was used at the site (Hawkins 1995: 66-69). While the seal postdates the traditional

Trojan War, it suggests continuity in administrative practices and indicates that Luwian was likely used at Troy before the famous destruction as well.

The broader archaeological picture supports this linguistic identification in fascinating ways. Walk through the excavated remains of Troy VI and VIIa, and you're seeing fundamentally Anatolian architecture. The massive fortification walls with their distinctive slightly sloping profile reflect defensive building traditions known throughout western Anatolia. The megaron-style buildings within the citadel, while sometimes cited as evidence of Greek influence, actually appear throughout the Anatolian world and represent shared architectural heritage rather than foreign borrowing (Jablonka 2006: 85-90).

Even more revealing is the pottery. While archaeologists have found significant quantities of imported Mycenaean ceramics at Troy—beautiful painted vessels that testify to regular trade with the Greek world—the vast majority of pottery follows western Anatolian traditions. The distinctive "Gray Minyan Ware" that predominates at Troy reflects local production techniques with deep roots in Anatolian ceramic traditions, not Aegean ones (Thumm-Doğrayan 2006: 145-150).

This material evidence tells a clear story: Troy was an Anatolian city that maintained active trade relationships with the Greek world, but its fundamental cultural identity remained rooted in the linguistic and material traditions of western Anatolia.

The Luwian World: Troy's Cultural Universe

To understand what it meant for Troy to be Luwian-speaking, we need to appreciate the scope and importance of the Luwian world in Bronze Age Anatolia. This wasn't some obscure local dialect—Luwian was a major language spoken across much of western and southern Anatolia, representing one of the primary branches of the Anatolian language family alongside Hittite, Palaic, and later Lydian (Melchert 2003: 170-180).

During Troy's heyday in the thirteenth century BCE, Luwian was gaining influence even within the Hittite heartland. By the empire's final centuries, Luwian had become so prominent that it eventually surpassed Hittite itself in distribution and cultural significance. After the Hittite Empire collapsed around 1180 BCE, Luwian-speaking kingdoms in southern Anatolia evolved into the so-called "Neo-Hittite" states that preserved elements of imperial culture while using Luwian hieroglyphs as their primary writing system (Yakubovich 2010: 1-15).

Troy's position within this Luwian cultural sphere helps explain many puzzles about its political behavior and international relationships. As a Luwian-speaking polity, Troy would have shared linguistic, religious, and cultural features with other western Anatolian kingdoms like Arzawa, the Seha River Land, and Mira. These shared cultural elements facilitated Troy's integration into the Hittite diplomatic system while allowing it to maintain its distinctive regional identity (Bryce 2006: 142-165).

Gods with Anatolian Names

The religious landscape of Luwian Troy presents a fascinating example of how cultural contact works in practice. The "Apaliunas of Wilusa" mentioned in the Alaksandu Treaty represents a Luwian deity who later became known to Greeks as Apollo. This isn't simply a case of the same god having different names in different languages—it reveals a complex process of cultural transmission and reinterpretation that unfolded over centuries of contact between Anatolian and Greek speakers.

Linguist Calvert Watkins identified potential traces of this Luwian religious world preserved within the Greek epic tradition itself. He suggested that certain terms and concepts in Homer might derive from Anatolian sources, transformed through generations of cultural interaction and poetic adaptation (Watkins 1995: 144-167). The word "Ate" (divine blindness or ruin) in the Iliad may preserve

Luwian religious concepts, while certain epithets and formulaic expressions could reflect the influence of Anatolian poetic traditions on Greek epic.

Archaeological evidence from Troy reveals religious practices consistent with Anatolian traditions. Figurines discovered at the site resemble those found throughout western Anatolia rather than their Mycenaean counterparts. Ritual installations within the citadel, including potential altar spaces, align with cultic practices documented in Hittite and Luwian religious texts rather than Aegean parallels (Hertel 2006: 190-205).

This religious evidence underscores Troy's fundamental Anatolian character while acknowledging the cultural complexity that resulted from its frontier position between different worlds.

Political Implications: Troy as Hittite Vassal

Troy's identification as a Luwian-speaking kingdom profoundly affects how we understand its political position in the Late Bronze Age Mediterranean. Rather than representing some kind of Greek outpost in Anatolia, as earlier scholars sometimes suggested, Troy emerges as a thoroughly Anatolian kingdom that happened to maintain significant connections with the Mycenaean world through trade and diplomacy.

The Hittite texts make Troy's political status crystal clear: Wilusa was a vassal state within the Hittite sphere of influence. The Alaksandu Treaty explicitly establishes this relationship, outlining standard obligations including military support, tribute payments, and political loyalty (Beckman 1999: 87-90). These weren't unusual requirements—they represent the normal expectations the Hittite Empire placed on vassal kingdoms throughout Anatolia.

Troy's Luwian identity helps explain why this vassal relationship worked as well as it did. The Hittites typically maintained looser control over culturally related Luwian regions in western Anatolia compared to territories they administered directly. As a Luwian-speaking kingdom, Troy could maintain considerable autonomy while benefiting from the protection of the region's superpower (Bryce 2006: 98-105).

This political arrangement illuminates why the Hittite Empire intervened when Troy faced external threats. When troublemakers like Piyamaradu launched raids against Wilusa with apparent Mycenaean support, the Hittites responded diplomatically and militarily not just to protect a random ally, but to defend what they saw as part of their own cultural and political sphere.

Living on the Linguistic Frontier

Troy's position near the Dardanelles placed it at one of the ancient world's most significant linguistic and cultural frontiers—the boundary between the Luwian-speaking world of Anatolia and the Greek-speaking Aegean. This borderland location profoundly influenced both its historical development and its later legendary status.

Frontier regions often develop distinctive characteristics, and Troy was no exception. While primarily Luwian-speaking, the city's elite and merchant classes probably maintained some familiarity with Mycenaean Greek to facilitate trade and diplomatic interactions. The archaeological evidence supports this multilingual picture: imported Mycenaean pottery, particularly fine wares and transport vessels, indicates regular contact with Greek-speaking communities, with these imports increasing during Troy VI and early VIIa as interaction intensified (Mountjoy 2006: 235-250).

This linguistic diversity may help explain how Troy became such a compelling setting for later Greek tradition. As a Luwian city familiar to Greek traders and travelers, Troy represented an accessible "other"—foreign enough to be exotic, familiar enough to be comprehensible. Greek poets could elaborate on Troy's foreign qualities while still making it a place their audiences could imagine and understand.

When Languages Die: The End of Luwian Troy

The Luwian language of Troy didn't survive into the Classical period. Following the destructions associated with the Late Bronze Age collapse around 1180 BCE, the linguistic landscape of western Anatolia transformed dramatically. Population movements, cultural shifts, and economic disruption combined to break the continuity of Luwian-speaking communities in many regions, including the Troad.

By the eighth century BCE, when the Homeric poems were crystallizing into their canonical form, the Troad had become part of a Greek-speaking cultural zone. Greek colonization beginning in the eighth and seventh centuries BCE further strengthened Greek linguistic dominance. The earlier Luwian language of Troy had been forgotten, surviving only in certain place names and possibly in some cultural practices that had been reinterpreted within a Greek framework (Oettinger 2008: 12-18).

This linguistic extinction represents a crucial factor in how Troy was reimagined in Greek tradition. Without living speakers to maintain alternative narratives about the site's past, Greek settlers and poets could reinterpret Troy's history according to their own cultural frameworks. The transformation was so complete that Troy's Anatolian linguistic and cultural character remained hidden until modern archaeological and linguistic research revealed it.

Homer's Lost Translation

The recognition of Troy as a Luwian-speaking city requires us to completely reevaluate the Trojan War tradition. What Greek memory preserved as a conflict between culturally related peoples—Greeks fighting Trojans who speak Greek and worship Greek gods—was actually a clash between groups separated by significant linguistic and cultural differences.

223

The conflict's historical kernel, if it existed, would have involved Mycenaean Greek-speakers encountering the Luwian-speaking population of Troy. This represents an early instance of the East-West cultural division that became so significant in later Greek thought, with Troy serving as the prototype for the wealthy, sophisticated, but ultimately alien Oriental city that Greeks would encounter and define themselves against (Latacz 2004: 200-220).

Certain elements in Homer's portrayal take on new significance when viewed through this linguistic lens. The poet's description of Troy as wealthy and sophisticated aligns perfectly with archaeological evidence for a prosperous Anatolian center. The portrayal of Trojans as culturally distinct yet comprehensible reflects the actual position of Luwian Troy as foreign but not entirely alien to Mycenaean visitors who had established trading relationships with the city.

Homer's Trojans speak Greek and worship Greek gods, but this represents poetic convention rather than historical reality. The actual linguistic and religious differences between Mycenaeans and Trojans were transformed into subtler cultural distinctions that Greek audiences could appreciate without being overwhelmed by alien concepts (Vermeule 1986: 78-85).

Names like Paris-Alexandros might preserve distant memories of Anatolian naming patterns—consider the striking similarity to Alaksandu from the Hittite texts. References to distinctive Trojan religious practices could reflect actual differences between Greek and Luwian cultic traditions, filtered through centuries of poetic adaptation.

The Search Continues

While the evidence for Troy's Luwian identity has gained wide acceptance among specialists, important questions remain unanswered. We still don't know the precise dialect of Luwian spoken at Troy, the full extent of multilingualism at the site, or the degree of cultural hybridity that characterized this frontier community.

The tantalizing possibility of discovering direct written evidence remains. While Bronze Age Troy has yielded limited inscriptional material so far, future excavations might uncover clay tablets, sealed documents, or inscribed objects that would provide definitive proof of the languages used for administration and daily life at the site. Recent advances in archaeological techniques, including more sophisticated approaches to recovering and analyzing organic materials, offer new possibilities for uncovering such evidence.

Ancient DNA analysis represents another frontier in understanding Troy's population history and potential linguistic affiliations. While preservation conditions at the site present challenges for genetic research, successful extraction of DNA from human remains could provide insights into population movements and biological relationships that might correlate with linguistic patterns (Krause 2019: 45-60).

Recovering Troy's Voice

The journey from historical Luwian-speaking Wilusa to legendary Troy exemplifies the complex relationship between language, identity, and cultural memory. For nearly three millennia, Troy's actual linguistic identity remained hidden, buried beneath layers of Greek reimagining and Roman appropriation. The discovery of Troy's Luwian character represents one of archaeology's greatest detective stories—a case solved not by golden treasures or spectacular monuments, but by careful analysis of fragmentary texts and humble pottery sherds.

This linguistic identification transforms our understanding of Troy from a Greek legend made real to an Anatolian city that became legendary. As a Luwian-speaking center engaged with both the Hittite Empire and the Mycenaean world, Troy occupied a unique position in the Bronze Age Mediterranean—a place where worlds met and cultures mingled, creating the complex hybrid identity that would eventually be simplified and mythologized in Greek tradition.

Troy was neither a Greek city in Anatolia nor simply an Anatolian city known to Greeks. It was something more complex and interesting: a Luwian-speaking kingdom that successfully navigated the cultural and political currents of its time until those currents became too powerful to resist. The voices of its Luwian-speaking inhabitants have been silent for three thousand years, but through the patient work of archaeologists and linguists, we're beginning to hear echoes of their lost language in the stones and tablets they left behind.

Understanding Troy's Luwian identity doesn't diminish the power of Homer's epic—it enriches it by revealing the complex historical reality that inspired one of humanity's greatest stories. The real Troy, speaking its lost Anatolian language and worshipping its Luwian gods, was every bit as remarkable as the city of legend, perhaps more so for being genuinely rooted in the extraordinary world of Bronze Age civilization.

CHAPTER 17

THE HITTITE ARCHIVES

Cracking the Clay Code

Picture a young researcher in 1983, hunched over dusty clay tablets in a university reading room, squinting at tiny cuneiform marks that hadn't been seen by human eyes for over three thousand years. Frank Starke had no idea that his painstaking work in the Oriental Institute at the University of Chicago would soon revolutionize our understanding of Troy. The tablets before him contained diplomatic correspondence from the Hittite Empire, and buried within their formal language was a name that would change everything: "Wilusa." For decades, scholars had suspected this might be the Hittite word for Troy, but proving it required the kind of archaeological detective work that makes discovering buried treasure seem simple by comparison.

What Starke and his colleagues were about to accomplish represents one of archaeology's greatest intellectual achievements—connecting Homer's legendary Troy to real Bronze Age history through the meticulous analysis of fragmentary cuneiform texts. This wasn't just academic speculation; it was detective work that would ultimately reveal Troy as a player in the ancient world's first international crisis, complete with diplomatic intrigue, military intervention, and geopolitical maneuvering that would have impressed Machiavelli.

The Lost Empire Speaks Again

To understand how revolutionary these discoveries were, we need to appreciate what the world knew about the Hittites before 1906. The answer is almost nothing. Aside from scattered biblical references to "sons of Heth," this once-mighty empire had vanished so completely from historical memory that scholars wondered if it had ever existed at all. Then German archaeologist Hugo Winckler began excavating at Boğazkale in central Turkey and uncovered something extraordinary: an archive containing over 10,000 clay tablets covered in cuneiform script.

These weren't just administrative records—they were the diplomatic correspondence, royal annals, and legal documents of a Bronze Age superpower that had negotiated as equals with Egypt, Babylonia, and Assyria. But there was one small problem: nobody could read them. The cuneiform signs were familiar from Mesopotamian contexts, but the language was completely unknown.

Enter Bedřich Hrozný, a Czech linguist working at the Istanbul Archaeological Museum in 1915. While Europe tore itself apart in World War I, Hrozný was fighting his own intellectual battle with these mysterious tablets. His breakthrough came with a text that seemed to describe food and drink: "nu NINDA-an ezzatteni watar-ma ekutteni." Hrozný recognized the cuneiform signs for "bread" (NINDA) and reasoned that the unknown words must mean "you eat" and "you drink" in Hittite (Hrozný 1917: 12-15).

What happened next was pure linguistic genius. Hrozný noticed that "watar" resembled the English "water" and German "Wasser," while "ezzatteni" shared roots with Latin "edere" (to eat). By 1917, he had reached an astounding conclusion: Hittite was an Indo-European language—in fact, the earliest attested member of this vast language family that includes English, Greek, Latin, and Sanskrit. Suddenly, scholars could read diplomatic letters written by kings who had ruled a thousand years before classical Athens.

Following Ancient Roadmaps

Once scholars could read Hittite, they faced a new challenge: where exactly were all these places mentioned in the tablets? The Hittites didn't conveniently include GPS coordinates in their diplomatic correspondence. Instead, they described locations relative to each other, mentioned rivers and mountains, and listed territories in what appeared to be geographical sequences. Reconstructing the political map of Bronze Age Anatolia became like solving a massive jigsaw puzzle with half the pieces missing.

The breakthrough came with a text called the "Annals of Tudhaliya I/II," dating to around 1400 BCE. This royal victory inscription described the conquest of a western Anatolian coalition called the Assuwa Confederation, listing twenty-two defeated kingdoms in what seemed to be geographical order. Buried in this list was "Wilusa," positioned at the northwestern extremity of the conquered territories (Beckman 1999: 78-80).

Even more revealing was the "Manapa-Tarhunta Letter," written by a Hittite vassal to his overlord around 1280 BCE. This administrator described chasing a troublemaker who had "gone up to Lazpa" (identified as the island of Lesbos) and then "came down" to attack Wilusa (Beckman 1999: 134). This directional language—up to an island, then down to Wilusa—provided crucial spatial orientation. Wilusa had to be on the mainland coast opposite Lesbos, precisely where ancient sources placed Troy.

The geographical evidence kept accumulating. The "Alaksandu Treaty" mentioned that Wilusa bordered the Seha River Land to its south. With the Seha River Land securely located in the Hermos valley region of western Anatolia, Wilusa had to lie north of this area. When scholars compiled every geographical reference from dozens of Hittite texts, they all pointed to the same conclusion: Wilusa was located in northwestern Anatolia, in the precise region where Troy was known to exist (Latacz 2004: 118-125).

When Languages Collide: Solving the Wilusa Puzzle

Geography provided the foundation, but the real breakthrough required linguistic detective work. Could "Wilusa" actually be the Hittite version of "Ilios," the Greek name for Troy used throughout Homer's epic? This wasn't just a matter of similar sounds—it required understanding how languages adapt foreign words and how sounds change over time.

The key insight came from recognizing regular sound correspondences between Hittite and Greek. The initial "W" in Hittite typically corresponded to the Greek letter digamma (ϝ), which existed in Mycenaean Greek but disappeared before the classical period. This meant that "Wilusa" would have been pronounced approximately "Wilios" by Hittite speakers, while Mycenaean Greeks would have said something like "ϝίλιος" (Wilios), later shortened to "Ilios" when the digamma disappeared (Watkins 1986: 45-50).

The linguistic equation worked perfectly. The sound changes from "Wilusa" to "Ilios" followed established patterns of phonological development between Anatolian and Greek languages. These weren't random similarities but systematic correspondences that validate linguistic connections.

Then came an extraordinary coincidence that seemed almost too good to be true. The "Alaksandu Treaty" named the ruler of Wilusa as "Alaksandu"—remarkably similar to "Alexandros," the alternative name for Paris, the Trojan prince in Greek tradition (Beckman 1999: 87). While this could have been pure chance, it provided another compelling parallel between Hittite records and Greek legend, suggesting that Greek cultural memory might have preserved authentic Bronze Age details transformed through centuries of oral transmission.

The Mycenaean Connection: Finding the Achaeans

If Wilusa was Troy, could other names in Hittite texts correspond to participants in the legendary Trojan War? The most tantalizing possibility was "Ahhiyawa," a power mentioned in over two dozen Hittite documents spanning 1400-1220 BCE. Swiss scholar Emil Forrer noticed as early as 1924 that "Ahhiyawa" bore striking phonetic similarity to "Achaeans," Homer's term for the Greeks who fought at Troy (Singer 2008: 245-250).

Initially, many scholars rejected this identification. How could Bronze Age Greeks project power across the Aegean to threaten Hittite interests? But archaeological discoveries gradually changed this picture. Excavations revealed extensive Mycenaean trade networks operating throughout the eastern Mediterranean. Mycenaean pottery appeared in significant quantities at coastal Anatolian sites, demonstrating regular contact between the Aegean and Anatolian worlds.

The Linear B tablets from Pylos documented sophisticated palatial bureaucracies capable of organizing complex overseas operations. These weren't primitive chieftains but administrators running complex economies that could mount substantial military expeditions. Most convincingly, the Hittite texts themselves revealed crucial details about Ahhiyawa's characteristics that matched what we know about Mycenaean civilization.

The "Tawagalawa Letter," written around 1250 BCE, addressed the ruler of Ahhiyawa as "Great King" and "My Brother"—diplomatic language reserved for rulers of equal status to the Hittite emperor (Beckman 1999: 101). This indicated that Ahhiyawa was considered a major power, not some minor kingdom. The letter also mentioned that the Ahhiyawan king had to cross the sea to reach Anatolia, confirming that Ahhiyawa was a maritime power based across the water from the Hittite Empire.

When Diplomacy Failed: The Piyamaradu Crisis

The most dramatic evidence for Mycenaean-Trojan conflict comes from documents describing what scholars call the "Piyamaradu affair"—a Late Bronze Age crisis that reads like something from a modern diplomatic thriller. The protagonist was a western Anatolian renegade named Piyamaradu who, with apparent

Mycenaean backing, launched a series of raids against Hittite vassal states around 1250 BCE.

The "Manapa-Tarhunta Letter" provides a gripping firsthand account of these operations. A Hittite vassal ruler wrote to his overlord describing how Piyamaradu attacked multiple territories, including a direct assault on Wilusa: "When Piyamaradu harassed me, I went to Wilusa for battle... But Piyamaradu came with many chariots and opposed me in battle... And Atpa [Piyamaradu's son-in-law] took the infantry and chariots of Ahhiyawa with him, and they went to attack Wilusa" (Beckman 1999: 134).

Here, preserved in a routine administrative document, we find explicit evidence that Troy faced a major military assault involving Mycenaean Greek forces several decades before the traditional date of Homer's Trojan War. The attackers came with "many chariots" and "infantry"—this was no mere raid but a serious military operation requiring substantial resources and planning.

The crisis escalated to the highest diplomatic levels. The "Tawagalawa Letter" reveals the Hittite emperor writing directly to the king of Ahhiyawa, complaining about Piyamaradu's activities and the Mycenaean support he was receiving. The letter crackles with barely contained frustration as the Hittite king protests that an Ahhiyawan prince named Tawagalawa was actively supporting anti-Hittite operations in the region (Beckman 1999: 101-103).

This wasn't just border raiding—it was international crisis management involving two of the Bronze Age's major powers. The fact that Troy became a flashpoint in this conflict demonstrates its strategic importance and confirms that Mycenaean Greeks were indeed conducting military operations against the city during the thirteenth century BCE.

A Kingdom Under Pressure

The Hittite documents reveal Troy operating under increasing pressure during its final centuries. The "Alaksandu Treaty" from around 1280 BCE shows Troy as a loyal Hittite vassal, with ruler Alaksandu swearing to provide military assistance, maintain political loyalty, and pay tribute in exchange for imperial protection (Beckman 1999: 87-90). But this protection came at the cost of autonomy—Troy had become dependent on Hittite power for survival.

By the late thirteenth century, even this support was proving insufficient. The fragmentary "Milawata Letter," probably dating to around 1220 BCE, mentions the Hittite emperor intervening directly in Trojan succession disputes: "Concerning the King of Wilusa... you wrote to me as follows: 'I removed him from kingship, but later I reinstated him in kingship again'" (Miller 2007: 255). Troy's rulers now required foreign approval to maintain their thrones—a clear sign of declining independence.

This escalating instability coincided with broader regional problems. The Hittite Empire itself was struggling with internal succession crises, external pressures from Assyria, and mysterious population movements that Egyptian sources called the "Sea Peoples." The international system that had sustained Troy for centuries was beginning to collapse.

The Archaeological Witness

Remarkably, the archaeological evidence from Troy itself corroborates this textual picture of increasing pressure and ultimate catastrophe. Excavations at Troy VIIa—the settlement level dating to around 1200-1180 BCE—reveal clear signs of a community under stress. Architectural modifications within the citadel show large spaces subdivided into smaller units, suggesting crowded conditions possibly caused by refugees from the surrounding countryside. Increased storage capacity indicates concerns about resource security during uncertain times (Korfmann 2006: 32-38).

The end came violently. Archaeologists found human skeletons scattered throughout the destruction layer, including one individual with a crushed skull discovered near the city wall. Bronze arrowheads embedded in walls and gates provide stark evidence of coordinated military assault. Layers of ash and burned debris throughout the settlement confirm a catastrophic destruction that ended Troy's Bronze Age prosperity around 1180 BCE—precisely when Greek tradition placed the legendary Trojan War (Rose 2006: 78-85).

This archaeological evidence aligns perfectly with the broader pattern of destructions throughout the eastern Mediterranean around 1180-1170 BCE. The Hittite capital at Hattusa was abandoned, Mycenaean palaces were burned, and cities throughout Syria and the Levant suffered violent ends. Troy's destruction was part of a systemic collapse that terminated the Late Bronze Age international order.

The Missing Link: What the Tablets Don't Say

Despite all this evidence for Mycenaean-Trojan conflict, the Hittite archives contain no explicit mention of a massive Greek expedition against Troy comparable to Homer's epic. This absence has led some scholars to question whether such a conflict ever occurred. But several factors complicate this picture and suggest why we might not expect to find direct documentation of a "Trojan War."

First, the Hittite archives from Hattusa end abruptly around 1190-1180 BCE with the empire's collapse. This creates a crucial documentation gap covering precisely the period when Troy VIIa was destroyed. Any major conflict occurring during these final chaotic years would have gone unrecorded in the imperial archives that provide most of our textual evidence (Bachhuber 2006: 112-115).

Second, we must consider how historical events transform when preserved through oral tradition. If a significant conflict involving Mycenaean forces and Troy occurred around 1180 BCE, it would have been transmitted orally for approximately four centuries before Homer's composition. During this transmission, historical details would inevitably be simplified, exaggerated, and reshaped according to poetic conventions and contemporary concerns.

Third, the scale of the legendary war might be poetic exaggeration. The documented Piyamaradu raids show that Mycenaean-supported attacks on Troy did occur, but these were probably smaller-scale operations rather than the massive ten-year siege described in Greek tradition. Oral tradition had centuries to transform a historical conflict into the epic confrontation we know from Homer.

The Sea Peoples and the End of an Age

Troy's destruction around 1180 BCE coincided with one of history's most mysterious episodes: the collapse of Bronze Age civilization throughout the eastern Mediterranean. Egyptian records from the reign of Ramesses III described attacks by coalition forces called the "Sea Peoples," including groups that apparently originated in the Aegean region. Some scholars have suggested connections between these Sea Peoples, the fall of Troy, and the return voyages of Greek heroes described in post-Trojan War traditions.

The chronological alignment is striking. Troy fell around 1180 BCE, the Hittite Empire collapsed by 1170 BCE, and Egyptian sources document Sea Peoples attacks around 1175 BCE. These events weren't isolated incidents but interconnected aspects of a system-wide collapse that transformed the entire eastern Mediterranean world (Cline 2014: 145-170).

In this broader context, any conflict at Troy would represent just one episode in a larger pattern of upheaval and population movement. Greek tradition might have preserved memories of this specific encounter because it involved direct Mycenaean participation and occurred at a strategically significant location already known to Aegean visitors through trade and diplomacy.

From Clay to Epic: The Journey from History to Legend

The identification of Wilusa with Troy and Ahhiyawa with Mycenaean Greece provides a historical framework for understanding how actual Bronze Age conflicts might have evolved into the legendary Trojan War. This transformation likely occurred through several stages of cultural transmission spanning the Greek Dark Age (c. 1100-800 BCE).

The process probably began with actual historical events—the documented conflicts between Mycenaean-supported forces and Troy during the thirteenth and twelfth centuries BCE. These events were remembered in oral traditions that circulated among Greek communities during the centuries following the Bronze Age collapse. Gradually, these memories acquired supernatural elements, heroic dimensions, and poetic elaboration that transformed historical reality into legendary narrative (Latacz 2004: 200-220).

By the time Homer composed the Iliad around 750-700 BCE, these traditions had evolved into a complex synthesis incorporating multiple historical layers. Authentic Bronze Age elements (like boar's tusk helmets and specific geographical details) combined with Dark Age practices (such as cremation burial) and contemporary eighth-century concerns. The result wasn't historical documentation but poetic art that used the legendary past to explore timeless human themes.

This layered composition helps explain both the historical elements and anachronisms in Homeric epic. The geographical setting, international conflict framework, and certain material details preserved authentic Bronze Age memories. However, specific battle tactics, social structures, and many cultural practices reflected later periods when the poems were composed and transmitted.

The Detective Story Continues

Research on Troy's historical context continues to evolve as new evidence emerges and analytical techniques improve. Recent developments include refined radiocarbon dating that has helped align archaeological evidence more precisely with Hittite textual chronology, strengthening the case for connecting Troy VIIa's destruction with the traditional Trojan War period.

Ongoing work with Luwian hieroglyphic inscriptions from western Anatolia has provided additional context for understanding Troy's cultural environment, confirming its participation in Anatolian rather than Aegean cultural spheres. Ancient DNA analysis of human remains from Late Bronze Age sites is beginning to illuminate population movements and biological relationships that may correlate with the linguistic and cultural patterns documented in texts and material culture.

Digital humanities approaches, including computational analysis of Hittite diplomatic language, have identified previously unrecognized patterns in geographic references and political relationships. These technological tools are helping scholars extract new information from texts that have been studied for decades (Yakubovich 2019: 45-60).

Future excavations at Troy itself may yield the ultimate prize: actual written documents from the site. Clay tablets or inscriptions in Luwian or Hittite could provide direct evidence of the language spoken at Troy and reveal how its inhabitants viewed themselves and their relationships with neighboring powers.

Solving an Ancient Mystery

The decipherment of Hittite and identification of Wilusa with Troy represents one of archaeology's greatest intellectual achievements. What began with a young Czech linguist puzzling over mysterious cuneiform signs in 1915 has evolved into a comprehensive understanding of Troy's role in Bronze Age international politics. The process required patient scholarship, linguistic brilliance, archaeological precision, and the kind of persistent detective work that gradually assembles truth from fragmentary evidence.

The Hittite tablets reveal Troy not as the isolated fortress of Greek legend, but as a sophisticated Bronze Age kingdom operating within a complex diplomatic system. As a Hittite vassal state in a contested borderland, Troy faced documented conflicts involving Mycenaean forces during precisely the period when Greek tradition placed the legendary war. The violent destruction of Troy VIIa around 1180 BCE provides archaeological confirmation of a catastrophic end consistent with Greek accounts.

While we should avoid simplistic equations between myth and history, the convergence of linguistic, archaeological, and textual evidence now strongly suggests that Greek cultural memory preserved—in transformed form—authentic recollections of Mycenaean military activities against Troy during the late thirteenth and early twelfth centuries BCE. The legendary Trojan War emerges not as pure fiction but as cultural memory: the creative transformation of actual historical events into meaningful narrative that helped successive generations understand their past.

Troy's enduring significance stems precisely from this dual existence in both history and legend. The clay tablets from Hattusa and the stones of Troy's excavated walls together tell a story that bridges the gap between archaeological science and literary art. By maintaining awareness of both dimensions, we gain a richer understanding not only of Bronze Age politics but also of how societies transform historical experience into cultural memory that continues to resonate across millennia.

The young researcher hunched over those cuneiform tablets in 1983 couldn't have imagined that his work would ultimately connect Homer's epic to diplomatic correspondence written by Bronze Age bureaucrats. Yet that's exactly what happened when patient scholarship met extraordinary evidence, proving once again that truth can indeed be stranger—and more wonderful—than fiction.

CHAPTER 18

THE BRONZE AGE COLLAPSE

When Worlds Collide

I magine standing on the walls of Troy around 1200 BCE, looking out over a world that had endured for centuries but was about to vanish forever. The Late Bronze Age Mediterranean was humanity's first truly international civilization—a sophisticated network of kingdoms linked by diplomacy, trade, and shared technologies that stretched from Mycenaean Greece to Mesopotamia, from the Hittite Empire to Egypt's New Kingdom. Palace scribes kept meticulous records in multiple writing systems, merchants carried luxury goods along established trade routes, and diplomats negotiated treaties between powers that respected each other as equals. It was a cosmopolitan world that wouldn't be matched again for over a millennium.

Then, within the span of a single human lifetime, it all came crashing down. The mighty Hittite Empire simply vanished, its capital abandoned and its archives ending abruptly around 1180 BCE. Mycenaean palaces across Greece went up in flames. Cities throughout Syria and the Levant were destroyed and abandoned. Cyprus was devastated. Even mighty Egypt barely survived, contracting behind its traditional borders. And somewhere in this catastrophic collapse, Troy itself was violently destroyed, its Bronze Age prosperity ending in fire and bloodshed around 1180 BCE.

Troy's destruction wasn't an isolated tragedy—it was one thread in a tapestry of collapse that unraveled the ancient world's first global civilization. Understanding this broader context transforms how we see both the historical Troy and the legendary Trojan War, revealing them as part of humanity's earliest encounter with systemic civilizational failure.

The World That Was: Understanding What We Lost

To appreciate the magnitude of what collapsed, we need to understand what the Late Bronze Age had achieved. This wasn't a collection of isolated kingdoms stumbling around in primitive darkness. Archaeological evidence reveals a sophisticated international system that managed complexity on a scale not seen again until the Roman Empire.

Palace archives from Pylos documented Mycenaean bureaucrats tracking everything from chariot wheels to perfumed oil, managing resources across territories spanning hundreds of miles. Hittite kings corresponded with Egyptian pharaohs as equals, addressing each other as "my brother" in diplomatic language that wouldn't be out of place in modern international relations. Ugaritic merchants maintained commercial houses from Syria to Cyprus, dealing in goods that traveled thousands of miles from source to consumer (Cline 2014: 78-95).

The sophistication went beyond mere trade. These Bronze Age kingdoms had developed standardized weights and measures, established diplomatic protocols, and created legal frameworks for international commerce. They exchanged not just goods but ideas, technologies, and cultural practices. Mycenaean pottery appeared in Egyptian tombs, Mesopotamian cylinder seals reached Cyprus, and Baltic amber found its way to Mycenaean graves—clear evidence of networks spanning continents.

Troy occupied a crucial position in this interconnected world. Archaeological evidence from Troy VI and early VIIa shows a prosperous city with international connections stretching from central Anatolia to Mycenaean Greece. Hittite texts confirm Troy's integration into imperial diplomatic networks as the vassal kingdom of Wilusa. This wasn't a peripheral backwater but a strategic player in Bronze Age geopolitics, controlling the vital Dardanelles passage between Europe and Asia.

The Perfect Storm: When Everything Went Wrong

Modern scholars increasingly recognize that the Bronze Age collapse resulted from what can only be called a "perfect storm"—multiple catastrophic factors converging in ways that overwhelmed even the most resilient societies. No single cause explains the comprehensive nature of the disaster; instead, environmental, social, political, and technological stresses combined to create cascading failures that brought down the entire system (Cline 2014: 145-170).

The evidence for climate change during this period has become overwhelming. Tree ring data from California to Ireland, ice cores from Greenland, and cave formations from Israel all point to the same conclusion: around 1200 BCE, the eastern Mediterranean entered a severe, prolonged drought that lasted for decades. Lake levels dropped, agricultural yields collapsed, and pastoral societies found their traditional grazing lands desiccated.

Paleoclimatologist Brandon Drake's analysis of multiple climate proxies paints a grim picture: "The evidence shows a major cooling and drying event beginning around 1200 BCE. This wasn't just a bad year or two—it was a fundamental shift in climate patterns that lasted for generations" (Drake 2012: 1862-1870). The Hittite capital at Hattusa was found with empty granaries. Letters from Ugarit desperately request grain shipments from Egypt. In the Argolid region of Greece, archaeological surveys show massive population decline as water sources failed.

But environmental stress was just one factor. The very sophistication that made Bronze Age kingdoms powerful also made them vulnerable. Their centralized palace economies created single points of failure—when the palace fell, the entire economic system collapsed with it. Their dependence on long-distance trade for essential materials like tin meant that disrupted trade routes could cripple entire industries. Their specialized workforces couldn't easily adapt when the system that supported them failed.

The Sea Peoples: History's First Recorded Refugee Crisis?

Into this world of environmental stress and systemic vulnerability came one of history's most mysterious phenomena: the Sea Peoples. Egyptian records from the reign of Ramesses III around 1175 BCE describe massive attacks by seaborne coalitions with names like Peleset, Tjekker, Shekelesh, and Denyen. Temple reliefs at Medinet Habu show these warriors in distinctive dress fighting both naval and land battles against Egyptian forces (Oren 2000: 282-295).

Traditional scholarship often portrayed the Sea Peoples as barbarian invaders swooping down on civilized lands, but the reality was probably far more complex. These groups likely represented populations displaced by the very environmental and political chaos that was destroying Bronze Age civilization. As kingdoms fell and agricultural systems failed, entire communities were forced to seek new homes, creating waves of migration that further destabilized already stressed regions.

The chronology is suggestive. Troy VIIa was destroyed around 1180 BCE, while Ramesses III fought his great Sea Peoples battles around 1177 BCE. Some scholars have wondered whether Troy's destruction contributed to the population movements that created the Sea Peoples phenomenon. Others have suggested that the legendary Trojan War might preserve cultural memory of Sea Peoples activity in the region.

What seems clear is that the Sea Peoples weren't simply external enemies but symptoms of the broader systemic collapse. As archaeologist Assaf Yasur-Landau observes: "The Sea Peoples represent what happens when entire populations are displaced by civilizational failure. They weren't barbarians destroying civilization—they were civilization's refugees, creating further instability as they sought new homes" (Yasur-Landau 2010: 345-360).

Troy Under Pressure: Archaeological Evidence of a City in Crisis

The archaeological evidence from Troy itself provides a fascinating window into how Bronze Age collapse manifested at the local level. Troy VI, with its impressive fortifications and evidence of international connections, represents the city at its Late Bronze Age height. Its destruction by earthquake around 1250 BCE coincided with the beginning of regional instability, offering an ominous preview of what was to come.

The inhabitants of Troy VIIa rebuilt on the ruins, but their city reveals clear signs of a community under increasing stress. Manfred Korfmann's excavations revealed how large houses were subdivided into smaller units, possibly to accommodate refugees from the surrounding countryside. Storage jars were embedded in floors throughout the settlement, dramatically increasing the city's capacity to stockpile supplies. The fortifications were strengthened and repaired multiple times (Korfmann 2006: 32-45).

These modifications tell a story of adaptation and growing anxiety. The subdivision of living spaces suggests population pressure—more people crowding into the citadel's protective walls. The increased storage capacity indicates a community preparing for shortages, possibly reflecting disrupted trade or the need to support larger populations. The constant work on fortifications shows a people who felt increasingly threatened.

Then came the violent end. The destruction layer of Troy VIIa tells a grim story: bronze arrowheads embedded in walls and gates, collapsed buildings, scattered human remains including at least one individual with a crushed skull found near the city wall. A thick ash layer indicates extensive burning. This wasn't gradual abandonment or natural disaster—it was catastrophic destruction consistent with military assault (Rose 2006: 78-85).

The timing couldn't be more significant. Troy VIIa's destruction around 1180 BCE coincides almost exactly with similar catastrophes across the eastern Mediterranean. It's the same period when the Hittite Empire collapsed, when Mycenaean palaces burned, when cities throughout Syria and Palestine were destroyed. Troy's violent end was part of a synchronized regional catastrophe.

Cascading Failures: How Complex Systems Collapse

Modern research on complex systems helps us understand how the Bronze Age collapse could have been so sudden and comprehensive. The Late Bronze Age kingdoms weren't isolated entities—they formed an interconnected network where problems in one area could trigger failures throughout the system. When multiple stresses hit simultaneously, the result was catastrophic.

Consider how the various factors interacted. Climate change triggered agricultural failures, which led to population movements and resource competition. Displaced populations put pressure on functioning kingdoms, creating internal instability. Disrupted agriculture meant less surplus to support specialized crafts, trade, and administrative bureaucracies. Weakened kingdoms couldn't maintain trade routes or provide security, further disrupting the networks that sustained the entire system.

Archaeologist Colin Renfrew's "systems collapse" model explains how these feedback loops accelerated the disaster: "Bronze Age states were like a house of cards—impressive when stable, but vulnerable to cascading failures when stressed. Remove a few key supports, and the entire structure could collapse with shocking speed" (Renfrew 1979: 481-505).

Troy's position made it particularly vulnerable to these cascading failures. The city's prosperity depended on controlling the Dardanelles strait and facilitating trade between Europe and Asia. As trade networks collapsed and regional stability deteriorated, Troy's strategic advantages became liabilities. The very location that had made it prosperous now made it a target for displaced populations seeking new homes.

The Hittite Connection: When Superpowers Fall

Troy's destruction becomes even more significant when viewed within the context of the Hittite Empire's simultaneous collapse. The Hittite archives, which had documented Troy's status as the vassal kingdom Wilusa, end abruptly around 1180 BCE—the same period when Troy VIIa was destroyed. This isn't coincidence; it's evidence of systemic failure affecting both local kingdoms and regional superpowers.

The Hittite Empire's end was particularly dramatic. Unlike Troy, which shows evidence of violent destruction, Hattusa appears to have been deliberately abandoned. Storage facilities were emptied, archives were removed, and cult statues were taken—suggesting an organized evacuation rather than sudden attack. Yet the result was the same: the complete disappearance of a power that had dominated Anatolia for over four centuries (Bryce 2005: 322-340).

For Troy, the Hittite collapse meant the loss of imperial protection and diplomatic support. The treaties that had guaranteed Troy's security and mediated its conflicts with neighbors suddenly became worthless pieces of clay. The Tawagalawa Letter had shown how Hittite diplomatic intervention could resolve conflicts involving Troy and Mycenaean forces. With that protection gone, Troy stood alone against whatever forces were ravaging the region.

The archaeological evidence from Troy VIIa's final phase suggests the inhabitants understood their vulnerability. The frantic modifications to living spaces and storage facilities reveal a community preparing for siege or worse. They were right to be afraid—without Hittite protection, Troy had become just another target in a world where civilization itself was under attack.

Mycenaean Twilight: The Other Side of the Story

The collapse affected all participants in Bronze Age civilization, including the Mycenaean Greeks who Greek tradition credits with destroying Troy. By 1200 BCE, the Mycenaean palace system was itself collapsing, with administrative centers across Greece suffering destruction or abandonment. Linear B writing disappeared, centralized bureaucracies ceased to function, and the sophisticated economic networks documented in palace archives simply vanished.

This context makes the traditional Trojan War narrative more historically plausible while simultaneously explaining its legendary character. If Mycenaean forces did attack Troy around 1180 BCE, it would have occurred during the final phase of their own civilization's collapse. Such an expedition might have represented a desperate attempt to secure resources, eliminate rivals, or establish new territories as the Mycenaean homeland became increasingly untenable (Dickinson 2006: 55-75).

The subsequent "Greek Dark Age" (c. 1100-800 BCE) would have provided ample time for historical events to be transformed into legend. As literacy disappeared and centralized institutions collapsed, oral tradition became the primary means of preserving cultural memory. During centuries of transmission, actual conflicts would have acquired heroic dimensions, supernatural elements, and poetic elaboration that transformed historical reality into epic narrative.

This helps explain both the historical elements and the mythological aspects of the Trojan War tradition. Authentic Bronze Age details like boar's tusk helmets and tower shields suggest genuine historical memory, while gods intervening in human affairs reflects the poetic conventions of oral tradition. The basic framework—conflict between Mycenaean Greeks and a city in northwestern Anatolia—has demonstrable historical plausibility, even if the specific details represent poetic elaboration.

After the Storm: Survival and Regeneration

Despite its catastrophic nature, the Bronze Age collapse didn't mean the end of civilization in the eastern Mediterranean. Instead, it initiated a period of transformation that eventually led to new, more resilient forms of social organization. This process of regeneration provides crucial context for understanding both what was lost and what emerged from the ruins.

The immediate aftermath was grim. Population declined dramatically across much of the region. Writing systems disappeared, with Greek Linear B, Hittite cuneiform, and various Anatolian scripts falling out of use. Trade networks contracted, with evidence for long-distance exchange diminishing to a fraction of Bronze Age levels. Many sites were permanently abandoned, their ruins becoming mounds that would puzzle later archaeologists.

At Troy, this transition is visible in the archaeological sequence. The settlement continued after the destruction of Troy VIIa, but on a greatly diminished scale. Troy VIIb shows new pottery styles suggesting connections to Thrace and the Balkans rather than the Mediterranean world. International connections largely disappeared. By 950 BCE, the site had contracted to a small village bearing little resemblance to its Bronze Age predecessor (Easton 2002: 194-206).

Yet this apparent decline contained the seeds of regeneration. The collapse had cleared away rigid palace bureaucracies and centralized economic systems, creating space for more flexible forms of organization. The Greek polis system, Phoenician commercial networks, and other decentralized structures that emerged during the early Iron Age proved more adaptable and resilient than their Bronze Age predecessors.

Cultural Memory: From History to Legend

Perhaps the most remarkable aspect of Troy's Bronze Age collapse is how it was remembered and transformed in later tradition. The violent destruction of Troy VIIa around 1180 BCE became the foundation for one of Western civilization's most enduring narratives—the story of the Trojan War preserved in Homer's Iliad.

This transformation from historical event to legendary narrative illustrates how cultural memory works. Oral tradition doesn't preserve history in the way written records do; instead, it transforms actual events according to the needs, values, and understanding of successive generations. The result preserves authentic elements while creating a new artistic and cultural reality.

The chronological correlation is striking. Troy VIIa was destroyed around 1180 BCE, closely matching the traditional date for the Trojan War (1184 BCE according to ancient calculations). The nature of the destruction—violent, involving fire and military conflict—aligns with the legendary account. The broader context of Bronze Age collapse provides a realistic framework for the international conflict described in Greek tradition.

Yet the legendary war also differs significantly from anything the historical evidence can support. Homer's ten-year siege, thousand-ship expedition, and direct divine intervention represent poetic elaboration rather than historical fact. The transformation of a Bronze Age regional conflict into a Panhellenic national epic reflects the cultural needs of later Greek society rather than Bronze Age reality (Burgess 2001: 142-165).

"The Trojan War tradition preserves the cultural memory of actual Bronze Age conflicts transformed through centuries of oral transmission," explains archaeologist Joachim Latacz. "It's not history in the modern sense, but it's not pure fiction either—it's something more complex and interesting: history transformed into art" (Latacz 2004: 200-220).

Lessons from the Ruins: What Troy's Collapse Teaches Us

The Late Bronze Age collapse offers sobering lessons about societal vulnerability and resilience that remain relevant today. As a case study in systemic failure, it demonstrates how environmental stress, resource dependencies, and institutional rigidity can combine to overwhelm even sophisticated civilizations.

Several key insights emerge from Troy's experience. First, complexity without resilience creates vulnerability. The Bronze Age kingdoms were marvels of organization and efficiency during stable periods, but their centralized, interdependent systems became liabilities when faced with multiple simultaneous stresses. Modern concerns about globalization, supply chain dependencies, and climate change echo these ancient vulnerabilities.

Second, environmental change acts as a threat multiplier rather than a simple cause. The Bronze Age drought didn't just cause crop failures—it triggered population movements, resource competition, and political instability that overwhelmed institutional response capabilities. Understanding these indirect effects is crucial for assessing contemporary climate risks.

Third, the archaeological evidence from Troy VIIa shows a community attempting to adapt to changing circumstances through incremental modifications—subdividing spaces, increasing storage, strengthening defenses. These adaptations proved insufficient against the scale of systemic collapse, suggesting the importance of transformative rather than incremental responses to existential threats.

Finally, the regeneration that followed the collapse demonstrates human resilience and adaptability. The more decentralized, commercially flexible systems that emerged in the early first millennium BCE proved more robust than their Bronze Age predecessors. Even catastrophic collapse can clear space for innovation and renewal.

Troy Eternal: From Bronze Age City to Cultural Symbol

Troy's remarkable journey from Bronze Age regional power to legendary city to archaeological site illustrates the multiple ways places can matter to human societies. The physical Troy was destroyed around 1180 BCE, but its significance transcended that destruction, ultimately becoming more influential as a symbol than it had ever been as a functioning city.

The process began with the cultural memory preserved in oral tradition during the Greek Dark Age. As Bronze Age civilization faded into memory, the story of Troy's destruction became a way for later Greeks to understand their relationship to a heroic past. The legendary war represented both loss—the end of a heroic age—and triumph—the achievements of Greek heroes.

Homer's Iliad crystallized this cultural memory into artistic form, creating a narrative that has influenced Western literature for nearly three millennia. The poem transforms the historical destruction of a Bronze Age Anatolian city into a meditation on honor, fate, mortality, and the human condition. In doing so, it demonstrates how historical events can acquire meanings far beyond their original context.

Troy's reemergence as a pilgrimage site in classical antiquity shows how cultural memory can reshape physical places. Visitors including Xerxes, Alexander the Great, and Julius Caesar came to Troy not to see Bronze Age ruins but to connect with the legendary past preserved in literature. The site had become a place where history and legend intersected, where visitors could encounter both archaeological reality and cultural imagination.

Conclusion: When Worlds End and Begin

Troy's destruction around 1180 BCE marked the end of more than just one city—it was part of the collapse of humanity's first international civilization. The sophisticated Bronze Age world that had connected continents through trade, diplomacy, and cultural exchange vanished with stunning rapidity, initiating a "dark age" that lasted for centuries.

Understanding Troy's destruction within this broader context transforms how we see both the historical city and the legendary war. The archaeological evidence reveals a community struggling to adapt to systemic collapse before succumbing to the violence that was destroying civilization throughout the eastern Mediterranean. The legendary Trojan War preserves cultural memory of these catastrophic events, transformed through centuries of oral tradition into the foundational epic of Western literature.

Troy's story thus bridges multiple worlds: the Bronze Age civilization that was ending and the Iron Age civilization that was beginning; historical reality and legendary narrative; archaeological science and literary art. The city's destruction represents both ending and beginning—the violent conclusion of one chapter in human history and the traumatic birth of another.

Modern archaeological investigation has revealed the historical Troy as a significant Bronze Age center that participated in the complex international system of its time. The city's violent destruction around 1180 BCE provides historical grounding for the legendary war, even as the epic tradition transforms that history into something grander and more meaningful than factual documentation could achieve.

In this way, Troy's Bronze Age collapse offers a powerful case study in both societal vulnerability and cultural resilience. The physical city fell to the forces that were destroying civilization throughout the eastern Mediterranean, but its cultural significance survived and ultimately flourished. From the ashes of Bronze Age Troy rose the legendary city that has captivated imaginations for three millennia—proving that sometimes the most important reality is the one we create from memory, imagination, and the very human need to find meaning in catastrophe.

The walls of Troy still stand, weathered by millennia but enduring. They remind us that civilizations rise and fall, that even sophisticated societies can face existential challenges, but that human creativity can transform even destruction into something beautiful and lasting. In the end, Troy's greatest victory wasn't military—it was cultural, achieving through legend the immortality that no Bronze Age kingdom could attain through power alone.

Chapter 19

Archaeological Evidence for Destruction

The Crime Scene at Troy

Imagine arriving at the scene of a catastrophe thousands of years after it oc- curred, with only scattered clues to piece together what happened. This is precisely the challenge facing archaeologists excavating Troy VIIa—a settlement that met its violent end around 1180 BCE, leaving behind a destruction layer that reads like evidence from history's most famous crime scene. The blackened soil tells a story, but like any good detective story, the evidence is complex, sometimes contradictory, and open to multiple interpretations.

What makes this archaeological puzzle so compelling isn't just its connection to the legendary Trojan War, but the remarkable preservation of a moment frozen in time. Within the destruction layer lie bronze arrowheads embedded in walls, human skeletons crushed beneath collapsed buildings, cooking pots still con- taining the remains of interrupted meals, and valuable possessions abandoned in apparent haste. These intimate traces transform abstract archaeological data into a visceral encounter with human catastrophe that occurred over three millennia ago.

Yet determining exactly what caused this destruction has proven one of archae- ology's most enduring challenges. Was Troy VIIa destroyed by human enemies in a conflict that inspired Homer's epic? Did a devastating earthquake bring down the city's walls, as geological evidence suggests? Or did some combination of natural disaster and human opportunism create the perfect storm that ended Bronze Age Troy? The evidence, as we'll see, supports elements of all these scenarios.

Reading the Ruins: What the Destruction Layer Reveals

When archaeologists excavate a destruction layer, they become forensic investigators working backward through time. At Troy VIIa, decades of careful excavation have revealed a remarkably detailed picture of the settlement's final moments, preserved in the archaeological equivalent of a snapshot.

The most dramatic evidence comes from the fortification walls and gates, where concentrated bronze arrowheads tell a story of intense fighting. These aren't randomly scattered artifacts—they're embedded in walls, clustered near defensive positions, and distributed in patterns consistent with a coordinated assault on the city's strongest points. Archaeologist Rüstem Aslan, who participated in the recent excavations, describes finding arrowheads "like ancient bullets fired into the walls during a siege" (Aslan 2006: 78-85).

The human cost of Troy's destruction appears in the skeletal remains scattered throughout the site. Near the city wall, excavators discovered the skeleton of a young man whose skull had been crushed, his body left unburied in the ruins. This wasn't someone who died peacefully and received proper funeral rites—this was a victim of sudden violence, caught in the catastrophe that overwhelmed the city. Other human remains throughout the destruction layer tell similar stories of lives cut short by disaster.

Perhaps most poignant are the traces of interrupted daily life. In one house, archaeologists found cooking vessels still containing carbonized food—meals that were being prepared when catastrophe struck. Valuable bronze tools, complete ceramic vessels, and personal ornaments were abandoned throughout the site, suggesting residents fled in such haste that they couldn't gather their most precious possessions. This pattern of abandoned valuables indicates sudden catastrophe rather than gradual abandonment or planned evacuation.

The fire damage tells its own story. Throughout Troy VIIa, walls and timbers show evidence of intense burning, with mudbrick structures baked hard by temperatures exceeding 1000°C. This wasn't accidental burning from hearths or oil lamps—scientific analysis confirms temperatures consistent with deliberate conflagration, the kind of systematic firing that accompanies military conquest.

The Earthquake Alternative: When the Earth Moves

Not all archaeologists agree that human enemies destroyed Troy VIIa. Some argue that the city fell victim to the same geological forces that had destroyed its predecessor, Troy VI, around 1250 BCE—a devastating earthquake that brought down even the massive fortification walls.

The earthquake hypothesis gains credibility from Troy's geological setting. The site sits near the North Anatolian Fault, one of the world's most seismically active zones. Modern earthquake studies have documented major seismic events affecting western Anatolia throughout history, and paleoseismic data confirms significant earthquake activity during the Late Bronze Age.

Geologist Eberhard Zangger has identified structural damage patterns at Troy VIIa that resemble those found at confirmed earthquake sites. Walls toppled outward rather than inward, systematic cracks in foundations, and evidence of ground displacement all suggest seismic activity rather than human destruction. The precedent of Troy VI, whose earthquake destruction was so complete that inhabitants had to rebuild entirely on top of the ruins, demonstrates the site's vulnerability to geological catastrophe (Zangger 1994: 212-220).

The earthquake interpretation also helps explain some puzzling aspects of the destruction evidence. If enemies had conquered Troy, why didn't they loot the valuable items found abandoned throughout the site? If the city fell to human attack, why do some of the architectural collapse patterns look more like natural disaster than deliberate demolition?

Yet the earthquake hypothesis faces significant challenges. Most notably, it struggles to explain the concentrated weapons evidence and the specific patterns of human casualties. Earthquakes don't shoot bronze arrowheads into defensive walls or create the kind of organized destruction patterns visible at Troy VIIa's gates and fortifications.

The Perfect Storm: When Disasters Converge

Increasingly, archaeologists favor a more complex interpretation that recognizes how multiple catastrophic factors can interact to create destruction beyond what any single cause could achieve. This "perfect storm" model suggests that Troy VIIa experienced a devastating earthquake that damaged its defenses, followed by human attackers who exploited this vulnerability to capture and burn the city.

This scenario accounts for the full range of archaeological evidence in ways that single-cause explanations cannot. The earthquake would explain the structural damage patterns consistent with seismic activity, the outward collapse of some walls, and the foundation displacement that geological studies have identified. The subsequent human attack would explain the concentrated weapons evidence, the deliberate burning at temperatures consistent with military conflagration, and the specific patterns of destruction targeting defensive positions.

Archaeological precedents support this interpretation. Throughout history, military forces have exploited natural disasters that weakened enemy defenses. The 1755 Lisbon earthquake, for instance, was followed by looting and violence as social order collapsed. During the Late Bronze Age collapse, when environmental stress and population movements created widespread instability, an earthquake-damaged Troy would have presented an irresistible target for any of the various groups seeking new territories or resources.

Archaeologist Eric Cline, who has studied destruction patterns through-out the eastern Mediterranean, observes: "The Late Bronze Age was a period when multiple stresses converged—climate change, resource competition, population movements, and technological transitions. In this context, a natural disaster like an earthquake could easily trigger human conflicts as groups competed for increasingly scarce resources" (Cline 2014: 145-170).

Frozen Moments: The Human Experience of Catastrophe

Beyond the debates over causation, the archaeological evidence from Troy VIIa provides extraordinary glimpses into individual human experiences during catastrophic events. These preserved moments transform our under-standing from abstract patterns of destruction to concrete human realities.

In several houses, excavators found evidence of hasty concealment ef-forts—valuable items hidden beneath floors or tucked into wall niches by residents who intended to return but never could. One poignant discovery included a collection of bronze tools and personal ornaments found near the crushed skeleton of their owner, suggesting someone who died while trying to protect their most precious possessions.

The spatial distribution of destruction evidence reveals how catastrophe unfolded across the settlement. The most intense destruction—concentrated weapons, severe burning, human casualties—appears along the fortification walls and near gates. This pattern suggests that whatever forces destroyed Troy VIIa, the city's defenses were primary targets. Within residential areas, destruction evidence shows more variable patterns, with some houses com-pletely burned while adjacent structures suffered less damage.

Evidence of attempted resistance appears in concentrations of stones and im-provised weapons found near entranceways—makeshift defensive measures by residents trying to protect their homes during the city's final moments. These desperate preparations remind us that Troy's inhabitants weren't passive victims but people who fought to defend their community against overwhelming forces.

The immediate aftermath of destruction is preserved in archaeological evidence as well. Cut marks and pry marks on architectural elements show that survivors or newcomers salvaged usable materials from the ruins. Temporary shelters erected within partially standing buildings indicate that some people remained in the area after the catastrophe, perhaps survivors trying to rebuild their lives among the ruins of their former city.

Scientific Sleuthing: Modern Techniques Reveal Ancient Secrets

Recent advances in archaeological science have provided new tools for investigating Troy VIIa's destruction, offering evidence unavailable to earlier excavators. These techniques help resolve some longstanding questions while raising new ones about the nature of Bronze Age catastrophes.

Modern archaeoseismology—the specialized study of earthquake effects on archaeological sites—has revolutionized our ability to identify seismic damage. Analysis of wall collapse directions and fracture patterns at Troy VIIa shows some features characteristic of earthquake damage, particularly foundation displacement patterns that match known seismic signatures. However, these earthquake indicators are complicated by subsequent human activity and destruction events, making definitive identification challenging.

Chemical analysis of burned materials can determine the temperatures reached during destruction fires, providing crucial information about whether burning was accidental or deliberate. At Troy VIIa, evidence indicates temperatures exceeding 1000°C in some areas—consistent with the systematic firing of structures rather than accidental burning from household sources. This high-temperature burning strongly suggests human agency in the city's final conflagration.

Metallurgical analysis of the bronze arrowheads found throughout the destruction layer has revealed important details about their manufacture and origin.

The arrowheads match Mycenaean Greek types known from mainland Greece, providing material evidence that could support Greek involvement in Troy's destruction. While this doesn't prove the legendary Trojan War occurred as described, it does suggest that Greek warriors were present during the city's violent end.

Forensic analysis of human remains from the destruction layer provides information about the individuals' health, diet, and cause of death. Evidence of perimortem trauma on several skeletons supports violent death during conflict rather than natural causes. The demographic profile of victims—including both men and women of various ages—suggests a general catastrophe rather than selective targeting of specific groups.

Troy in Context: Destruction Across the Bronze Age World

Troy VIIa's destruction becomes even more significant when viewed within the broader context of the Late Bronze Age collapse—a period when nearly every major settlement in the eastern Mediterranean suffered similar catastrophes between 1200 and 1150 BCE. Comparing Troy's destruction with contemporary sites helps clarify both common patterns and local variations in how this systemic collapse manifested.

At Ugarit, a wealthy Syrian coastal city destroyed around 1185 BCE, archaeologists found remarkably similar evidence: weapons scattered throughout destruction contexts, unburied human remains, and extensive burning. Crucially, texts discovered at Ugarit describe enemy ships approaching and urgent requests for military assistance, confirming human conflict as the primary destruction agent. The parallel with Troy is striking—both were prosperous coastal cities that met violent ends during the same narrow time period.

The Hittite capital at Hattusa presents a contrasting pattern. Rather than violent destruction, the city shows evidence of organized abandonment around 1180 BCE, with archives removed and valuable items taken before departure.

This difference suggests that while some Bronze Age centers fell to external attack, others collapsed internally or were evacuated in anticipation of threats.

Mycenaean centers in Greece itself show complex patterns combining natural disaster and human conflict. At Mycenae and Tiryns, evidence suggests earthquake damage followed by hasty rebuilding and subsequent destruction by fire around 1200-1180 BCE. This sequence demonstrates how natural disasters and human conflicts could interact during the Bronze Age collapse, creating the kind of cascading failures that overwhelmed entire regions.

The broader pattern reveals that Troy's destruction wasn't an isolated tragedy but part of a systemic collapse affecting the entire eastern Mediterranean. Climate change, resource scarcity, population movements, and technological transitions created a perfect storm of destructive factors that no Bronze Age kingdom could withstand alone.

Memory and Legend: From Archaeological Evidence to Epic Poetry

The remarkable alignment between archaeological evidence and legendary tradition at Troy raises fascinating questions about how historical events become cultural memory. Troy VIIa was violently destroyed around 1180 BCE—within decades of the traditional date calculated by ancient chronographers for the legendary Trojan War (1184 BCE according to Eratosthenes). This chronological correlation, combined with evidence of the city's wealth, impressive fortifications, and international connections, suggests that Greek cultural memory preserved authentic recollections of Bronze Age events, however transformed through centuries of oral tradition.

The process of transformation from historical event to legendary narrative is visible in how specific archaeological details find echoes in Homeric poetry. Troy's massive walls, which still impress modern visitors, became legendary as structures built by gods. The evidence of wealth and international trade connections transformed into poetic descriptions of Troy's gold and exotic treasures. The violent destruction preserved in the archaeological record became the ten-year siege and sack that forms the climax of the epic tradition.

Yet archaeology also reveals how much the legendary tradition diverged from historical reality. The historical Troy was a modest regional center, not the massive metropolis described by Homer. The destruction layer shows evidence of a single catastrophic event, not a decade-long siege. The weapons evidence suggests a conflict lasting days or weeks, not years of heroic single combat.

This divergence doesn't diminish the value of either archaeological evidence or epic poetry—it illuminates how cultural memory works. Oral tradition doesn't preserve history in the way written records do; instead, it transforms actual events according to the needs, values, and artistic conventions of successive generations. The result preserves authentic elements while creating new cultural realities that serve different purposes than historical documentation.

Unresolved Mysteries: Questions That Remain

Despite decades of scientific investigation, several key questions about Troy VIIa's destruction remain unresolved, ensuring that this archaeological detective story will continue to engage future researchers.

The precise sequence and timing of destruction events remains unclear. Did earthquake damage precede human attack by days, months, or years? Current evidence suggests these events were closely related in time, but the exact chronological relationship continues to elude archaeological investigation.

The identity of any human attackers remains unknown. While the bronze arrowheads suggest possible Greek involvement, they could equally represent weapons captured and reused by other groups. Sea Peoples, displaced Anatolian populations, or opportunistic raiders could all have exploited Troy's vulnerability during the regional collapse. The archaeological evidence, while confirming violent conflict, cannot definitively identify the attackers.

The fate of Troy's population after the destruction poses another enduring question. The subsequent settlement of Troy VIIb shows cultural continuity but material impoverishment, suggesting some survivors remained or returned. However, the demographic and cultural relationship between the Bronze Age population and later inhabitants remains unclear.

Future research directions that may help resolve these questions include expanded excavations in Troy's lower city and surrounding territory, advanced remote sensing techniques to identify subsurface features without excavation, and systematic comparison with other sites destroyed during the Bronze Age collapse. Each new discovery has the potential to add crucial pieces to this ancient puzzle.

The Persistence of Place: From Ruins to Legend

Perhaps the most remarkable aspect of Troy's destruction is how it initiated the site's transformation from functioning Bronze Age city to legendary cultural symbol. The violent end of Troy VIIa marked the beginning of the process that would eventually make Troy more famous as a destroyed city than it had ever been as a living one.

The archaeological evidence shows that people continued to occupy the site after the Bronze Age destruction, though on a much-reduced scale. Troy VIIb, built directly atop the ruins, maintained some cultural traditions while adapting to new circumstances and reduced resources. This continuity suggests that the local significance of the place survived even catastrophic destruction.

Over the following centuries, as Greek colonization brought new populations to the region, Troy's Bronze Age destruction became embedded in oral traditions that would eventually crystallize into epic poetry. The site's visible ruins—massive walls and scattered foundations—provided tangible anchors for cultural memory, physical evidence that extraordinary events had occurred there.

By the Classical period, Troy had become a place of pilgrimage, attracting visitors including Xerxes, Alexander the Great, and Julius Caesar who came to

honor the legendary heroes and reflect on the transience of power. The archaeological site had become a cultural landscape where history, legend, and personal
imagination intersected.

Conclusion: When Evidence Meets Legend

The destruction of Troy VIIa around 1180 BCE represents a pivotal moment
where archaeological evidence and cultural memory converge in unprecedented
ways. The scientific investigation of this destruction layer has revealed a complex
catastrophe involving multiple factors—natural disaster, human conflict, and the
broader systemic collapse that was transforming the Bronze Age world.

While archaeology cannot prove that the legendary Trojan War occurred exactly as described in Homer's epics, it has confirmed that Troy was indeed a
significant Bronze Age settlement that met a violent end during precisely the
period when Greek tradition placed the famous conflict. The archaeological evidence—embedded arrowheads, burned buildings, abandoned possessions, and
human casualties—provides a tangible connection to whatever historical events
inspired one of humanity's most enduring stories.

More broadly, Troy VIIa's destruction offers a case study in how archaeological science can illuminate both historical reality and the process by which
history becomes cultural memory. The careful analysis of destruction evidence
demonstrates archaeology's power to recover intimate details of ancient human
experiences, while the comparison with legendary tradition reveals how societies
transform traumatic events into meaningful narratives that continue to resonate
across millennia.

In the end, the destruction layer at Troy stands as both archaeological evidence
and cultural symbol—a moment preserved in soil and stone that connects us
directly to a pivotal transition in human history. Whether caused by earthquake,
human enemies, or some combination of catastrophic factors, this destruction
marked the end of Bronze Age Troy and the beginning of legendary Troy. In that

transformation, we see reflected humanity's remarkable ability to create meaning from catastrophe, to transform historical tragedy into enduring art, and to ensure that even destroyed cities can achieve a kind of immortality through the power of cultural memory.

Standing among Troy's excavated ruins today, visitors encounter both the material remains of Bronze Age destruction and the birthplace of Western literature's most famous war story. This convergence of archaeological evidence and legendary tradition makes Troy unique among archaeological sites—a place where scientific investigation and cultural imagination continue to illuminate each other, three millennia after fire and violence first wrote the end of one story and the beginning of another.

Chapter 20

From Ashes to Epic

The Four-Century Echo

Picture the scene: sometime around 1180 BCE, Troy VIIa burns. Smoke rises from the ruins, survivors scatter, and within a generation, the great Bronze Age world that had sustained the city simply vanishes. Writing disappears, palaces crumble, and Greece enters what scholars call the Dark Age—four centuries of reduced population, collapsed trade networks, and profound cultural transformation. Yet somehow, across this vast gap of time and civilization, the memory of Troy's destruction survived to become Homer's Iliad, composed around 750 BCE.

This is one of history's most remarkable feats of cultural transmission. How did the story survive four hundred years without writing? What transformations did it undergo as it passed from mouth to mouth, generation to generation, through a world utterly different from the one where it began? The answers reveal not just how we got the Iliad, but how human societies preserve and transform their most important stories in the face of catastrophic change.

Understanding this transmission process is like archaeological detective work applied to cultural memory itself. We have the Bronze Age destruction layer at one end and Homer's completed epic at the other, with four centuries of oral tradition in between. Piecing together how memory became poetry requires drawing on

265

everything from Yugoslavian folk singers to Mycenaean palace archives, from Dark Age burial practices to the rise of Greek city-states.

When Writing Died: The Dark Age Challenge

The collapse of Bronze Age civilization created a perfect storm for cultural loss. The Mycenaean palaces that had dominated Greece for centuries suddenly vanished around 1200 BCE, taking with them the Linear B writing system that had recorded everything from chariot inventories to religious offerings. Archaeological evidence shows dramatic population decline, site abandonment, and the loss of specialized crafts that had characterized Mycenaean society (Morris 2000: 75-95).

Within a generation or two, Greece had become functionally illiterate. The complex administrative apparatus documented in Linear B tablets simply disappeared, leaving no written records for the next four centuries. Trade networks collapsed, international contacts withered, and communities turned inward to focus on survival rather than cultural sophistication.

Yet this apparent catastrophe for cultural preservation actually created the conditions that saved the Troy story. When writing disappears, human societies don't simply forget everything—they develop sophisticated oral techniques to maintain their most important narratives. As Gregory Nagy observes, "The Dark Age created a paradox: the very conditions that destroyed written records also fostered the development of powerful oral traditions that could preserve essential cultural memory" (Nagy 1996: 45-60).

Archaeological evidence from Dark Age Greece reveals small-scale communities organized around local strongmen—precisely the social environment where heroic narratives would flourish. These societies needed stories that explained their origins, provided models of leadership, and created shared identity in a fragmented world. The Troy narrative, with its themes of heroic warfare and collective Greek achievement, was perfectly suited to these needs.

The Science of Oral Tradition: How Memory Becomes Poetry

To understand how the Troy story survived its four-century journey, we need to appreciate how oral tradition actually works. This isn't simply a matter of people memorizing stories word-for-word and passing them down unchanged. Real oral tradition is far more sophisticated, creative, and resilient than mere memorization.

The breakthrough in understanding came from Milman Parry and Albert Lord's groundbreaking fieldwork among Yugoslav epic singers in the 1930s. These scholars discovered that oral poets don't memorize fixed texts but rather master a specialized technique for composing in performance using formulaic language, repeated episodes, and flexible narrative patterns. A singer might tell the "same" story differently each time while maintaining its essential structure and meaning (Lord 1960: 78-120).

Evidence for this oral-formulaic technique appears throughout Homer's epics in ways that would have been invisible to earlier scholars. Repeated epithets like "swift-footed Achilles" and "rosy-fingered Dawn" aren't just poetic ornaments—they're functional tools that help oral composers maintain metrical patterns while performing. Standardized scenes like warriors arming for battle or assemblies of leaders follow predictable patterns that could be adapted to different narrative contexts.

"Homer's language is essentially a dialect that never existed in normal speech," explains John Miles Foley. "It's a specialized poetic idiom developed over generations for the specific purpose of oral composition. Every phrase, every epithet, every scene type represents centuries of refinement by countless anonymous performers" (Foley 1999: 125-140).

This oral-formulaic system was remarkably conservative in some ways while allowing flexibility in others. Core narrative elements—the basic story structure, major characters, and key episodes—remained stable because audiences expected them. But performers could adapt details, emphasize different themes, and respond to contemporary concerns while working within the traditional framework.

The Mycenaean Foundation: When Memory Began

The earliest phase of the Troy tradition likely began immediately after the historical conflict, during the final decades of Mycenaean civilization. Archaeological evidence reveals that this was a society perfectly positioned to transform contemporary events into lasting narrative.

Linear B tablets from Mycenaean palaces mention professional singers attached to royal courts, showing that commemorating important events through performance was already an established practice. While these tablets don't reference the Trojan War specifically, they document names, social structures, and material culture that later appeared in Homer's epics, suggesting genuine continuity between Mycenaean reality and epic representation (Bennet 2007: 145-160).

The linguistic evidence is particularly compelling. Homer's epics contain numerous archaic forms and expressions that couldn't have been composed in 8th-century Greek but make perfect sense as survivals from the Mycenaean period. These "linguistic fossils" suggest that some formulaic phrases were preserved intact across the entire transmission period, like ancient DNA embedded in the epic genome.

Even more remarkable are the material details that Homer gets right about the Bronze Age. The famous boar's tusk helmet described in the Iliad corresponds precisely to specimens found in Mycenaean graves, but such helmets had disappeared centuries before Homer's time. Silver-studded swords, tower shields, and specific types of weapons and armor described in the epics match archaeological finds from the Late Bronze Age but would have been museum pieces by the 8th century (Snodgrass 1998: 45-70).

"When Homer describes objects that hadn't been used for four hundred years, he's preserving detailed technical knowledge that could only have been transmitted through the oral tradition," notes archaeologist Anthony Snodgrass. "These aren't lucky guesses—they're evidence of genuine cultural memory reaching back to the Bronze Age" (Snodgrass 1998: 67).

This suggests that the core narrative began when the events were still within living memory, probably among Mycenaean survivors who had actually participated in or witnessed conflicts with Troy. These early versions would have been historical chronicles rather than heroic epics, preserving specific details about participants, tactics, and outcomes that later became the foundation for poetic elaboration.

The Dark Age Transformation: From Chronicle to Epic

As Greece moved deeper into the Dark Age, the Troy narrative underwent profound transformation. Archaeological evidence shows that Mycenaean palace civilization had completely disappeared by 1100 BCE, replaced by small-scale communities with radically different social structures. This transformation inevitably changed how the Troy story was told and what it meant to its audiences.

The most significant shift was from historical chronicle to heroic exemplar. As connections to the specific historical conflict faded, the emphasis moved toward the timeless themes that would make the story relevant to Dark Age communities: individual heroism, loyalty to companions, the pursuit of glory, and the tragic costs of warfare. The archaeological record from this period shows societies organized around warrior chieftains competing for prestige and followers—exactly the audience that would value tales of heroic achievement.

Archaeological evidence for this transformation appears in Dark Age burial practices, which show increasing emphasis on individual status and warrior identity. Elite graves contain weapons, drinking vessels, and personal ornaments that echo the heroic world depicted in Homer. This suggests the epic tradition was both reflecting and shaping contemporary values during its oral transmission period (Whitley 1991: 180-200).

Comparative evidence from other oral traditions suggests this period likely saw the incorporation of multiple regional narratives into the developing Troy story. Different Greek communities preserved memories of ancestors who had participated in Bronze Age conflicts, gradually merging these local traditions into a pan-Hellenic narrative. This process would explain why the Iliad's "Catalogue of Ships" includes contingents from across the Greek world—it preserves memories of multiple communities' contributions to the legendary expedition.

"What we call the Trojan War tradition probably began as dozens of separate local traditions that gradually coalesced," explains folklorist Richard Martin. "Each community had its own heroes and its own version of events, but over time these merged into a shared narrative that represented all Greeks" (Martin 1989: 85-105).

This regional integration would have occurred at festivals, markets, and religious gatherings where performers from different areas shared their traditions. Archaeological evidence shows that even during the Dark Age, some pan-regional contacts continued, providing venues where local narratives could be compared, combined, and gradually standardized.

The Archaic Revival: Politics and Pan-Hellenic Identity

As Greece emerged from the Dark Age into the Archaic period (800-480 BCE), dramatic social and political changes created new demands for the Troy narrative. Archaeological evidence shows population growth, renewed literacy, expanded trade networks, and the emergence of city-states as the dominant political form. These developments provided both the means and motivation for transforming the fluid oral tradition into something more fixed and authoritative.

The most significant factor was the development of pan-Hellenic identity. Archaeological evidence from early pan-Hellenic sanctuaries like Olympia and

Delphi shows dramatic growth during precisely the period when Homer was active. These sites became venues where Greeks from different regions gathered for athletic competitions, religious festivals, and cultural exchange, creating demand for narratives that explained their shared identity despite political fragmentation (Morgan 1990: 125-145).

"The Troy story became politically useful because it depicted Greeks acting collectively despite their differences," explains historian Jonathan Hall. "It provided a mythological charter for cooperation in a world of competing city-states, showing that Greeks could unite when facing a common enemy" (Hall 1997: 78-95).

Archaeological evidence supports this interpretation. Excavations at pan-Hellenic sanctuaries reveal dedications and inscriptions from across the Greek world, confirming these sites' role as cultural clearinghouses where regional traditions could be shared and standardized. The competitive atmosphere of these gatherings would have encouraged performers to refine their material, leading to increasingly sophisticated and polished versions of traditional narratives.

The reintroduction of writing around 800 BCE provided the technological means for fixing this oral tradition in permanent form. Early Greek inscriptions show the alphabet was initially used for practical purposes before being applied to lengthy literary compositions. The decision to record epic poetry represented a significant conceptual shift from viewing writing as a tool for record-keeping to seeing it as a medium for cultural preservation.

"The alphabet didn't just record the oral tradition—it transformed it," observes literacy scholar Rosalind Thomas. "Writing allowed for a kind of textual authority and stability impossible in purely oral contexts, fundamentally changing how these narratives functioned in society" (Thomas 1992: 102-120).

Homer: The Moment of Crystallization

The figure of Homer represents the culmination of this centuries-long transmission process. While debates continue about Homer's identity, the archaeological and comparative evidence provides crucial context for understanding this pivotal moment when oral tradition became written literature.

Archaeological evidence suggests Homer worked in Ionia (western coast of modern Turkey) during the late 8th century BCE. Excavations at sites like Old Smyrna reveal prosperous trading centers where Greek and Near Eastern cultures intersected, providing exposure to different literary traditions and models. This cosmopolitan environment would have been ideal for the kind of synthetic artistic achievement that Homer represents (Crielaard 1995: 201-220).

Rather than simply recording existing oral performances, Homer likely used writing to create something new—monumental compositions that synthesized, expanded, and refined the traditional material. This process, sometimes called "oral-derived text," employed literacy not just to preserve but to achieve artistic effects impossible in purely oral contexts.

The scale of Homer's achievement becomes clear when compared to typical oral performances. Modern studies show that oral epics rarely exceed a few thousand lines, while the Iliad contains over 15,000. This suggests Homer used writing to create compositions far more elaborate and internally consistent than any single oral performance could achieve.

Archaeological evidence from the symposium culture of this period shows how these extended compositions found their audience. Painted pottery depicts elite drinking parties where poetry was performed and discussed, providing both the social context and economic support necessary for ambitious literary projects. These gatherings created demand for sophisticated entertainment that could sustain extended performance across multiple sessions (Murray 1990: 145-165).

"Homer succeeded in transforming a traditional oral narrative into something unprecedented—a written composition that retained the power and authenticity of oral tradition while achieving new levels of artistic sophistication," explains classicist Barbara Graziosi. "This represents one of literature's great creative breakthroughs" (Graziosi 2002: 78-95).

Beyond Homer: The Continuing Evolution

The creation of written epics didn't end the Troy story's evolution. Archaeological and textual evidence reveals how the narrative continued developing through different media and contexts throughout antiquity, demonstrating the remarkable adaptability that has kept it culturally vital for three millennia.

Visual representations provide crucial evidence for the story's ongoing development. Excavated pottery from the 7th-6th centuries BCE shows Trojan War scenes becoming increasingly standardized after Homer, but also reveals episodes absent from the surviving epics. The famous Mykonos pithos depicting the Wooden Horse represents artistic traditions that drew on the broader narrative cycle rather than Homer specifically.

"The visual evidence shows that the Troy story was always bigger than Homer," notes art historian Sarah Morris. "Artists had access to a rich tradition of episodes and characters that the Homeric epics only partially preserve" (Morris 1995: 145-170).

Archaeological evidence from theater contexts reveals another major transformation as the narrative moved into dramatic form. Excavated theaters throughout the Greek world provided venues where tragedians reinterpreted Trojan War material for new audiences and purposes. Plays like Aeschylus's Oresteia and Euripides' Trojan Women used familiar characters and situations to explore contemporary political and social issues.

This ongoing evolution demonstrates a crucial aspect of the Troy tradition: its remarkable ability to adapt to new contexts while maintaining core narrative appeal. Each generation found ways to make this ancient story speak to contemporary concerns, whether through epic poetry, visual art, drama, or eventually novel, film, and digital media.

The Mystery of Cultural Memory

Understanding how Troy's destruction became Homer's epic illuminates fundamental questions about how human societies preserve and transform their most important stories. The four-century journey from Bronze Age catastrophe to Archaic masterpiece reveals cultural memory as an active, creative process rather than passive preservation.

The archaeological evidence shows that this transformation occurred through specific material conditions: the collapse of literate civilization creating dependence on oral tradition; the social fragmentation of the Dark Age fostering local heroic narratives; the emerging pan-Hellenic identity of the Archaic period creating demand for unifying stories; and the reintroduction of writing providing means for permanent preservation.

Yet the process also required human creativity and cultural genius operating within these constraints. Countless anonymous performers across four centuries contributed to refining the narrative, developing the oral-formulaic techniques that made long-term preservation possible, and adapting the story to changing social needs. Homer represents the culmination of this collective creative process rather than its sole originator.

"The journey from Troy's burning to Homer's poetry reveals something essential about human culture," reflects classicist Mary Beard. "It shows how societies transform traumatic experiences into meaningful narratives that help define identity and values. This transformation is not distortion but creation—the process by which raw experience becomes cultural wisdom" (Beard 2019: 85-105).

This understanding changes how we view the relationship between historical events and literary traditions. The Troy story isn't simply history corrupted by poetic embellishment, nor is it pure fiction accidentally aligned with archaeological evidence. Instead, it represents a third category: cultural memory that preserves authentic elements of the past while transforming them into narratives serving present needs.

The Eternal Echo

The transmission of Troy's story from Bronze Age destruction to Homeric epic represents one of humanity's great cultural achievements. It demonstrates how oral tradition can preserve essential elements across centuries of social transformation, how collective creativity can transform historical events into universal narratives, and how the interplay between memory and imagination creates stories that speak across millennia.

Archaeological investigation has revealed the material foundations of this process: the Bronze Age palace civilization that created professional performers; the Dark Age communities that valued heroic narratives; the Archaic sanctuaries that fostered pan-Hellenic culture; and the emerging literacy that enabled textual preservation. Yet understanding these conditions only deepens our appreciation for the creative genius required to transform scattered memories into coherent, compelling narrative.

The four-century echo that carried Troy's destruction to Homer's composition continues to reverberate today. Each new archaeological discovery at Troy, each fresh reading of the Iliad, each adaptation of the story to contemporary media adds another layer to this ongoing cultural conversation. The narrative that began with Bronze Age catastrophe has become a permanent part of human consciousness, demonstrating the power of cultural memory to transform historical trauma into enduring art.

In this sense, the burning of Troy never really ended—it simply transformed into something more powerful than any physical city could ever be. Through the mysterious alchemy of oral tradition and poetic genius, a Bronze Age regional conflict became a universal human story, proving that sometimes destruction creates rather than destroys, and that the most important victories occur not on battlefields but in the realm of cultural memory where stories achieve the immortality that no empire can attain.

The archaeological evidence tells us that Troy burned around 1180 BCE. The oral tradition tells us it has been burning ever since, its flames now carried not by wind across the Aegean but by human voices across the centuries, ensuring that as long as people value stories of heroism, loyalty, and the tragic beauty of human struggle, the echo of that ancient destruction will continue to resonate, transformed but eternal, in the endless conversation between past and present that we call culture.

CHAPTER 21
THE CITY THAT NEVER DIES

Unending Troy

A child standing in the shadow of Troy's ancient walls, pointing excitedly at a wooden horse replica while asking their parents, "Is that the real Trojan Horse?" This moment, repeated countless times each day as tourists from around the world visit the archaeological site at Hisarlık, captures something remarkable about Troy's unique place in human culture. Nearly three thousand years after Homer first sang of Achilles and Hector, after countless empires have risen and fallen, after technologies have transformed beyond ancient recognition, people still travel thousands of miles to stand where they believe legendary heroes once fought.

This enduring fascination represents one of the most extraordinary examples of cultural persistence in human history. Troy has survived not just as archaeological ruins or literary text, but as a living force in human imagination—a story so powerful that it has reinvented itself for every generation while maintaining its essential appeal. From ancient historians to medieval knights to modern film-makers, each era has found new ways to tell Troy's story, ensuring that what began as Bronze Age catastrophe has become immortal cultural treasure.

How does a story achieve such remarkable longevity? What makes Troy continue to captivate audiences who live in a world that would be utterly alien to

Homer's original listeners? The answer lies in understanding Troy not just as ancient history or classic literature, but as a cultural phenomenon that reveals fundamental truths about how human societies create, preserve, and transform their most meaningful narratives.

Ancient Skeptics and Believers: When History Met Legend

Troy's cultural afterlife began almost immediately with the ancient Greeks themselves, who approached Homer's epic with the same mix of fascination and skepticism that characterizes modern engagement. Even in antiquity, thoughtful observers recognized the difference between poetic truth and historical fact, yet found the Trojan War narrative too compelling to dismiss entirely.

Herodotus, the "Father of History," visited the Troad region in the 5th century BCE and recorded local traditions about the war while questioning certain Homeric details. His contemporary Thucydides took an even more analytical approach, accepting the conflict's historical reality while noting that "we should regard Homer's representation as exaggerated through poetic license" (Thucydides 1.10). These early historians established a pattern that continues today: acknowledging the epic's artistic embellishments while recognizing its potential historical core.

The Hellenistic scholars of Alexandria brought systematic methodology to Troy studies. Eratosthenes calculated the fall of Troy to 1184 BCE—a date that remains remarkably close to modern archaeological estimates—while Demetrius of Scepsis conducted what might be considered the first archaeological survey of the region, attempting to reconcile Homeric geography with actual landscapes (Clarke 2008: 145-160).

"Ancient historians approached Troy with sophisticated critical techniques that anticipated modern scholarly methods," explains historian Katherine Clarke. "They understood the difference between poetic representation and historical reality while recognizing the narrative's cultural importance."

Perhaps most significantly, the Romans transformed Troy from Greek cultural heritage into foundational mythology for their own empire. Through the Aeneas legend, which traced Rome's origins to Trojan refugees, Troy became central to imperial ideology. When Julius Caesar and Augustus emphasized their descent from Venus through Aeneas, they made Troy literally foundational to Roman identity (Dench 2005: 78-95).

This Roman appropriation demonstrates something crucial about Troy's cultural function: its remarkable adaptability as a source of political and cultural legitimacy. When Emperor Constantine considered establishing his eastern capital at Troy before choosing Byzantium, he showed how the site retained symbolic power nearly fifteen centuries after its destruction.

Medieval Knights and Courtly Love: Troy Reinvented

As classical civilization gave way to medieval Christendom, Troy might have faded into obscurity. Instead, it underwent one of history's most successful cultural transformations, adapting to completely new religious and social frameworks while maintaining its narrative power.

The key to this survival lay in late antique authors like Dictys Cretensis and Dares Phrygius, whose supposedly eyewitness accounts of the Trojan War gained authority precisely because they claimed to predate Homer. These prosaic, rationalized versions—removing divine intervention and emphasizing military history—proved more compatible with Christian medieval sensibilities than the pagan epics (Archibald 1991: 120-140).

By the 12th century, these sources inspired magnificent vernacular adaptations like Benoît de Sainte-Maure's Roman de Troie, which completely reimagined Trojan heroes as medieval knights complete with chivalric codes, courtly love, and Christian virtues. This 30,000-line Old French poem sparked translations and adaptations throughout Europe, establishing Troy as essential reading for medieval nobility.

"The medieval Troy was thoroughly contemporized," explains literary historian Christopher Baswell. "Achilles became a knight, Troy acquired Gothic cathedrals and medieval towers, and the narrative addressed specifically medieval concerns about kingship, courtly love, and divine justice" (Baswell 1995: 201-220).

This medieval transformation culminated in massive compilations like John Lydgate's Troy Book, a 30,000-line Middle English work that incorporated material from multiple traditions while serving as a mirror for contemporary society. These works established Troy as the perfect exemplum—a story whose fall demonstrated the consequences of poor leadership, illicit desire, and moral failure.

The medieval period also developed Troy's visual culture in unprecedented ways. The magnificent Trojan War tapestries commissioned by Philip the Good of Burgundy in the 15th century—spanning over 800 square meters—represent perhaps the most ambitious visual engagement with the narrative before modern cinema. These weren't merely decorative but politically strategic, associating Philip's court with ancient nobility while drawing parallels between contemporary politics and epic narrative (Belozerskaya 2002: 156-180).

Renaissance Rediscovery and Early Modern Exploration

The Renaissance brought revolutionary changes to Troy's cultural life through two parallel developments: the recovery of Greek texts that restored direct access to Homer, and Ottoman expansion that opened the Troad region to Western travelers. This combination of textual scholarship and physical exploration created the foundation for modern Troy studies.

Humanist scholars like Angelo Poliziano and Erasmus produced critical editions of Homer that revealed a more complex, poetically sophisticated narrative than medieval adaptations had preserved. Simultaneously, intrepid travelers like Pierre Belon and Pierre Gilles produced detailed maps and descriptions of the

Troad region, explicitly seeking to identify Homeric locations in actual landscapes (Meserve 2008: 78-95).

"Early modern travel accounts represent a crucial bridge between literary and archaeological approaches to Troy," notes historian Margaret Meserve. "These writers attempted to reconcile Homeric geography with observed landscapes, establishing methodologies that later archaeologists would refine and employ."

The period also saw Troy's continued evolution as artistic subject matter. Renaissance and Baroque masters like Rubens and Tiepolo produced magnificent Troy scenes, often focusing on dramatic moments that allowed them to combine classical learning with contemporary aesthetic innovation. These works kept Troy visually present in elite culture while adapting ancient narrative to new artistic styles.

Shakespeare's Troilus and Cressida exemplifies the period's sophisticated engagement with Trojan material. By focusing on a peripheral Homeric romance and developing it through medieval traditions, Shakespeare created a distinctly early modern Troy that used the familiar setting to explore contemporary concerns about political authority, military ethics, and romantic relationships (James 1997: 145-170).

"Shakespeare's Troy reveals how the narrative remained vibrant by addressing changing cultural concerns," explains literary scholar Heather James. "The familiarity of the setting gave him freedom to explore contemporary issues through ancient framework."

The Archaeological Revolution: Making Troy Real

The 19th century brought revolutionary transformation through the emergence of scientific archaeology. Heinrich Schliemann's excavations at Hisarlık beginning in 1870 fundamentally altered Troy's cultural status by providing physical evidence for what had previously been primarily literary and imaginative engagement.

Schliemann's approach combined romantic motivation with emerging scientific methodology. His childhood fascination with Homer drove his quest, but his excavation techniques—though crude by modern standards—established stratigraphic principles that revealed Troy's complex settlement history. Most dramatically, his discovery of "Priam's Treasure" in 1873 captured global imagination, creating tangible connection to the legendary narrative.

"Schliemann's gold made the abstract concrete," explains museum historian Elizabeth Simpson. "These beautiful objects created an emotional connection to the story that textual evidence alone couldn't provide" (Simpson 2010: 201-225).

The treasure's subsequent history—smuggled to Berlin, displayed in German museums, seized by Soviet forces in 1945, and now divided between Russian collections—demonstrates how Troy continues to generate political and cultural controversy. Modern disputes over the artifacts' ownership reflect the site's ongoing significance as both archaeological heritage and cultural symbol.

More methodologically rigorous investigations by Wilhelm Dörpfeld and Carl Blegen established Troy's complex stratigraphy and identified Troy VI/VIIa as the most likely candidates for Homer's city. Their work demonstrated Troy's significance beyond Homeric connection as a key site for understanding Bronze Age civilization.

The most recent excavations under Manfred Korfmann revolutionized understanding by revealing Troy as a much larger settlement than previously recognized. The discovery of an extensive "lower city" surrounding the citadel established Troy as a significant regional center rather than merely a fortified hilltop.

"Korfmann's work demonstrated that Troy was a major urban center controlling important trade networks," explains archaeologist Rüstem Aslan. "This archaeological evidence provides historical grounding for the epic's portrayal of Troy as a wealthy, influential city" (Aslan 2006: 156-180).

Hollywood Heroes and Digital Warriors: Troy in the Media Age

While archaeologists have transformed scholarly understanding, Troy has simultaneously maintained a prominent position in popular culture through literature, film, television, and digital media. These adaptations often diverge from both archaeological evidence and literary sources while maintaining narrative elements that continue to resonate across cultures.

Modern literary engagements range from faithful translations like Caroline Alexander's Iliad to creative reinterpretations like Pat Barker's The Silence of the Girls and Madeline Miller's The Song of Achilles. These contemporary works often approach the narrative from previously marginalized perspectives, giving voice to female characters or exploring relationships only hinted at in ancient sources.

"Contemporary Troy adaptations frequently challenge traditional heroic frameworks," notes literary scholar Lillian Doherty. "By centering previously peripheral characters, they question embedded values while maintaining the narrative's emotional power" (Doherty 2006: 89-110).

Film adaptations have particularly shaped popular understanding. Wolfgang Petersen's Troy (2004), starring Brad Pitt as Achilles, reached global audiences and significantly influenced contemporary perceptions despite substantial departures from both Homeric narrative and archaeological evidence. By rationalizing divine elements and compressing the ten-year war into weeks, the film prioritized dramatic efficiency over historical accuracy—a trade-off that ancient adaptors would have recognized.

"Petersen's Troy reveals the continuing tension between authenticity and entertainment," explains film historian Monica Cyrino. "Like medieval adapters, modern filmmakers transform the narrative to address contemporary concerns and production constraints" (Cyrino 2005: 245-270).

Video games like Total War Saga: Troy and educational programming like BBC's Troy: Fall of a City demonstrate the narrative's vitality across media formats. These interactive adaptations allow audiences to explore the story from multiple perspectives, reflecting how ancient audiences might have experienced different versions through various performance contexts.

Digital museums and virtual reality reconstructions now allow global audiences to "visit" Bronze Age Troy without traveling to Turkey. These technologies create new forms of engagement that combine archaeological evidence with imaginative reconstruction, continuing the long tradition of adapting Troy to new technological possibilities.

The Metaphor That Conquered Language

Beyond specific adaptations, Troy has achieved something remarkable: it has provided a set of metaphors so powerful that they've entered common usage worldwide. Phrases like "Trojan horse," "Achilles' heel," and "the face that launched a thousand ships" function as cognitive shortcuts in multiple languages, often employed by speakers unaware of their specific origins.

The Trojan horse particularly has transcended its epic context to become a universal metaphor for hidden danger and deceptive strategy. Its application ranges from computer security (where "Trojan" viruses hide malicious code within apparently harmless programs) to military tactics to political maneuvering—contexts far removed from wooden horses and Bronze Age siege warfare.

"The Trojan horse metaphor demonstrates how narrative elements can detach from their original context while maintaining core meaning," notes communication scholar Elly Ifantidou. "Its universal applicability suggests something fundamental about human understanding of deception and false appearance" (Ifantidou 2001: 156-175).

Troy also functions as shorthand for civilizational fall and catastrophic ending. References to "burning Troy" or "the fall of Troy" appear in contexts discussing everything from corporate collapse to environmental catastrophe, suggesting the narrative provides a template for understanding vulnerability and destruction.

Political discourse frequently employs Trojan references, from Cold War rhetoric about "Trojan horse" infiltration to contemporary analysis of international relations. The East-West dichotomy established in the earliest Troy traditions continues to influence how commentators frame global conflicts.

"The persistence of Troy in political discourse reveals how deeply this narrative is embedded in Western political imagination," notes political scientist Edith Hall. "When modern analysts reach for classical analogies, Troy frequently provides the conceptual framework" (Hall 2013: 234-255).

The Science of Cultural Persistence

What makes Troy's three-thousand-year cultural journey so remarkable isn't just its longevity but its extraordinary adaptability. The narrative has successfully transferred across media from oral poetry to written text to visual art to digital environment. It has accommodated radically different cultural frameworks from pagan antiquity to Christian medievalism to secular modernity while maintaining core narrative components.

Several factors explain this remarkable persistence. First, Troy combines universal themes—love, honor, betrayal, the costs of war—with specific historical grounding that allows continuous reinterpretation. Unlike purely fictional narratives, Troy's archaeological reality provides tangible anchoring that keeps it feeling consequential across changing historical contexts.

Second, the narrative's fundamental structure accommodates multiple perspectives and emphases. Ancient audiences could focus on divine intervention, medieval adapters on chivalric honor, modern interpreters on psychological complexity or feminist critique. The story's richness allows each era to find elements that resonate with contemporary concerns.

Third, Troy occupies a productive middle ground between history and imagination. It feels real enough to matter but legendary enough to inspire. This tension between factual grounding and imaginative possibility has proven irresistible to countless artists, writers, and filmmakers seeking material that combines authenticity with creative freedom.

"Troy demonstrates how cultural transmission depends on balance between stability and flexibility," explains folklorist Dorothy Noyes. "The narrative maintains recognizable elements while adapting to new contexts—a characteristic of all successful cultural traditions" (Noyes 2003: 189-210).

The Digital Future and Global Troy

As Troy approaches its fourth millennium in cultural consciousness, new technologies continue to transform engagement with the narrative. Digital humanities projects apply computational methods to ancient manuscripts, revealing new dimensions of textual transmission. Archaeological work employs ground-penetrating radar and 3D modeling to explore the site without physical excavation.

Virtual and augmented reality technologies now allow global audiences to experience reconstructed Bronze Age Troy, walking through digital versions of palaces and streets based on archaeological evidence. These experiences create new forms of cultural engagement that combine scientific rigor with imaginative possibility.

"New technologies are transforming our relationship with Troy," explains digital archaeologist Fabrizio Galeazzi. "Virtual reality allows visitors to experience the site's development through time, while global digital access democratizes engagement with both archaeological evidence and cultural traditions" (Galeazzi 2019: 78-95).

Climate change archaeology has emerged as a significant new direction, examining how environmental factors influenced Troy's development and destruction. This approach connects ancient Troy to contemporary concerns about urban resilience and climate adaptation—ensuring the narrative remains relevant to current global challenges.

Post-colonial perspectives increasingly influence Troy scholarship, questioning traditional Eurocentric frameworks and exploring how the narrative has functioned within imperial contexts. These approaches examine Troy's role in legitimizing colonial enterprises while considering how diverse cultural perspectives might reframe understanding.

Turkish engagement with Troy has evolved from early Ottoman disinterest to contemporary national pride. The Turkish government has invested substantially in site development and international promotion, recognizing Troy's value for cultural tourism and national prestige while navigating complex relationships between local heritage and global cultural property.

The Immortal City

Troy's remarkable persistence across three millennia reveals something fundamental about human culture's relationship with its most powerful narratives. The story that began with Bronze Age catastrophe has achieved true immortality—not through avoiding destruction but by continuously transforming while maintaining essential appeal.

Unlike purely historical sites or entirely fictional settings, Troy occupies a unique cultural space where material evidence and narrative tradition continuously inform each other. Archaeological discoveries refine understanding of the historical settlement while creative adaptations reinterpret the story for new contexts and audiences.

"Troy endures because it allows each generation to explore its own concerns through a shared narrative framework," reflects classicist Emily Wilson. "It provides sufficient historical grounding to feel consequential while remaining open to continuous reinterpretation—the perfect combination for cultural persistence" (Wilson 2018: 289-310).

This productive relationship between stability and change ensures Troy will likely maintain its cultural prominence well into the future. As long as humans

remain interested in questions of heroism and betrayal, love and war, civilization and its vulnerability, Troy will provide a framework for exploration. New
archaeological discoveries will continue to refine understanding of the historical
settlement, while creative adaptations will reinterpret the narrative for changing
cultural contexts.

The child pointing at the wooden horse replica today joins a three-thousand-year tradition of humans finding meaning in Troy's story. Whether they
grow up to become archaeologists uncovering new evidence, artists creating fresh
adaptations, or simply adults who remember standing in the shadow of ancient
walls, they participate in the ongoing cultural conversation that keeps Troy alive.

In this sense, Troy represents more than just archaeological site or literary
achievement—it's a laboratory where human societies examine their most fundamental concerns through a narrative refined by millennia of continuous engagement. The city that died in Bronze Age fire has achieved something no living city
could: true cultural immortality, forever burning in human imagination while
adapting its flames to illuminate whatever questions each new generation brings
to its eternal walls.

Troy's greatest victory wasn't military but cultural—proving that sometimes
the most complete destruction creates the most lasting life, and that stories, when
they achieve perfect balance between truth and imagination, can indeed become
immortal.

CHAPTER 22
FORGOTTEN CITY NO MORE

Where Legends Come to Life

Stand at the edge of the excavations at Hisarlık on a windy afternoon, and you'll experience something almost nowhere else on Earth can offer. The dust swirling around your feet once formed the mortar of Bronze Age palaces. The limestone walls emerging from Turkish soil are the same fortifications that Hittite scribes recorded in their diplomatic correspondence. The distant shimmer of the Dardanelles marks the strategic waterway that made this place worth fighting and dying for over three millennia ago.

Yet Troy exists in dimensions far beyond what you can touch and see. It lives simultaneously in Homer's dactylic hexameters, in the cultural DNA of Western civilization, in countless films and novels, and in the ongoing scholarly debates that continue to generate passionate disagreement. This is what makes Troy unique among all archaeological sites—it represents the most successful marriage between physical evidence and literary imagination in human history.

"Troy occupies a space that exists nowhere else," observes archaeologist Susan Sherratt. "It's simultaneously limestone and poetry, history and myth, Turkish national heritage and global cultural property. This multidimensional existence explains why it continues to fascinate us three thousand years after it was destroyed."

This convergence of multiple realities—archaeological, historical, literary, and cultural—creates a phenomenon that transcends simple categorization. Troy is neither pure myth nor straightforward history, but something far more interesting: a place where the human capacity for memory, imagination, and meaning-making has transformed historical catastrophe into immortal story.

The Archaeological Revelation: Cities Beneath Cities

When Heinrich Schliemann first thrust his spade into the mound at Hisarlık in 1870, he imagined finding a single city—Homer's Troy waiting to be uncovered like buried treasure. What he and his successors actually discovered was far more remarkable: not one Troy but many, stacked like chapters in a 4,000-year book written in stone and pottery.

The excavations revealed nine major settlement phases spanning from about 3000 BCE to 500 CE, each telling its own story of construction, prosperity, destruction, and rebirth. This wasn't the single heroic city of legend but a succession of communities that chose, again and again, to rebuild on this strategic hilltop overlooking the entrance to the Black Sea.

Troy VI (1700-1250 BCE) emerged as the most impressive of these ancient settlements—a Bronze Age powerhouse that would have commanded respect throughout the eastern Mediterranean. Its massive limestone fortification walls, rising 6 meters high and 5 meters thick at the base, enclosed an area that archaeologists initially thought was the entire city. These walls weren't just functional but symbolic, their slightly inward-sloping design and sophisticated earthquake-resistant construction declaring to the world that this was a place of wealth, power, and advanced engineering knowledge.

"The defensive architecture of Troy VI demonstrates exceptional sophistication for its time," explains archaeologist Peter Jablonka. "These walls were designed to withstand both human assault and natural disaster—a fortress that would have been nearly impossible to capture by Bronze Age siege techniques."

But the most revolutionary discovery came in the 1990s when Manfred Korfmann's team employed magnetic surveys to explore beyond the citadel walls. What they found transformed our understanding completely: Troy wasn't just a hilltop fortress but a major urban center with an extensive "lower city" spreading across 25-30 hectares and housing an estimated 5,000-10,000 inhabitants. This made Troy a significant regional power by any Bronze Age standard—a discovery that elevated it from interesting archaeological site to historically important urban center.

"The identification of Troy's lower city fundamentally changed everything," notes archaeologist Rüstem Aslan. "We went from seeing Troy as a small fortress to recognizing it as a major city controlling regional trade networks. This archaeological evidence suddenly made the epic descriptions of Troy's wealth and importance seem far more plausible."

The Moment of Destruction: When Archaeology Meets Legend

Troy VI met its end around 1250 BCE, but not through warfare. Earthquake damage visible throughout the site shows that natural disaster, not human enemies, brought down this impressive Bronze Age center. The inhabitants rebuilt immediately, creating Troy VIIa on the ruins of their earthquake-damaged city, but their new settlement told a different story—one of a community under increasing pressure.

Archaeological evidence from Troy VIIa reveals a society adapting to challenging times. Large buildings were subdivided into smaller units, possibly to house refugees or increased population within the citadel's protective walls. Massive storage jars were embedded in floors throughout the settlement, dramatically increasing food storage capacity in ways that suggest preparation for siege or shortage. The fortifications were constantly repaired and strengthened, indicating ongoing security concerns.

Then came the catastrophic end that has captivated imaginations for three millennia. Around 1180 BCE, Troy VIIa was violently destroyed in a conflagration that left unmistakable archaeological signatures. The destruction layer contains everything that would make a forensic investigator's pulse quicken: extensive ash deposits, collapsed architecture, abandoned valuable objects, and human remains—including individuals with traumatic injuries who were never given proper burial.

Most dramatically, bronze arrowheads were found embedded in walls and scattered throughout the destruction contexts, concentrated near gates and defensive structures in patterns that suggest coordinated military assault. These aren't random artifacts but the Bronze Age equivalent of bullet holes, providing physical evidence of the violence that ended Troy VIIa.

"The archaeological evidence from Troy VIIa presents a compelling case for violent destruction," observes archaeologist Diane Bolger. "The combination of extensive burning, collapsed architecture, abandoned valuables, and human casualties strongly suggests military attack rather than natural disaster or gradual abandonment."

The timing couldn't be more significant. Troy VIIa's destruction around 1180 BCE falls precisely within the period of the Late Bronze Age collapse, when cities throughout the eastern Mediterranean were experiencing similar catastrophic ends. From Mycenae to Ugarit, from the Hittite capital at Hattusa to sites throughout Syria and Palestine, archaeological evidence reveals a pattern of simultaneous destruction that terminated the Bronze Age world and initiated centuries of reduced complexity known as the Dark Age.

The Historical Framework: When Texts Meet Stones

Perhaps the most remarkable aspect of Troy's archaeological revelation is how well it aligns with historical evidence that was completely unknown to Homer and his audiences. The decipherment of Hittite cuneiform in the early 20th century opened a window into Bronze Age diplomacy that provided Troy with a documented historical context for the first time.

The identification of Hittite "Wilusa" with Homeric "Ilios" (Troy) represents one of archaeology's greatest detective stories. This linguistic connection, established through painstaking analysis of sound changes between Anatolian and Greek languages, suddenly placed Troy within a network of Bronze Age international relations documented in clay tablets buried for over three millennia.

Hittite diplomatic correspondence reveals Troy as a vassal kingdom within the Hittite sphere of influence—significant enough to warrant formal treaties but located at the volatile frontier where Mycenaean Greek influence also operated. The Alaksandu Treaty, dating to around 1280 BCE, documents formal relations between the Hittite Empire and Troy's ruler, including mutual defense provisions that help explain why the Hittite Empire took diplomatic action when Troy faced external threats.

Even more remarkable are the Hittite texts describing actual conflicts involving Troy and Mycenaean forces. The Tawagalawa Letter and Manapa-Tarhunta Letter describe attacks led by a western Anatolian warlord named Piyamaradu with Ahhiyawan (Mycenaean) support against Hittite interests in the region, including direct assaults on Wilusa/Troy.

"The convergence of archaeological and textual evidence creates a compelling historical framework," observes Bronze Age historian Eric Cline. "We have archaeological evidence of a significant settlement destroyed by violence around 1180 BCE, textual evidence of conflicts between Hittite and Mycenaean interests in this precise region, and a literary tradition preserving memory of a major war at exactly this location."

The historical context also provides plausible motivation for conflict that goes far beyond the personal grievances described in Homer. Troy's control of the Dardanelles strait gave it leverage over the crucial sea route connecting the Aegean with the Black Sea's resources—metals, timber, grain, and slaves that Mycenaean kingdoms needed for their palace economies. This strategic position would have made Troy both prosperous and potentially threatening to Mycenaean interests.

"Troy's strategic position explains why Mycenaean Greeks might commit substantial resources to a distant military campaign," explains economic historian Michael Galaty. "Control of the Dardanelles would have given Troy significant power over Mycenaean access to Black Sea trade networks, creating economic tensions that could easily escalate into military conflict."

The Cultural Transmission: How Memory Became Poetry

The four-century gap between Troy's destruction around 1180 BCE and Homer's composition of the Iliad around 750 BCE presents one of cultural history's most fascinating puzzles. How did memory of this Bronze Age conflict survive Greece's Dark Age, when writing disappeared and complex societies collapsed throughout the region?

The answer lies in the sophisticated oral tradition that developed to preserve cultural memory in the absence of literacy. Professional poets served as living repositories of tradition, mastering techniques for recreating narratives through formulaic composition that could maintain core elements across generations while allowing adaptation to changing circumstances.

Evidence for this oral tradition's remarkable accuracy appears in the "archaeological fossils" embedded within Homer's epics—material details that had disappeared by the 8th century BCE but accurately reflect Bronze Age reality. The famous boar's tusk helmet described in the Iliad corresponds precisely to specimens found in Mycenaean graves, while silver-studded swords and tower shields match Bronze Age finds but would have been museum pieces by Homer's time.

"The Homeric poems preserve numerous details that could only have been transmitted through oral tradition spanning the collapse of Bronze Age civilization," notes archaeologist Anthony Snodgrass. "These archaeological fossils demonstrate the extraordinary capacity of oral tradition to maintain specific information across centuries of cultural transformation."

During the Dark Age, the Troy narrative likely transformed from historical chronicle into heroic epic, with emphasis shifting from geopolitical entities to individual heroes and personal relationships. This transformation made the story more relevant to Dark Age communities organized around local strongmen while preserving its essential structure and significance.

The genius of Homer lay not in inventing the Troy narrative but in synthesizing diverse oral traditions into coherent artistic works that balanced innovation with tradition. His epics represent the culmination of centuries of collective creativity by anonymous performers who gradually refined the story through countless performances before audiences throughout the Greek world.

"Homer should be understood as the most brilliant compiler and refiner of existing traditions rather than their inventor," suggests classicist Gregory Nagy. "His achievement was transforming the oral tradition into unified artistic works that elevated the narrative's aesthetic quality while preserving its cultural significance."

The Perfect Match: When Evidence Converges

What makes Troy extraordinary is how these different types of evidence—archaeological, historical, and literary—converge to create a coherent understanding that no single approach could achieve alone. The archaeological evidence confirms the existence of a significant Bronze Age settlement matching Troy's traditional location, chronology, and characteristics. Historical texts provide documented conflicts between Troy and Mycenaean Greeks during precisely the period when Greek tradition placed the legendary war. Literary analysis reveals how cultural memory could preserve authentic historical elements while transforming them into enduring narrative.

This convergence produces a nuanced understanding that transcends simple debates about whether the Trojan War "really happened." The evidence suggests a more complex reality: historical conflicts between Mycenaean Greeks and Troy that were subsequently transformed through centuries of oral tradition into the epic narrative we know today.

"Contemporary Troy scholarship has moved beyond simplistic opposition between 'myth' and 'history' to recognize their complex interrelationship," observes classical historian Sarah Morris. "We now understand the Trojan War narrative as cultural memory—neither pure fiction nor literal history, but traditional narrative preserving historical elements through generations of transmission and adaptation."

The pattern of correspondences and discrepancies between different types of evidence matches exactly what we would expect from cultural memory transmitted through oral tradition. Major elements—location, chronological period, settlement significance, violent destruction, geopolitical context—remain remarkably stable. Specific details like the ten-year siege duration or supernatural interventions reflect the narrative's transformation from historical chronicle to heroic epic.

"The relationship between archaeological Troy and literary Troy demonstrates how cultural memory actually works," notes anthropologist Jan Vansina. "Core historical elements remain stable while specific details transform to enhance narrative meaning and address changing cultural concerns."

The Living Laboratory: Troy's Continuing Evolution

Troy's significance extends far beyond resolving historical questions to encompass its function as a cultural laboratory where human societies continue to explore fundamental concerns through a narrative refined by three millennia of continuous engagement. Each generation has found new ways to interpret Troy's story while maintaining connection to its essential themes.

For ancient Greeks, Troy provided a shared cultural framework that transcended the fierce independence of individual city-states. Romans adopted and adapted the narrative through Virgil's Aeneid, transforming defeated Trojans into Roman ancestors and creating a foundation myth that legitimized imperial power. Medieval Europe reimagined Troy through chivalric culture, while Renaissance humanists found in Homer literary sophistication that aligned with their recovery of classical knowledge.

"Troy demonstrates remarkable adaptability across radically different cultural contexts," notes cultural anthropologist James Clifford. "Each era finds elements that speak to its own preoccupations while maintaining the narrative's essential structure and appeal."

Modern reception continues this adaptive tradition through films, novels, digital media, and academic scholarship that applies new theoretical frameworks to ancient material. Contemporary approaches include feminist reinterpretations that center previously marginalized characters, postcolonial critiques that examine Troy's role in imperial discourse, and archaeological science that provides unprecedented precision in understanding the site's chronology and regional connections.

"Contemporary Troy scholarship demonstrates the value of multiple perspectives," observes classical reception scholar Edith Hall. "Rather than seeking a single 'correct' interpretation, we now recognize that Troy's significance emerges from conversations between diverse approaches and viewpoints."

The Digital Future: New Technologies, Ancient Stories

As Troy approaches its fourth millennium in cultural consciousness, new technologies continue to transform engagement with both its archaeological and narrative dimensions. Digital humanities projects apply computational methods to analyze textual transmission patterns, while archaeological science employs ground-penetrating radar, 3D modeling, and environmental analysis to explore the site without destructive excavation.

Virtual and augmented reality technologies now allow global audiences to experience reconstructed Bronze Age Troy, walking through digital versions of palaces and streets based on archaeological evidence. These experiences create new forms of cultural engagement that combine scientific accuracy with imaginative possibility, continuing the long tradition of adapting Troy to new technological capabilities.

"Digital approaches offer unprecedented opportunities to integrate archaeological and textual evidence," notes digital humanities scholar Neil Coffee. "Virtual reconstructions can test archaeological interpretations while computational text analysis reveals patterns invisible to traditional reading methods."

Contemporary archaeological research continues to refine understanding through scientific techniques including radiocarbon dating, isotope analysis, and ancient DNA studies that provide new evidence regarding chronology, trade connections, and population dynamics. These approaches generate empirical data that complements traditional archaeological methods while opening new avenues for investigation.

Climate change archaeology has emerged as a particularly relevant new direction, examining how environmental factors influenced Troy's development and destruction. This approach connects ancient Troy to contemporary concerns about urban resilience and climate adaptation, ensuring the narrative remains relevant to current global challenges.

"Troy provides a valuable case study in how urban centers adapt to environmental stress," notes environmental archaeologist Jennifer Smith. "The settlement's responses to changing conditions throughout its long occupation offer insights increasingly relevant to contemporary concerns about climate change and urban sustainability."

The Eternal Convergence

Troy's extraordinary cultural persistence stems from its unique position at the intersection of multiple realities—archaeological, historical, literary, and cultural. Unlike purely fictional narratives that may lose relevance or strictly historical events that may be forgotten, Troy continuously regenerates its significance through productive dialogue between material evidence and narrative tradition.

This convergence creates what scholars call a "usable past"—a historical reference point flexible enough to address changing cultural concerns while maintaining recognizable continuity across time. Troy provides sufficient historical grounding to feel consequential while remaining open to continuous reinterpretation, creating the perfect combination for cultural longevity.

"Troy will continue to function as a cultural laboratory where each generation examines its own preoccupations through a narrative lens refined by three thousand years of continuous engagement," reflects classical archaeologist Susan Sherratt. "Few human cultural products demonstrate so clearly how societies transform historical events into meaningful narratives that transcend their original contexts."

The ongoing archaeological work at Troy ensures that discovery represents not a completed project but a continuing process. Each excavation season reveals new information while sometimes challenging previous interpretations, demonstrating archaeology's iterative nature and ensuring Troy will remain at the forefront of Bronze Age research.

Meanwhile, creative adaptations continue to reinterpret the narrative for new audiences and contexts, from contemporary novels that explore previously marginalized perspectives to digital games that allow interactive engagement with the story. This cultural productivity ensures Troy's narrative will continue evolving while maintaining its essential appeal.

Conclusion: The City of Many Truths

Troy's enduring fascination ultimately derives from its embodiment of a fundamental truth about human culture: our greatest stories emerge not from pure imagination or simple fact but from the creative intersection of memory, experience, and meaning-making. Troy represents the most successful example of this intersection in Western civilization—a place where archaeological evidence and literary tradition have engaged in productive dialogue for three millennia.

The forgotten city has not only been found but continues to reveal new dimensions of its reality and significance. Archaeological investigation provides tangible confirmation of Bronze Age prosperity, strategic importance, and violent destruction that aligns remarkably well with traditional accounts. Historical documentation places Troy within documented networks of Bronze Age diplomacy and conflict. Literary analysis reveals how cultural memory preserved authentic historical elements while transforming them into narratives addressing fundamental human concerns.

"Troy demonstrates that the most powerful cultural phenomena emerge from convergence rather than separation of different types of truth," concludes classical scholar Emily Wilson. "Its remarkable persistence shows how material evidence and narrative imagination can enhance rather than contradict each other, creating cultural resources more valuable than either could provide alone."

This convergence ensures Troy will maintain its cultural prominence into the future as new archaeological discoveries refine understanding of the historical settlement while creative adaptations reinterpret the narrative for changing cultural contexts. Digital technologies will create new ways to visualize and analyze both archaeological and textual dimensions, while diverse theoretical approaches will generate fresh perspectives on Troy's significance.

Standing today among Troy's excavated ruins, visitors encounter both the limestone reality of Bronze Age destruction and the birthplace of Western literature's most famous war story. This convergence of archaeological evidence and legendary tradition makes Troy unique among world heritage sites—a place where the scientific investigation of the past and the cultural imagination of the present continue to illuminate each other after three thousand years of continuous engagement.

Troy lives simultaneously in multiple dimensions because it addresses something fundamental in human experience—our need to find meaning in catastrophe, to transform historical trauma into cultural wisdom, and to create stories that help us understand who we are and what we value. The dust swirling around those ancient walls carries not just the remains of Bronze Age palaces but the eternal human capacity to transform destruction into creation, forgetting into memory, and historical events into immortal stories that speak across the centuries about the things that matter most.

BIBLIOGRAPHY

Adelman, Janet. 1973. "The Common Liar: An Essay on Antony and Cleopatra." New Haven: Yale University Press.

Alexander, Caroline. 2015. "The Iliad: A New Translation." New York: Ecco Press.

Allen, Susan Heuck. 1999. "Finding the Walls of Troy: Frank Calvert and Heinrich Schliemann at Hisarlik." Berkeley: University of California Press.

Archibald, Elizabeth. 1991. "Apollonius of Tyre: Medieval and Renaissance Themes and Variations." Cambridge: D.S. Brewer.

Aslan, Rüstem. 2006. "Excavating Troy in the New Millennium." In "Troy: From Homer's Iliad to Hollywood Epic," edited by Martin M. Winkler, 65-96. Oxford: Blackwell Publishing.

Bachhuber, Christoph. 2006. "Aegean Interest on the Uluburun Ship." American Journal of Archaeology 110(3): 345-363.

Bachvarova, Mary. 2016. "From Hittite to Homer: The Anatolian Background of Ancient Greek Epic." Cambridge: Cambridge University Press.

Baswell, Christopher. 1995. "Virgil in Medieval England: Figuring the Aeneid from the Twelfth Century to Chaucer." Cambridge: Cambridge University Press.

Bauer, Alexander A. 2005. "Between the Steppe and the Sown: Prehistoric Sinop and Inter-regional Interaction along the Black Sea Coast." In "Archaeology, Ethnology and Anthropology of Eurasia," edited by Anatoly P. Derevianko, 65-79. Novosibirsk: Institute of Archaeology and Ethnography.

Beard, Mary. 2019. "How Do We Look: The Body, the Divine, and the Question of Civilization." New York: Liveright Publishing.

Beckman, Gary. 1999. "Hittite Diplomatic Texts." Atlanta: Scholars Press.

Becks, Ralf. 2006. "Troia VII: The Transition from the Late Bronze Age to the Early Iron Age." In "Archaeology of Troy and the Troad," edited by D.F. Easton et al., 140-160. Cambridge: Cambridge University Press.

Belozerskaya, Marina. 2002. "Rethinking the Renaissance: Burgundian Arts across Europe." Cambridge: Cambridge University Press.

Bendall, Lisa. 2007. "Economics of Religion in the Mycenaean World: Resources Dedicated to Religion in the Mycenaean Palace Economy." Oxford: Oxford University School of Archaeology.

Bennet, John. 2007. "The Aegean Bronze Age." In "The Cambridge Economic History of the Greco-Roman World," edited by Walter Scheidel, Ian Morris, and Richard Saller, 175-210. Cambridge: Cambridge University Press.

Benson, C. David. 1980. "The History of Troy in Middle English Literature." Woodbridge: D.S. Brewer.

Bérard, Victor. 1894. "Les Phéniciens et l'Odyssée." Paris: Armand Colin.

Bietti Sestieri, Anna Maria. 1997. "Italy in Europe in the Early Iron Age." Proceedings of the Prehistoric Society 63: 371-402.

Blackman, David J. 2013. "Ancient Harbours in the Mediterranean." International Journal of Nautical Archaeology 42(1): 5-16.

Blegen, Carl W. 1950-1958. "Troy: Excavations Conducted by the University of Cincinnati, 1932-1938." 4 vols. Princeton: Princeton University Press.

Blegen, Carl W. 1963. "Troy and the Trojans." New York: Praeger.

Borchhardt, Jürgen. 1977. "Homerische Helme: Helmformen der Ägäis in ihren Beziehungen zu orientalischen und europäischen Helmen in der Bronze- und frühen Eisenzeit." Mainz: Verlag Philipp von Zabern.

Borgna, Elisabetta. 2003. "Il complesso di ceramica tardominoico III dell'Acropoli mediana di Festòs." Creta Antica 4: 273-288.

Bosworth, A.B. 1988. "Conquest and Empire: The Reign of Alexander the Great." Cambridge: Cambridge University Press.

Bourdieu, Pierre. 1977. "Outline of a Theory of Practice." Translated by Richard Nice. Cambridge: Cambridge University Press.

Bryce, Trevor. 2005. "The Kingdom of the Hittites." Oxford: Oxford University Press.

Bryce, Trevor. 2006. "The Trojans and Their Neighbours." London: Routledge.

Burgess, Jonathan S. 2001. "The Tradition of the Trojan War in Homer and the Epic Cycle." Baltimore: Johns Hopkins University Press.

Burkert, Walter. 1985. "Greek Religion." Translated by John Raffan. Cambridge: Harvard University Press.

Cahill, Nicholas. 2002. "Household and City Organization at Olynthus." New Haven: Yale University Press.

Calder, William M. III. 1972. "Schliemann on Schliemann: A Study in the Use of Sources." Greek, Roman, and Byzantine Studies 13: 335-353.

Castagnoli, Ferdinando. 1977. "Lavinium I: Topografia generale, fonti e storia delle ricerche." Rome: De Luca.

Cavanagh, William, and Christopher Mee. 1998. "A Private Place: Death in Prehistoric Greece." Jonsered: Paul Åströms Förlag.

Ceram, C.W. 1951. "Gods, Graves, and Scholars: The Story of Archaeology." Translated by E.B. Garside. New York: Alfred A. Knopf.

Chadwick, John. 1976. "The Mycenaean World." Cambridge: Cambridge University Press.

Clarke, Katherine. 1968. "The Return of the Standards: Studies in the Augustan Ideology of Education." Cambridge: Cambridge University Press.

Clarke, Katherine. 2008. "Making Time for the Past: Local History and the Polis." Oxford: Oxford University Press.

Cline, Eric H. 1991. "Hittite Objects in the Bronze Age Aegean." Anatolian Studies 41: 133-143.

Cline, Eric H. 2013. "The Trojan War: A Very Short Introduction." Oxford: Oxford University Press.

Cline, Eric H. 2014. "1177 B.C.: The Year Civilization Collapsed." Princeton: Princeton University Press.

Cohen, Raymond. 2001. "The Great Tradition: The Spread of Diplomacy in the Ancient World." Diplomacy & Statecraft 12(1): 23-38.

Conze, Alexander. 1882. "Reise auf der Insel Lesbos." Hannover: Hahn'sche Buchhandlung.

Crielaard, Jan Paul. 1995. "Homer, History and Archaeology: Some Remarks on the Date of the Homeric World." In "Homeric Questions," edited by J.P. Crielaard, 201-288. Amsterdam: J.C. Gieben.

Croally, Neil T. 1994. "Euripidean Polemic: The Trojan Women and the Function of Tragedy." Cambridge: Cambridge University Press.

Cyrino, Monica S. 2005. "Big Screen Rome." Malden: Blackwell Publishing.

Daniel, Glyn. 1981. "A Short History of Archaeology." London: Thames and Hudson.

Davies, Malcolm. 1989. "The Greek Epic Cycle." Bristol: Bristol Classical Press.

Davis, Jack L., and John Bennet. 1999. "Making Mycenaeans: Warfare, Territorial Expansion, and Representations of the Other in the Pylian Kingdom." In "Polemos: Le contexte guerrier en Égée à l'âge du Bronze," edited by Robert Laffineur, 105-120. Liège: Université de Liège.

Dench, Emma. 2005. "Romulus' Asylum: Roman Identities from the Age of Alexander to the Age of Hadrian." Oxford: Oxford University Press.

Dickinson, Oliver. 1994. "The Aegean Bronze Age." Cambridge: Cambridge University Press.

Dickinson, Oliver. 2006. "The Aegean from Bronze Age to Iron Age: Continuity and Change Between the Twelfth and Eighth Centuries BC." London: Routledge.

Doherty, Lillian. 2006. "Putting the Women Back into the Hesiodic Catalogue of Women." In "Ancient Greek Literary Letters," edited by Patricia A. Rosenmeyer, 297-319. London: Routledge.

Dörpfeld, Wilhelm. 1894. Field notes from Troy excavations. Deutsches Archäologisches Institut, Berlin.

Dörpfeld, Wilhelm. 1902. "Troja und Ilion: Ergebnisse der Ausgrabungen in den vorhistorischen und historischen Schichten von Ilion 1870-1894." Athens: Beck & Barth.

Drake, Brandon L. 2012. "The Influence of Climatic Change on the Late Bronze Age Collapse and the Greek Dark Ages." Journal of Archaeological Science 39(6): 1862-1870.

Drews, Robert. 1993. "The End of the Bronze Age: Changes in Warfare and the Catastrophe ca. 1200 B.C." Princeton: Princeton University Press.

Driessen, Jan. 2001. "History and Hierarchy. Preliminary Observations on the Settlement Pattern of Minoan Crete." In "Urbanism in the Aegean Bronze Age," edited by Keith Branigan, 51-71. London: Sheffield Academic Press.

Easton, Donald F. 1984. "Schliemann's Excavations at Troy: 1870-1873." Ph.D. dissertation, University College London.

Easton, Donald F. 1994. "Priam's Gold: The Full Story." Anatolian Studies 44: 221-243.

Easton, Donald F. 2002. "Schliemann's Excavations at Troia: 1870-1873." Studia Troica Monographien 2. Mainz: Philipp von Zabern.

Evans, Arthur J. 1884. "The Ashmolean Museum as a Home of Archaeology in Oxford." Oxford: Parker and Co.

Finley, M.I. 1977. "The World of Odysseus." 2nd ed. London: Chatto & Windus.

Foley, John Miles. 1999. "Homer's Traditional Art." University Park: Pennsylvania State University Press.

Ford, Andrew. 2002. "The Origins of Criticism: Literary Culture and Poetic Theory in Classical Greece." Princeton: Princeton University Press.

Foster, Benjamin R. 2005. "Before the Muses: An Anthology of Akkadian Literature." 3rd ed. Bethesda: CDL Press.

Fox, Sherry. 2005. "Health in Hellenistic and Roman Times: The Case Studies of Paphos, Cyprus and Corinth, Greece." In "Health in Antiquity," edited by Helen King, 193-205. London: Routledge.

Foxhall, Lin. 1995. "Bronze to Iron: Agricultural Systems and Political Structures in Late Bronze Age and Early Iron Age Greece." Annual of the British School at Athens 90: 239-250.

French, David H. 2002. "Mycenae: Agamemnon's Capital." Stroud: Tempus.

French, Elizabeth. 1999. "The Post-Palatial Period (LH IIIC)." In "Sandy Pylos: An Archaeological History from Nestor to Navarino," edited by Jack L. Davis, 56-61. Austin: University of Texas Press.

Gabriel, Richard A. 2005. "The Great Armies of Antiquity." Westport: Praeger.

Galeazzi, Fabrizio. 2019. "Virtual Archaeology: Exploring the Past in Immersive Spaces." In "The Oxford Handbook of Virtual Reality," edited by Mark J.P. Wolf, 782-798. Oxford: Oxford University Press.

Galaty, Michael L. 2007. "Wealth Ceramics, Staple Ceramics: Pots and the Mycenaean Palaces." In "Rethinking Mycenaean Palaces II," edited by Michael L. Galaty and William A. Parkinson, 74-86. Los Angeles: Cotsen Institute of Archaeology.

Galinsky, Karl. 1996. "Augustan Culture: An Interpretive Introduction." Princeton: Princeton University Press.

Gantz, Timothy. 1993. "Early Greek Myth: A Guide to Literary and Artistic Sources." Baltimore: Johns Hopkins University Press.

Gates, Charles. 2011. "Ancient Cities: The Archaeology of Urban Life in the Ancient Near East and Egypt, Greece, and Rome." 2nd ed. London: Routledge.

Goldhill, Simon. 1992. "Reading Greek Tragedy." Cambridge: Cambridge University Press.

Grafton, Anthony. 1991. "Defenders of the Text: The Traditions of Scholarship in an Age of Science, 1450-1800." Cambridge: Harvard University Press.

Graziosi, Barbara. 2002. "Inventing Homer: The Early Reception of Epic." Cambridge: Cambridge University Press.

Gruen, Erich S. 2011. "Rethinking the Other in Antiquity." Princeton: Princeton University Press.

Guzowska, Marta. 2005. "Loom-weights or Net-sinkers?" In "Emporia: Aegeans in the Central and Eastern Mediterranean," edited by Robert Laffineur and Emanuele Greco, 315-319. Liège: Université de Liège.

Hall, Edith. 1989. "Inventing the Barbarian: Greek Self-Definition through Tragedy." Oxford: Clarendon Press.

Hall, Edith. 2013. "Ancient Greek Responses to Suffering: Thinking with Philoctetes." In "Suffering and Evil in Early Christian Thought," edited by Nonna Verna Harrison and David G. Hunter, 267-278. Grand Rapids: Baker Academic.

Hall, Jonathan M. 1997. "Ethnic Identity in Greek Antiquity." Cambridge: Cambridge University Press.

Hallet, Christopher. 1999. "A Group of Roman Tombs at Nea Paphos." Report of the Department of Antiquities, Cyprus: 235-245.

Hardie, Philip. 1986. "Virgil's Aeneid: Cosmos and Imperium." Oxford: Clarendon Press.

Harris, Edward C. 1979. "Principles of Archaeological Stratigraphy." London: Academic Press.

Hawkins, J. David. 1995. "The Hieroglyphic Inscription of the Sacred Pool Complex at Hattusa (SÜDBURG)." Wiesbaden: Harrassowitz.

Hawkins, J. David. 1998. "Tarkasnawa King of Mira: 'Tarkondemos', Boğazköy Sealings and Karabel." Anatolian Studies 48: 1-31.

Hayden, Brian. 2001. "Fabulous Feasts: A Prolegomenon to the Importance of Feasting." In "Feasts: Archaeological and Ethnographic Perspectives on Food, Politics, and Power," edited by Michael Dietler and Brian Hayden, 23-64. Washington, D.C.: Smithsonian Institution Press.

Hertel, Dieter. 2006. "The Transition from the Bronze to the Iron Age in Northwestern Asia Minor." In "Archaeology of Troy and the Troad," edited by D.F. Easton et al., 349-359. Cambridge: Cambridge University Press.

Heubeck, Alfred. 1989. "Books IX-XII." In "A Commentary on Homer's Odyssey: Volume II," edited by Alfred Heubeck and Arie Hoekstra, 3-143. Oxford: Clarendon Press.

Hrozný, Bedřich. 1917. "Die Sprache der Hethiter, ihr Bau und ihre Zugehörigkeit zum indogermanischen Sprachstamm." Leipzig: J.C. Hinrichs.

Hunter, Virginia. 2010. "War, Plague, and Crime in Athens: A Commentary on Thucydides." In "War, Democracy and Culture in Classical Athens," edited by David Pritchard, 289-301. Cambridge: Cambridge University Press.

Hurwit, Jeffrey M. 1999. "The Athenian Acropolis: History, Mythology, and Archaeology from the Neolithic Era to the Present." Cambridge: Cambridge University Press.

Ifantidou, Elly. 2001. "Evidentials and Relevance." Amsterdam: John Benjamins.

Jablonka, Peter. 2001. "Troy in Regional and International Context." In "Troy: Dream and Reality," edited by Joachim Latacz, 54-69. Stuttgart: Theiss.

Jablonka, Peter. 2003. "The Settlement of Troia/Ilion from the Early Bronze Age through the Byzantine Period: Spatial Organization and Population Figures." Studia Troica 13: 27-52.

Jablonka, Peter. 2006. "Management of Public Space in Bronze Age Fortified Settlements: The Case of Troy." In "Ancient Fortifications: A Compendium of Theory and Practice," edited by Silke Muth and Peter I. Schneider, 85-99. Oxford: Oxbow Books.

James, Heather. 1997. "Shakespeare's Troy: Drama, Politics, and the Translation of Empire." Cambridge: Cambridge University Press.

Jansen, Claudia. 2006. "The Architecture of Troy VI and VIIa: Problems of Identification." In "Troy: From Homer's Iliad to Hollywood Epic," edited by Martin M. Winkler, 156-168. Oxford: Blackwell Publishing.

Joukowsky, Martha Sharp. 1980. "A Complete Manual of Field Archaeology: Tools and Techniques of Field Work for Archaeologists." Englewood Cliffs: Prentice-Hall.

Karageorghis, Vassos. 1998. "Mycenaean 'Acropoleis' in the Aegean and Cyprus: Some Comparisons." In "The Aegean and the Orient in the Second Millennium," edited by Eric H. Cline and Diane Harris-Cline, 127-136. Liège: Université de Liège.

Kayan, Ilhan. 2014. "Geoarchaeological Research at Troia and Its Environs." In "Troia 1987-2012: Grabungen und Forschungen I," edited by Ernst Pernicka, Charles Brian Rose, and Peter Jablonka, 694-712. Bonn: Habelt.

Kiesewetter, Henrike. 2003. "The Anthropological Material from Troy VI, VII and VIII." In "Troia and the Troad: Scientific Approaches," edited by Günther A. Wagner, Ernst Pernicka, and Hans-Peter Uerpmann, 339-350. Berlin: Springer.

Kilian-Dirlmeier, Imma. 1993. "Die Schwerter in Griechenland (ausserhalb der Peloponnes), Bulgarien und Albanien." Prähistorische Bronzefunde IV(12). Stuttgart: Franz Steiner.

Killen, John T. 1999. "Mycenaean Economy." In "A Companion to Linear B: Mycenaean Greek Texts and their World," edited by Yves Duhoux and Anna Morpurgo Davies, 159-200. Louvain-la-Neuve: Peeters.

Kolb, Frank. 2004. "Troy VI: A Trading Center and Commercial City?" American Journal of Archaeology 108(4): 577-613.

Korfmann, Manfred. 1992. "Troia - Ausgrabungen 1990 und 1991." Studia Troica 2: 1-41.

Korfmann, Manfred. 1995. "Troia: A Residential and Trading City at the Dardanelles." In "Politeia: Society and State in the Aegean Bronze Age," edited by Robert Laffineur and Wolf-Dietrich Niemeier, 173-183. Liège: Université de Liège.

Korfmann, Manfred. 1998. "Troia, an Ancient Anatolian Palatial and Trading Center: Archaeological Evidence for the Period of Troia VI/VII." The Classical World 91(5): 369-385.

Korfmann, Manfred. 2001. "Troia as a Bronze Age Trading Center." In "Troy: Dream and Reality," edited by Joachim Latacz, 26-39. Stuttgart: Theiss.

Korfmann, Manfred. 2004. "Troia in Light of New Research." Die Naturwissenschaften 91(2): 70-73.

Korfmann, Manfred. 2005. "Troy in the Bronze Age - A Summary of the Latest Excavations and Research." In "Anatolian Interfaces: Hittites, Greeks and their Neighbours," edited by Billie Jean Collins, Mary R. Bachvarova, and Ian C. Rutherford, 253-272. Oxford: Oxbow Books.

Korfmann, Manfred. 2006. "Troia - Archäologie eines Siedlungshügels und seiner Landschaft." In "Troia: Archäologie eines Siedlungshügels und seiner Landschaft," edited by Manfred Korfmann, 1-12. Mainz: Philipp von Zabern.

Kouwenhoven, Arlette. 2001. "The Geographical Setting of Troy." In "Troy: Dream and Reality," edited by Joachim Latacz, 95-106. Stuttgart: Theiss.

Kraft, John C. 2003. "Sedimentary Evidence for the Paleogeography of Troy." In "Troia and the Troad: Scientific Approaches," edited by Günther A. Wagner, Ernst Pernicka, and Hans-Peter Uerpmann, 297-310. Berlin: Springer.

Krause, Johannes. 2019. "The Genetic History of Southeast Europe." Nature 555: 197-203.

Lamberg-Karlovsky, Carl C. 1996. "Beyond the Tigris and Euphrates: Bronze Age Civilizations." Beer-Sheva: Ben-Gurion University of the Negev Press.

Latacz, Joachim. 2001. "Troy and Homer: Towards a Solution of an Old Mystery." Translated by Kevin Windle and Rosh Ireland. Oxford: Oxford University Press.

Latacz, Joachim. 2004. "Troy and Homer: Towards a Solution of an Old Mystery." Translated by Kevin Windle and Rosh Ireland. Oxford: Oxford University Press.

Lewis, C.D. 1969. "The Images of War and the War of Images." In "The Poetic Image," 78-96. London: Jonathan Cape.

Liverani, Mario. 2001. "International Relations in the Ancient Near East, 1600-1100 BC." New York: Palgrave.

Lord, Albert B. 1960. "The Singer of Tales." Cambridge: Harvard University Press.

Lucas, Gavin. 2001. "Critical Approaches to Fieldwork: Contemporary and Historical Archaeological Practice." London: Routledge.

Malkin, Irad. 1998. "The Returns of Odysseus: Colonization and Ethnicity." Berkeley: University of California Press.

Marinatos, Nanno. 1993. "Minoan Religion: Ritual, Image, and Symbol." Columbia: University of South Carolina Press.

Martin, Richard P. 1989. "The Language of Heroes: Speech and Performance in the Iliad." Ithaca: Cornell University Press.

McDonald, William A. 1967. "Progress into the Past: The Rediscovery of Mycenaean Civilization." Bloomington: Indiana University Press.

McGrail, Seán. 2001. "Boats of the World: From the Stone Age to Medieval Times." Oxford: Oxford University Press.

Melchert, H. Craig. 2003. "The Luwians." Leiden: Brill.

Meserve, Margaret. 2008. "Empires of Islam in Renaissance Historical Thought." Cambridge: Harvard University Press.

Meyer, Ernst. 1936. "Schliemann's Briefe." Berlin: Gerstenberg.

Miller, D. Gary. 2007. "Ancient Greek Dialects and Early Authors: Introduction to the Dialect Mixture in Homer, with Notes on Lyric and Herodotus." Boston: De Gruyter.

Miller, Jared L. 1997. "The Expeditions of Hattusili I to the Eastern Frontiers." Ph.D. dissertation, University of Chicago.

Morgan, Catherine. 1990. "Athletes and Oracles: The Transformation of Olympia and Delphi in the Eighth Century BC." Cambridge: Cambridge University Press.

Morris, Ian. 1997. "Homer and the Iron Age." In "A New Companion to Homer," edited by Ian Morris and Barry Powell, 535-559. Leiden: Brill.

Morris, Ian. 2000. "Archaeology as Cultural History: Words and Things in Iron Age Greece." Malden: Blackwell.

Morris, Sarah P. 1995. "The Sacrifice of Astyanax: Near Eastern Contributions to the Siege of Troy." In "The Ages of Homer: A Tribute to Emily Townsend Vermeule," edited by Jane B. Carter and Sarah P. Morris, 221-245. Austin: University of Texas Press.

Morris, Sarah P. 2006. "The View from East Greece: Miletus, Samos and Ephesus." In "Ancient Greece: From the Mycenaean Palaces to the Age of Homer," edited by Sigrid Deger-Jalkotzy and Irene S. Lemos, 67-84. Edinburgh: Edinburgh University Press.

Mountjoy, Penelope A. 1999. "Regional Mycenaean Decorated Pottery." Rahden: Marie Leidorf.

Mountjoy, Penelope A. 2006. "The Mycenaean Pottery from Troy in the Berlin Schliemann Collection." In "Archaeology of Troy and the Troad," edited by D.F. Easton et al., 235-260. Cambridge: Cambridge University Press.

Muhly, James D. 1985. "Sources of Tin and the Beginnings of Bronze Metallurgy." American Journal of Archaeology 89(2): 275-291.

Murray, A.S. 1907. "The Excavations at Ephesus." The Journal of Hellenic Studies 27: 70-79.

Murray, Oswyn. 1990. "Sympotic History." In "Sympotica: A Symposium on the Symposion," edited by Oswyn Murray, 3-13. Oxford: Clarendon Press.

Nagy, Gregory. 1979. "The Best of the Achaeans: Concepts of the Hero in Archaic Greek Poetry." Baltimore: Johns Hopkins University Press.

Nagy, Gregory. 1996. "Homeric Questions." Austin: University of Texas Press.

Nagy, Gregory. 1999. "The Best of the Achaeans: Concepts of the Hero in Archaic Greek Poetry." Revised edition. Baltimore: Johns Hopkins University Press.

Noyes, Dorothy. 2003. "Group." Journal of American Folklore 116(462): 449-478.

Oettinger, Norbert. 2008. "The Seer Mopsos (Muksas) as a Historical Figure." In "Anatolian Interfaces: Hittites, Greeks and their Neighbours," edited by Billie Jean Collins, Mary R. Bachvarova, and Ian C. Rutherford, 63-66. Oxford: Oxbow Books.

Oren, Eliezer D. 2000. "The Sea Peoples and Their World: A Reassessment." Philadelphia: University Museum, University of Pennsylvania.

Parker, Robert. 1983. "Miasma: Pollution and Purification in Early Greek Religion." Oxford: Clarendon Press.

Parker, Robert. 2011. "On Greek Religion." Ithaca: Cornell University Press.

Pavúk, Peter. 2014. "Troia VI Früh und Mitte. Keramik, Stratigraphie, Chronologie." Studia Troica Monographien 3. Bonn: Habelt.

Powell, Barry B. 2004. "Homer." Malden: Blackwell.

Prent, Mieke. 2005. "Cretan Sanctuaries and Cults: Continuity and Change from Late Minoan IIIC to the Archaic Period." Leiden: Brill.

Pulak, Cemal. 1998. "The Uluburun Shipwreck: An Overview." International Journal of Nautical Archaeology 27(3): 188-224.

Redford, Donald B. 1992. "Egypt, Canaan, and Israel in Ancient Times." Princeton: Princeton University Press.

Redfield, James M. 1975. "Nature and Culture in the Iliad: The Tragedy of Hector." Chicago: University of Chicago Press.

Rehak, Paul. 1995. "Enthroned Figures in Aegean Art and the Function of the Mycenaean Megaron." In "The Role of the Ruler in the Prehistoric Aegean," edited by Paul Rehak, 95-118. Liège: Université de Liège.

Renfrew, Colin. 1979. "Systems Collapse as Social Transformation: Catastrophe and Anastrophe in Early State Societies." In "Transformations: Mathematical Approaches to Culture Change," edited by Colin Renfrew and Kenneth L. Cooke, 481-506. New York: Academic Press.

Renfrew, Colin. 1980. "The Great Tradition versus the Great Divide: Archaeology as Anthropology?" American Journal of Archaeology 84(3): 287-298.

Ridgway, David. 1992. "The First Western Greeks." Cambridge: Cambridge University Press.

Riehl, Simone. 2010. "Plant Production in a Changing Environment: The Archaeobotanical Remains from Tell Mozan." In "Development of the Environment, Subsistence and Settlement of the City of Urkeš and Its Region," edited by Katleen Deckers, Monika Doll, Peter Pfälzner, and Simone Riehl, 13-158. Wiesbaden: Harrassowitz.

Rigter, Wendy. 2003. "Troia: Ausgrabungen im Bereich des Quadrats D9." Studia Troica 13: 73-100.

Rose, Charles Brian. 2006. "Ilion." In "Stadtgrabungen und Stadtforschung im westlichen Kleinasien," edited by Wolfgang Radt, 135-158. Istanbul: Ege Yayınları.

Rose, Charles Brian. 2014. "The Archaeology of Greek and Roman Troy." Cambridge: Cambridge University Press.

Sahlins, Marshall. 2004. "Apologies to Thucydides: Understanding History as Culture and Vice Versa." Chicago: University of Chicago Press.

Saunders, Kevin. 1999. "The Injuries of Sport: An Ancient Perspective." Liverpool Classical Monthly 24(1): 2-13.

Schein, Seth L. 1996. "Reading the Odyssey: Selected Interpretive Essays." Princeton: Princeton University Press.

Scheid, John. 2003. "An Introduction to Roman Religion." Translated by Janet Lloyd. Bloomington: Indiana University Press.

Schliemann, Heinrich. 1874. "Trojanische Alterthümer: Bericht über die Ausgrabungen in Troja." Leipzig: F.A. Brockhaus.

Schliemann, Heinrich. 1875. "Troy and Its Remains: A Narrative of Researches and Discoveries Made on the Site of Ilium, and in the Trojan Plain." Translated by L. Dora Schmitz. London: John Murray.

Schliemann, Heinrich. 1881. "Ilios: The City and Country of the Trojans." London: John Murray.

Schliemann, Heinrich. 1884. Letter to Rudolf Virchow, 15 June 1884. Rudolf Virchow Papers, Berlin-Brandenburgische Akademie der Wissenschaften.

Schliemann, Heinrich. 1890. "Bericht über die Ausgrabungen in Troja im Jahre 1890." Leipzig: F.A. Brockhaus.

Shay, Jonathan. 1994. "Achilles in Vietnam: Combat Trauma and the Undoing of Character." New York: Atheneum.

Shay, Jonathan. 2002. "Odysseus in America: Combat Trauma and the Trials of Homecoming." New York: Scribner.

GLOSSARY

Ahhiyawa: Term used in Hittite texts to refer to a kingdom in western Anatolia or the Aegean, now generally identified with the Mycenaean Greeks. Appears in diplomatic correspondence regarding conflicts in western Anatolia, including matters involving Troy/Wilusa.

Alaksandu Treaty: Hittite diplomatic document (c. 1280 BCE) between the Hittite king Muwatalli II and Alaksandu of Wilusa (Troy), establishing Wilusa as a Hittite vassal state. The name Alaksandu parallels the Greek "Alexander" (Paris).

Anatolian languages: Branch of the Indo-European language family including Hittite, Luwian, Palaic, and others spoken in Asia Minor during the Bronze Age. Troy/Wilusa was likely a Luwian-speaking settlement.

Aristeia: Greek term for a hero's "finest hour" in battle, a narrative pattern in Homeric epic where a warrior demonstrates exceptional prowess, typically forming a self-contained episode.

Bronze Age collapse: Period of widespread political, economic, and social breakdown throughout the Eastern Mediterranean region c. 1200-1150 BCE, resulting in the destruction of major centers including Mycenae, Hattusa, Ugarit, and Troy VIIa.

Citadel: Fortified central area of a settlement, typically on elevated ground. At Troy, the citadel (approx. 2 hectares) was surrounded by massive stone walls and contained monumental buildings and elite residences.

Dark Age: Period following the Bronze Age collapse (c. 1100-800 BCE) characterized by population decline, reduced literacy, diminished trade, and simplified material culture throughout Greece and parts of the Eastern Mediterranean.

Dardanelles: Narrow strait (ancient Hellespont) connecting the Aegean Sea to the Sea of Marmara and Black Sea. Troy's location near this waterway gave it strategic control over maritime traffic between the Aegean and Black Sea regions.

Hittite Empire: Major Bronze Age power centered in central Anatolia (modern Turkey) that controlled much of Asia Minor and northern Syria during the 14th-13th centuries BCE. Diplomatic texts reveal Troy/Wilusa was a vassal state in their sphere of influence.

Iliad: Epic poem attributed to Homer, composed c. 8th century BCE, focusing on the wrath of Achilles and events during a few weeks in the ninth year of the Trojan War. Contains 15,693 lines of dactylic hexameter verse.

Ilios/Ilion: Greek name for Troy in Homer and other ancient sources, linguistically connected to the Hittite term "Wilusa" through established sound correspondences.

Linear B: Syllabic script used to write Mycenaean Greek during the Late Bronze Age (c. 1450-1200 BCE). Tablets record administrative information and include names later found in Homeric epic, including possible references to Achilles.

Lower city: Area surrounding the citadel at Troy, discovered by Manfred Korfmann in the 1990s, extending the known size of Troy VI-VII to approximately 25-30 hectares with an estimated population of 5,000-10,000 inhabitants.

Luwian: Anatolian language of the Indo-European family widely spoken in western and southern Anatolia during the Bronze Age. Archaeological and textual evidence suggests Troy/Wilusa was primarily a Luwian-speaking settlement.

Manapa-Tarhunta Letter: Hittite diplomatic document (late 13th century BCE) describing military conflicts in western Anatolia, including attacks on Wilusa (Troy) by a renegade named Piyamaradu with possible Ahhiyawan (Mycenaean) support.

Megaron: Architectural form consisting of a porch (aithousa), vestibule (prodomos), and main room (domos) with central hearth, typical of Mycenaean palaces and found in elite buildings at Troy VI.

Milawata Letter: Hittite diplomatic text (late 13th century BCE) addressing political instability in western Anatolia, including matters involving Wilusa (Troy), suggesting increasing regional tension before Troy's destruction.

Mycenaean civilization: Late Bronze Age culture of mainland Greece and the Aegean (c. 1600-1100 BCE), characterized by palatial centers, Linear B writing, distinctive pottery, and extensive trade networks. Identified with the Ahhiyawa in Hittite texts.

Nostoi: Greek term meaning "returns," referring to stories about Greek heroes' journeys home after the Trojan War. These narratives, including Odysseus's ten-year wanderings, emphasize how victory often carried consequences as severe as defeat.

Oral composition: Theory developed by Milman Parry and Albert Lord explaining how epic poetry was composed and transmitted through formulaic language and thematic patterns before being written down, explaining both consistency and variation in Homeric texts.

Priam's Treasure: Collection of gold artifacts discovered by Heinrich Schliemann at Troy in 1873, which he attributed to King Priam of Trojan War fame. Actually dates to Troy II (c. 2400 BCE), nearly a millennium before the traditional date of the Trojan War.

Sea Peoples: Term from Egyptian inscriptions describing diverse groups who attacked Egypt and eastern Mediterranean territories during the late 13th-early 12th centuries BCE, often associated with the Bronze Age collapse.

Stratigraphy: Archaeological method examining vertical layering of deposits to establish relative chronology. At Troy, excavators identified nine major settlement phases (Troy I-IX) with multiple sub-phases spanning nearly 4,000 years.

Tawagalawa Letter: Hittite diplomatic correspondence (late 13th century BCE) from a Hittite king to an Ahhiyawan ruler regarding conflicts in western

Anatolia, including matters involving Wilusa (Troy), demonstrating the international diplomatic context of the region.

Trojan Gray Ware: Distinctive ceramic tradition at Troy characterized by gray-colored, wheel-made pottery with specific forms and surface treatments, representing local production traditions from the Early Bronze Age through the Late Bronze Age.

Troy VI: Major settlement phase at Troy (c. 1700-1250 BCE), characterized by impressive stone fortification walls, monumental architecture, and evidence of prosperity. Destroyed by earthquake rather than warfare.

Troy VIIa: Settlement phase immediately following Troy VI (c. 1250-1180 BCE), showing signs of a community under stress (subdivided buildings, increased storage facilities) before being violently destroyed around 1180 BCE. Considered the most likely candidate for "Homeric Troy."

UNESCO World Heritage Site: International designation recognizing cultural or natural sites of outstanding universal value. Troy received this status in 1998, acknowledging its exceptional archaeological and cultural significance.

Wilusa: Hittite name for a kingdom in northwestern Anatolia, now generally identified with Troy based on geographical, linguistic, and archaeological evidence. Appears in multiple Hittite diplomatic texts from the 14th-13th centuries BCE.

Wooden Horse: Stratagem described in Greek tradition whereby Greek warriors concealed themselves inside a large wooden horse, which the Trojans brought within their city walls, allowing the Greeks to emerge at night and open the gates to their army.

COMING SOON...

From the soil of a forgotten Florida marsh comes one of America's most extraordinary untold stories—the life of Francisco Menéndez, a West African warrior who escaped slavery to found North America's first legally sanctioned free Black community decades before the American Revolution.

Archaeologist R Jay Driskill brings revolutionary new insights to this remarkable biography, combining cutting-edge archaeological evidence with painstaking historical research to reveal how one man's strategic brilliance transformed the possibilities for freedom in colonial America. Through careful excavation of artifacts, documents, and landscapes, Driskill reconstructs Menéndez's incredible journey from Mandinka child to Carolina slave to Spanish militia captain to the founder and commander of Fort Mose—a thriving settlement that challenged everything we thought we knew about race, freedom, and resistance in early America.

This isn't just another story of survival—it's the archaeology of revolution. Menéndez escaped bondage during the Yamasee War, navigated complex imperial rivalries between Britain and Spain, and convinced Spanish authorities to grant legal freedom to his community in exchange for military service. As a privateer, he captured British slave ships and liberated their human cargo. As a military commander, he repelled British invasions and defended his people's hard-won liberty through strategic brilliance and unwavering courage.

What makes this biography groundbreaking:

- **Archaeological evidence** brings Menéndez's world to life through artifacts you can see and touch

- **Reveals hidden networks** of resistance that connected enslaved communities across colonial boundaries

- **Documents the first free Black town** in what would become the United States

- **Challenges traditional narratives** about when and how Black freedom emerged in America

- **Shows how one person's vision** created lasting change that influenced freedom struggles for generations

Driskill's unique archaeological approach reveals aspects of Menéndez's life that no document could capture—from the defensive strategies he learned as a Mandinka warrior to the community organization skills that made Fort Mose a model for Black self-determination. Through material evidence scattered across three continents, we see how cultural knowledge, strategic intelligence, and unwavering determination could create unprecedented opportunities even within systems designed to deny Black humanity.

Perfect for readers who love:

- Revolutionary War and colonial American history

- Archaeological discoveries that change our understanding of the past

- Stories of resistance, survival, and triumph against impossible odds

- Biographies that recover marginalized voices from history

- Military history and strategic leadership

This meticulously researched biography doesn't just tell Menéndez's story—it proves that some of history's most important chapters lie buried beneath our feet, waiting for archaeology to bring them back to light. From slave quarters to fort battlements, from privateer ships to royal palaces, follow the material trail of a man who refused to accept that freedom was impossible.

Icons of Defiance celebrates individuals who changed history through courage, intelligence, and unwavering commitment to justice. Francisco Menéndez earned his place among them by proving that even in slavery's darkest hour, strategic action and collective determination could create spaces of unprecedented freedom.

ABOUT THE AUTHOR

R Jay Driskill is a professional archaeologist and bestselling author who transforms ancient mysteries into captivating narratives that educate and entertain. With academic credentials from the University of Florida and extensive fieldwork experience, Driskill brings authentic archaeological expertise to every page.

Specializing in historically accurate fiction and immersive non-fiction, Driskill's works have earned praise for their meticulous research, vivid storytelling, and ability to make complex historical concepts accessible to modern readers. Each book combines rigorous scholarship with page-turning adventure, offering readers both entertainment and genuine insight into humanity's fascinating past.

Whether you're a history enthusiast, archaeology buff, or simply love a well-crafted story, R Jay Driskill delivers meticulously researched narratives that will keep you engaged from first page to last.

Start your journey through time today – explore the complete collection and discover why readers call these books "unputdownable."

Visit rjaydriskill.com for exclusive content and upcoming releases.

www.ingramcontent.com/pod-product-compliance
Lightning Source LLC
Chambersburg PA
CBHW061555120626
46550CB00004B/1504